P9-DEC-938

John Willard Brister
Library
Memphis State University
Memphis, Tennessee

WITHDRAWAL

Terminology of documentation

Terminologie de la documentation

Terminologie der Dokumentation

Терминология в области документации

Terminología de la documentación

Terminology of documentation
Terminologie de la documentation
Terminologie der Dokumentation
Терминология в области документации
Terminología de la documentación

A selection
of 1,200 basic terms
published in English,
French, German,
Russian and Spanish

Compiled by
Gernot Wersig
and
Ulrich Neveling

The Unesco Press   Paris 1976
Les Presses de l'Unesco
Unesco Verlag
Издательство Юнеско
Editorial de la Unesco

Published by The Unesco Press,
7 Place de Fontenoy, 75700 Paris
Printed by Imprimeries Populaires, Geneva

ISBN 92-3-001232-7

© Unesco 1975
Printed in Switzerland

Reference
Z
1006
W47

Preface

In 1970 Unesco concluded a contract with the German Society for Documentation for the preparation of this *Terminology of Documentation* to meet the need for a multilingual vocabulary covering various aspects of documentation activities, including: linguistic problems; communication; theory; documentary languages; systems analysis, design and evaluations; general concepts of electronic data processing.

This work has been prepared by Gernot Wersig, associate professor, Institute for Medical Statistics and Documentation, Berlin, who is a member of the Committee on Terminology and Linguistics Problems of the German Society for Documentation, and Ulrich Neveling, scientific assistant, Institute for Journalism at the Free University, Berlin. The Russian terms have been added by the All-Union Institute for Scientific and Technical Information (VINITI), Moscow. The Spanish terms have been added by Dr Armando M. Sandoval, director, Centro de Información Científica y Humanística, Universidad de México.

The *Terminology of Documentation* is intended to help standardize basic terminology in the rapidly developing field of documentation and thus to foster international co-operation. It should also be useful as a reference work for organizations and individuals working in the fields of documentation, libraries and information processing, to translators and to students in these fields.

Préface

En 1970, l'Unesco a chargé par contrat la Société allemande de documentation d'établir cette terminologie pour remédier à l'absence d'un vocabulaire multilingue portant sur divers aspects des activités de documentation : problèmes linguistiques; communication; théorie; langages documentaires; analyse, conception et évaluation de systèmes; principes fondamentaux du traitement électronique de l'information.

Ce répertoire a été compilé par Gernot Wersig, professeur associé à l'Institut de statistique et de documentation de Berlin, membre du Comité de la terminologie et des problèmes linguistiques de la Société allemande de documentation, et par Ulrich Neveling, assistant scientifique à l'Institut du journalisme de l'Université libre de Berlin. Les équivalents russes ont été fournis par l'Institut central d'information scientifique et technique (VINITI) de Moscou. Les équivalents espagnols ont été fournis par le Dr Armando M. Sandoval, directeur del Centro de Información Científica y Humanística de l'Université du Mexique.

La *Terminologie de la documentation* vise à faciliter la normalisation de la terminologie de base relative aux activités en voie d'expansion rapide qui ont trait à la documentation et à stimuler ainsi la coopération internationale. Elle devrait aussi fournir un utile instrument de travail aux organisations et aux individus qui s'occupent de la documentation, des bibliothèques et du traitement de l'information, aux traducteurs et aux étudiants qui se spécialisent dans ces domaines.

Vorwort

Um dem Bedürfnis nach einem mehrsprachigen Wörterbuch, das eine Reihe von Bereichen der Dokumentation abdeckt, abzuhelfen, hat 1970 Unesco einen Kontrakt mit der Deutschen Gesellschaft für Dokumentation (DGD) über die Erarbeitung dieser *Terminology of Documentation* abgeschlossen. Einbezogen werden sollten insbesondere: linguistische Probleme; Kommunikationstheorie; Dokumentationssprachen; Systemanalyse, -entwurf und -bewertung; allgemeine Begriffe der elektronischen Datenverarbeitung.

Diese Aufgabe wurde übernommen von Gernot Wersig, Assistenz-Professor, Institut für Medizinische Statistik und Dokumentation, Berlin, Mitglied des Komitees Terminologie und Sprachfragen der DGD, und Ulrich Neveling, Wissenschaftlicher Assistent, Institut für Publizistik, Berlin.

Die russischen Benennungen wurden vom Ael-Unions Institut für Wissenschaftliche und Technische Information (VINITI), Moskau, hinzugefügt. Die spanischen Benennungen sind von Dr. Armando M. Sandoval, dem Direktor des Centro de Información Científica y Humanística, Universidad de México, hinzugefügt worden.

Die *Terminology of Documentation* soll helfen, die grundlegende Terminologie in dem sich schnell entwickelnden Bereich der Dokumentation zu vereinheitlichen und dadurch die internationale Kooperation zu fördern. Sie soll weiterhin als ein Nachschlagewerk dienen für die Organisationen und Individuen, die im Bereich Dokumentation, Bibliothekswesen und Datenverarbeitung arbeiten, sowie für Übersetzer und Studenten dieser Bereiche.

Предисловие

В 1970 г. ЮНЕСКО заключила контракт с Германским обществом документации на подготовку настоящей терминологии в области документации, чтобы удовлетворить потребность в многоязычном словаре, охватывающем различные аспекты, связанные с документацией, включая: лингвистические проблемы; информацию; теорию; языки документации; анализ, проектирование и оценку систем, общие концепции электронной обработки данных.

Эта работа была подготовлена г-ном Гернотом Версигом, доцентом Института медицинской статистики и документации, Берлин, который является членом Комитета по терминологии и лингвистическим проблемам Германского общества документации, и г-ном Ульрихом Невелингом, научным сотрудником Института журналистики Свободного университета, Берлин.

Русские термины были представлены Всесоюзным институтом научно-технической информации (ВИНИТИ), Москва. Испанские термины — д-ром Армандо Д. Сандовалом, директором Центра информации по естественным и гуманитарным наукам Мексиканского национального автономного университета, Мехико.

Терминология в области документации имеет целью содействовать стандартизации основной терминологии в быстро развивающейся области документации и тем самым содействовать международному сотрудничеству. Данный словарь будет также полезен в качестве реферативного документа для организаций и лиц, работающих в таких областях как документация, библиотечное дело и обработка информации, для переводчиков и студентов, связанных с этими областями.

Prólogo

En 1970, la Unesco firmó un contrato con la Sociedad Alemana de Documentación para la preparación de esta *Terminología de la documentación*, con objeto de atender la necesidad de contar con un vocabulario plurilingüe que abarque diversos aspectos de las actividades de documentación: problemas de lingüística, comunicación, teoría, lenguajes documentales, evaluaciones, diseño y análisis de sistemas, y conceptos generales del tratamiento (procesamiento) electrónico de datos.

Esta obra ha sido preparada por los Sres. Gernot Wersig, profesor asociado del Instituto de Documentación y Estadísticas Médicas de Berlín y miembro del Comité de Terminología y Problemas Lingüísticos de la Sociedad Alemana de Documentación, y Ulrich Neveling, asistente científico, del Instituto de Periodismo de la Universidad Libre de Berlín. Los términos rusos han sido añadidos por el Instituto Pansoviético de Información Científica y Técnica (VINITI) de Moscû. Los términos españoles han sido añadidos por el doctor Armando M. Sandoval, director del Centro de Información Científica y Humanística de la Universidad de México.

Con esta *Terminología de la documentación* se pretende facilitar la normalización de la terminología básica de la documentación, que está en rápido desarrollo, y promover, por ende, la cooperación internacional. También ha de resultar útil como obra de consulta y referencia a las organizaciones y a los individuos que trabajan en los sectores de la documentación, las bibliotecas y el tratamiento de datos, y a los traductores y a los estudiantes de estas disciplinas y sectores.

Contents

Table des matières

Inhaltsverzeichnis   Содержание   Índice

Introduction

1   General

1.1 Background

In 1962, Anthony Thompson presented to the FID conference at Scheveningen a first draft of a *Vocabularium Documentationis* compiled under a contract concluded between Unesco and FID. A second draft was submitted in November 1963, a third in June 1974. The third draft, containing about 1,200 terms with their definitions in English and equivalents in German, Spanish, French and Russian, was discussed at the meeting of the FID Committee on Linguistic Problems held in September 1964 at Scheveningen, but it was never published.

In November 1970, Unesco made a second attempt to prepare a *Vocabularium Documentationis*. By that time the scene had changed completely. A number of compilations of definitions in the field of documentation had been published (see below, Bibliography). In several countries committees for the standardization of information and documentation terminology had been set up. Since 1969, a Working Group of Technical Committee 46 of ISO had been engaged in establishing international standards for information and documentation terminology.

1.2 Stages of work

In 1971, a preliminary version of the *Terminology of Documentation* was compiled under a Unesco contract containing about 1,200 English terms with definitions in English, as well as French and German equivalents. This preliminary version was distributed for comments to a large number of experts in the field. The comments received were then incorporated into the terminology, being revised under a further Unesco contract in 1973. The French equivalents were taken from other multilingual sources and corrected by AFNOR. The German equivalents were discussed with the Committee for Terminology and Linguistic Problems of the German Documentation Society. Under a Unesco contract, Russian equivalents were elaborated by VINITI and included without any alterations. The Spanish equivalents, added by A. Sandoval, were sent to a number of specialists whose comments have been incorporated in this final version.

1.3 Classification

Neither the Universal Decimal Classification nor the classification schemes developed by the ISO/TC 46 Working Group seemed entirely suitable for the presentation of the vocabulary.

It was therefore decided to adopt a middle course between alphabetic and detailed classified arrangement by grouping the terms pragmatically in broad classes and arranging them alphabetically within these classes. This provides access to terms of a broad subfield of information and documentation. A more detailed access to concept relations, which would be achieved by using a highly detailed classification scheme, was sought by other means (cf. para. 2.6).

For setting up the broad classes three aspects were essential:

first, bring together terms belonging to a particular area of a given subject field, e.g terms belonging to punched card systems;

second, bring together terms belonging to the same facet of a given subject field, e.g. terms denoting particular systems;

third, avoid too many terms in any one class. Hence it was decided that a group should not exceed approximately sixty terms.

A Universal Decimal Classification (UDC) index provides access by UDC notations.

1.4 Sources

The following sources proved to be a great help in searching out terms and definitions:

the eleven vocabularies compiled by Florence Casey for COSATI (B7);

the work of Subcommittee OC/20/12; Documentation Terminology, of Committee OC/20, Documentation Standards of the British Standards Institution (B6);

the work of Subcommittee 1, Vocabulary of Data Processing, of ISO Technical Committee 97, Computers and Information Processing (A10);

the work of Working Group 3, Terminology, of ISO Technical Committee 46, Documentation (A6, A7).

In addition, sources listed in section 4, 'Bibliography of Sources', were used.

The main sources of each group of the vocabulary are indicated below:

  1 Basic aspects of information and documentation.

 11 Sciences related to information and documentation: B7.

 12 Concepts: A6, A7, A16, D3, D20, D21 (1).

 13 Basic elements of representation: A5, A6, A10(01, 04), D3, D21(1).

 14 Elements of language: A6, A7, A10(01, 04), B19, D3, D20, D21(1).

 15 Types of languages: A7, A10(10), D4, D21(1).

 16 Representation of vocabularies: A6, A7, B19.

 17 Communication and information theory: A7, B7, D20, D21(2).

 18 Conversion and coding: A10(01, 04), B7.

 19 Dissemination of information: B6, B7.

110 Reprography and printing: A4, B6.

1.5 Definitions

Adding definitions to the vocabulary presented certain difficulties because:
many existing vocabularies offer varying definitions for the same term;
these definitions often differ not in subject but in wording;
there are very good compilations of definitions given in some of the most important
vocabularies;
vocabularies often adopt definitions from some other source without indicating this source.
The following course was chosen:
Out of the various definitions found in the literature the one that seemed to be correct
as to subject and clearest as to its wording was selected. Only in cases where different
subjects were denoted by the the same term were different definitions included.
For similar terms (e.g. terms denoting systems) a standard text was sought in which the
defining differences could be inserted.
For the sake of conciseness and clearness the wording of definitions was changed,
wherever possible, to include those terms already defined in the vocabulary.
Within a definition each term defined at some other place in the vocabulary is marked
accordingly.
Of course, this work could not be carried out consistently. The user may find a number
of instances where, in his judgement, definitions given in other sources are more intelli-

gible, better interrelated with others, and more systematic. But to our knowledge no similar attempt has been made on an international level to compile a vocabulary in this way. To a certain extent the present vocabulary may therefore be regarded as unique, and it is hoped it will serve the user in a more effective way than a traditional compilation of definitions would do.

1.6 Scope

Developments in recent years made it necessary to place particular emphasis on:
linguistic problems, because of the introduction of electronic data processing into the field of information and documentation;
communication theory, because of the ever growing influence of information sciences on practical work;
documentary languages, because the development of computerized information systems has created new problems in this area (e.g. thesauri);
systems analysis, design and evaluation, because these techniques, developed in recent years, are becoming increasingly important for practical work;
general concepts of electronic data processing, because many systems are now using such devices or will do so in the future.
It should be stressed that the present vocabulary is not and cannot be a substitute for existing vocabularies in the special fields of electronic data processing, linguistics, or cybernetics.
It aims at providing specialists in information and documentation with a tool which will enable them to participate in the technical communication of their field, and offering a means of orientation in the entire field of information and documentation.

1.7 Languages

The compilation of a technical vocabulary and at the same time a multilingual dictionary is not an easy task. From an analysis of existing vocabularies and pertinent literature it was realized that perfect synchronization even of two languages was not feasible. It was found that many terms of Anglo-American usage could not be translated into German and vice versa. Introducing other languages rendered the matter even more complicated.
It was therefore decided to select English as the guiding language because the majority of the sources available were in English.

2 Structure of the vocabulary

2.1 General remarks

In general, presentation of the vocabulary is patterned on the following three models:
the work proposed by A. Thompson in preparing the third draft in 1964;
the work done by ISO/TC 97/SC 1 in preparing the data processing vocabulary;
cross referencing within thesauri.
To produce a combination of a classified vocabulary and a multilingual dictionary it was necessary to adapt some of the essential elements of the models and implement a specific set of rules.

2.2 Entry

An entry in this vocabulary consists of
the leading term, i.e. the English term chosen for the alphabetical arrangement of entries
    within one group;
English terms considered to be synonymous with the leading term;
French equivalents;
German equivalents;
Russian equivalents;
Spanish equivalents;
one or more definitions of the leading term;
as many index numbers as there are definitions in an entry;
cross references to terms used in the definitions;
cross references to terms related to the definitions.

2.3 Terms

The following rules have been laid down:
The English and French terms are presented in the same spelling form in which they
    appear in a text, i.e. without capitalization.
The German terms are spelled in the same way as they appear in a text, i.e. capital
    letters are used to begin nouns.
Not all spelling variants (solid, open or hyphened compounds) are listed.
The leading term is always printed in bold.
In general, no distinction is made between preferred, tolerated and deprecated terms
(but the sequence gives an indication of the more personal preferences of the authors).
The terms of the respective language always begin at the same position.
The position of each language differs from that of the other languages and is indicated
    by indention.
The terms of languages other than English are marked by the following symbols:
    F = French;
    D = German;
    R = Russian;
    S = Spanish.
A special problem arises in the German vocabulary because of different usage in Austria,
    Switzerland, the Federal Republic of Germany and the German Democratic Republic.
    In most instances no distinction is made; only in cases where meanings differ consider-
    ably in the Federal Republic of Germany and the German Democratic Republic have
    symbols been placed in parentheses behind the term in question:
    (FRG) = preferred in the Federal Republic of Germany;
    (GDR) = preferred in the German Democratic Republic.
In some cases equivalents of the leading term cannot be referred to all definitions listed
    in an entry. In such cases the definition which applies to the term is indicated by the
    corresponding number enclosed in parentheses behind the term:
    (1) = definition   (1) applies;
    (2) = definition   (2) applies, etc.

2.4 Index numbers

The following rules have been followed:

Each definition has an index number of its own. The index number therefore does not identify the entry but a definition within the entry.

The index number consists of three parts: two (or three) digits indicating the group to which the defined term belongs; a hyphen as a separator; two digits indicating the current number of each definition within one group, starting with 01 for the first definition.

The index numbers are used for cross references within the vocabulary and references from indexes to entries.

2.5 Definitions

Efforts have been made to standardize definitions to a maximum degree. In some instances it was possible to render them more concise by using terms already defined at some other place in the vocabulary.

To facilitate access to terms used in the definitions two rules were established:

Terms used in the definition and defined within the same group are quoted (' '). No further cross reference is made to terms so indicated.

Terms used in the definition and defined in another group of the vocabulary are printed in italic.

Terms which are defined in the vocabulary as nouns and are used in another definition in adjectival or verbal form are not marked as such.

Parentheses within definitions indicate less important elements of the definition. The same applies to abbreviations, such as "i.e." (giving explanations) and "e.g." (giving examples).

2.6 Cross references to terms related to the definitions

As an aid to the user it seemed appropriate to indicate concept relations. These cross references are established according to general use, and not as in thesauri—according to necessities of indexing and retrieval. Cross references to other definitions are made according to the following rules:

The category itself is indicated by the symbol REF.

The symbol REF is followed by the leading terms and the index number of the related definition.

After each term and index number the following symbols are inserted to specify the relationship:

(BT) = broader term (in some way hierarchically superordinate);
(NT) = narrower term (in some way hierarchically subordinate);
(OT) = opposite term;
(RT) = related term (no specification of the kind of relationship).

The following order is established for terms to which cross references are made within this category:

(BT) (NT) (OT) (RT).

3   Indexes

The vocabulary has five alphabetical indexes: English, French, German, Russian, Spanish. In each index entries are made for:
each term appearing in the vocabulary, i.e. not only leading terms but also equivalent terms;
each element of the term, considered to be meaningful, i.e. the indexes are rotated indexes (the text following the entry word being in natural word order),
which means that in the English index, e.g., the term 'needle-operated punched card' will be listed as
"card, needle-operated punched";
"needle-operated punched card";
"punched card, needle-operated".

Each entry in the index consists of the term and the index number(s) assigned to the definition(s) of the term.

A separate index lists the UDC numbers which are related to the topics covered by the vocabulary. Each entry refers to the relevant group or entry within the main part of the vocabulary.

4   Bibliography of sources

The bibliography lists all those documents which were used directly or indirectly in the preparation of the vocabulary. Other sources which the user may find useful are included; however, no sources published prior to 1960 were consulted. The arrangement is according to the language and/or languages of the respective source document.

Introduction

1 Généralités

1.1 Historique

En 1962, Anthony Thompson avait présenté à la conférence de la FID, réunie à Scheveningen, l'avant-projet d'un *Vocabularium documentationis* établi en exécution d'un contrat conclu entre l'Unesco et la FID. Une deuxième et une troisième version de cet ouvrage furent présentées respectivement en novembre 1963 et juin 1964. La troisième version, qui contenait quelque 1 200 termes avec des définitions en anglais et des équivalents en allemand, espagnol, français et russe, fut examinée lors de la session tenue par le Comité de la FID sur les problèmes linguistiques en septembre 1964 à Scheveningen, mais elle n'a jamais été publiée.

En novembre 1970, l'Unesco prit une deuxième initiative en vue de l'élaboration d'un *Vocabularium documentationis*. Entre-temps, la situation avait changé du tout au tout. Un certain nombre de recueils de définitions en matière de documentation avaient paru (voir la bibliographie donnée page 47) et, dans plusieurs pays, des comités chargés de normaliser la terminologie de l'information et de la documentation avaient été constitués. Un groupe de travail du Comité technique 46 de l'ISO (ISO/TC 46) s'occupait depuis 1969 de mettre au point des normes internationales dans le domaine de la terminologie de l'information et de la documentation.

1.2 Étapes du travail

En 1971 une version préliminaire de la *Terminologie de la documentation* contenant quelque 1 200 termes anglais avec des définitions en anglais et des équivalents en français et en allemand a été établie sous contrat avec l'Unesco. Cette première version a été envoyée à un grand nombre d'experts pour examen et observations. Les observations reçues ont ensuite été incorporées à la terminologie au cours d'une révision entreprise en exécution d'un nouveau contrat conclu avec l'Unesco en 1973. Les équivalents français, puisés dans d'autres sources multilingues, ont été vérifiés par l'AFNOR.

Les équivalents allemands ont fait l'objet de discussions avec le Comité de la terminologie et des problèmes linguistiques de la Société allemande de documentation. Aux termes d'un contrat conclu avec l'Unesco, les équivalents russes ont été élaborés par le VINITI et incorporés à la terminologie sans aucune modification. Enfin, les équivalents espagnols, fournis par A. Sandoval, ont été communiqués à un certain nombre de spécialistes dont les observations ont été prises en considération pour mettre au point cette version définitive.

1.3 Classification

Pour présenter la terminologie, ni la classification universelle, ni les systèmes de classification mis au point par le groupe de travail ISO/TC 46 ne paraissaient convenir parfaitement.

On a donc opté pour une solution de compromis entre un classement alphabétique et un classement systématique détaillé: les termes ont été regroupés de façon pragmatique en un certain nombre de grandes classes et rangés par ordre alphabétique à l'intérieur de grande classe. Ce mode de présentation permet au lecteur d'avoir accès aux termes qui se rapportent à un vaste sous-secteur de l'information et de la documentation. L'analyse plus détaillée des relations entre concepts, qui exige normalement l'emploi d'un système de classification extrêmement complexe, a été assurée par d'autres moyens (voir paragraphe 2.6).

En vue de délimiter les grandes classes, on s'est fondé avant tout sur trois grands principes:

En premier lieu, regrouper les termes relatifs à un secteur particulier d'un domaine donné, par exemple ceux qui ont trait aux systèmes de cartes perforées.

Ensuite, regrouper les termes qui concernent une même facette d'un domaine particulier – ainsi les termes désignant tel ou tel système.

En troisième lieu, éviter de gonfler démesurément les classes. Il a été décidé, à cette fin, qu'aucune ne devrait comprendre plus d'une soixantaine de termes.

Un index de la Classification décimale universelle (CDU) permet de consulter le répertoire en utilisant les notations de la CDU.

1.4 Sources

Pour la recherche des termes et des définitions, on a utilisé avec grand profit la documentation ci-après:

Les onze vocabulaires établis par Florence Casey pour le COSATI (B7);

Les travaux du sous-comité OC/20/12 (terminologie de la documentation), du Comité OC/20 (normes en matière de documentation) de la British Standards Institution (B6);

Les travaux du sous-comité 1 (vocabulaire du traitement des données) du Comité technique 97 de l'ISO sur les ordinateurs et le traitement de l'information (A10);

Les travaux du groupe de travail 3 (terminologie) du Comité technique 46 de l'ISO sur la documentation (A6, A7).

On a tiré parti, en outre, des sources énumérées dans la section 4 (bibliographie).

Les principales sources des termes figurant dans chaque groupe sont indiquées ci-dessous:

1 Aspects fondamentaux de l'information et de la documentation

11 Sciences en rapport avec l'information et la documentation: B7

1.5 Définitions

L'incorporation de définitions dans le vocabulaire a posé un certain nombre de problèmes pour les raisons suivantes:

Le même terme est souvent défini de façon différente dans les vocabulaires existants;

Ces définitions diffèrent souvent non pas tant par leur substance que par leur rédaction;

Certains des principaux vocabulaires existants contiennent de très bons recueils de définitions;

Les vocabulaires donnent souvent des définitions tirées d'une autre source sans indiquer cette source.

La politique ci-après a été appliquée:
Parmi les diverses définitions données dans les ouvrages spécialisés, on a choisi celle
    qui paraissait correcte quant au fond et formulée de la façon la plus claire. C'est
    seulement lorsqu'un même terme désigne des notions différentes que plusieurs
    définitions différentes ont été fournies.
Pour les termes analogues (par exemple ceux qui désignent des systèmes), on s'est
    efforcé de mettre au point un texte unique auquel il serait possible d'ajouter dans
    chaque cas l'indication des particularités distinctives.
Dans un souci de concision et de clarté, on a modifié les définitions chaque fois que
    possible en vue d'y inclure des termes précédemment définis dans le vocabulaire.
Tout terme utilisé dans une définition qui est dans un autre endroit du vocabulaire
    est signalé comme tel.
Bien entendu, ces principes n'ont pu être strictement respectés. Le lecteur jugera peut-
être dans certains cas que des définitions données ailleurs sont plus claires, mieux reliées
aux autres et plus systématiques. Mais, à notre connaissance, c'est la première fois que
l'élaboration d'un vocabulaire de cette espèce est entreprise sur le plan international.
Le présent répertoire peut donc être considéré, dans une certaine mesure, comme
unique en son genre, et l'on espère qu'il rendra plus de services qu'un recueil de définitions de type classique.

1.6 Sujets couverts

Compte tenu de l'évolution observée ces dernières années, il est apparu nécessaire
d'insister tout particulièrement sur les éléments suivants:
Les problèmes linguistiques, en raison de l'introduction du traitement électronique
    des données dans le domaine de l'information et de la documentation;
La théorie de la communication, à cause de l'influence sans cesse croissante qu'exercent
    les sciences de l'information sur le plan pratique;
Les langages documentaires, parce que la mise au point de systèmes d'information
    automatiques a créé de nouveaux problèmes dans ce domaine (par exemple, à pro-
    pos des thesaurus);
Les techniques d'analyse, de conception et d'évaluation des systèmes élaborés depuis
    quelques années, parce qu'elles jouent un rôle d'une importance croissante sur le
    plan pratique;
Les notions fondamentales relatives au traitement électronique de l'information, parce
    que de nombreux systèmes utilisent déjà ou utiliseront ces procédés.
Il convient de souligner que le présent vocabulaire ne saurait en aucun cas remplacer
les vocabulaires spécialisés existants qui portent sur le traitement électronique de
l'information, la linguistique ou la cybernétique.
Il vise à fournir aux spécialistes de l'information et de la documentation un instrument qui leur permettra de participer aux échanges d'informations techniques sur les
sujets dont ils s'occupent, et à faciliter l'orientation de ceux qui s'intéressent aux divers
aspects de ce domaine d'activité.

1.7 Langues

Établir un vocabulaire technique qui soit en même temps un dictionnaire multilingue
n'est pas chose aisée. Une analyse des vocabulaires et de la littérature spécialisée existants
a montré qu'il est impossible de parvenir à une concordance parfaite, ne fût-ce qu'entre

deux langues. De nombreux termes anglo-américains sont intraduisibles en allemand, et inversement. L'introduction d'autres langues complique encore le problème.

Aussi a-t-il été décidé de choisir comme langue de base celle de la majorité des sources disponibles, c'est-à-dire l'anglais.

2 Structure de la terminologie

2.1 Observations générales

Dans l'ensemble, la structure du vocabulaire s'inspire des trois modèles suivants:
Le troisième projet de *Vocabularium documentationis*, établi par A. Thompson en 1964;
Le vocabulaire sur le traitement des données établi par l'ISO/TC/97/SC 1;
Les systèmes de renvoi utilisés dans les thesaurus.
Compte tenu de la nature du présent ouvrage, qui combine certaines caractéristiques d'un vocabulaire systématique avec celles d'un dictionnaire multilingue, il est apparu nécessaire de modifier certains des éléments fondamentaux des modèles et d'appliquer un ensemble particulier de règles.

2.2 Contenu des notices

Chacune des notices se compose des éléments ci-après:
Le terme principal, c'est-à-dire le terme anglais choisi pour figurer dans la liste alphabétique des notices que comprend le groupe dont il s'agit;
Les termes anglais considérés comme synonymes du terme principal;
Les équivalents français;
Les équivalents allemands;
Les équivalents russes;
Les équivalents espagnols;
Une ou plusieurs définitions du terme principal;
Autant d'indices qu'il y a de définitions par notice;
Des renvois aux termes employés dans les définitions;
Des renvois aux termes associés aux définitions.

2.3 Termes

On a suivi les règles ci-après:
Les termes anglais et français sont présentés sous la forme qu'ils revêtent dans un texte, c'est-à-dire entièrement en minuscules.
Les termes allemands sont présentés sous la forme qu'ils revêtent dans un texte, c'est-à-dire que la première lettre des substantifs est une majuscule.
Toutes les variantes orthographiques (mots composés d'éléments soudés, distincts ou reliés par un trait d'union) ne sont pas données.
Le terme principal est toujours en caractères gras.
En général, aucune distinction n'est faite entre les termes à employer de préférence, les termes tolérés et ceux qui sont déconseillés (l'ordre dans lequel ils sont cités fournit toutefois une indication quant aux préférences personnelles des auteurs).
Les termes dans une autre langue que l'anglais sont signalés par les symboles suivants:
F = français

D = allemand
R = russe
S = espagnol.

Le vocabulaire allemand pose un problème particulier du fait que les usages diffèrent
en Autriche, en Suisse, dans la République fédérale d'Allemagne et dans la République démocratique allemande. Dans la plupart des cas, aucune distinction n'est
faite; c'est seulement quand il existe des divergences considérables de sens entre
l'usage de la République fédérale d'Allemagne et celui de la République démocratique
allemande que les symboles ci-après ont été placés entre parenthèses après le terme
considéré:

(FRG) = terme préférentiel dans la République fédérale d'Allemagne;

(GDR) = terme préférentiel dans la République démocratique allemande.

Il arrive que certains équivalents du terme principal ne répondent pas à toutes les définitions figurant dans la notice. On précise alors quelle est la définition adéquate en
indiquant le numéro entre parenthèses après le terme, comme suit:

(1) = la définition (1) est valable;

(2) = la définition (2) est valable, etc.

2.4 Indices

Voici quelles ont été les règles suivies:

A chaque définition correspond un indice qui lui est propre. L'indice sert donc à identifier non la notice, mais une définition à l'intérieur de la notice.

L'indice est formé de trois éléments: deux (ou trois) chiffres indiquant le groupe auquel
appartient le terme défini; un trait d'union marquant une séparation; deux chiffres
qui constituent le numéro courant de chaque définition à l'intérieur du groupe, le
numéro de la première définition étant 01.

Les indices servent: de renvois à l'intérieur du vocabulaire; de renvois des index aux
notices.

2.5 Définitions

Les définitions ont été normalisées dans toute la mesure possible et dans certains cas
elles ont pu être abrégées grâce à l'emploi de termes définis précédemment dans le vocabulaire.

Pour faciliter l'accès aux termes utilisés dans les définitions, deux règles ont été
établies:

Les termes employés dans la définition et déjà définis dans le même groupe sont entre
guillemets (ex.: 'semiotics'). Ces termes ne font l'objet d'aucun nouveau renvoi.

Les termes employés dans la définition et définis dans un autre groupe sont en italique.
Les termes définis dans le vocabulaire en tant que substantifs qui sont employés dans
une autre définition sous une forme adjectivale ou verbale ne sont pas signalés comme
tels. Sont placés entre parenthèses, dans une définition, les éléments relativement moins
importants. Il en est de même des abréviations comme "i.e." (introduisant une expli-
cation) et "e.g." (introduisant un exemple).

2.6 Renvois à des termes associés aux définitions

On a jugé bon, pour aider l'utilisateur, d'indiquer certaines relations entre notions. Ces doubles renvois sont établis conformément à l'usage général, et non comme dans les thesaurus – où ils le sont en fonction des nécessités de l'indexation et de la recherche. Les doubles renvois aux autres définitions sont établis conformément aux règles suivantes:

La catégorie elle-même est indiquée par le symbole "REF". Ce symbole est suivi des termes principaux et de l'indice de la définition associée.

Chaque terme et chaque indice sont suivis des symboles ci-après, qui précisent la nature de la relation:

(BT) = terme générique (relation de supériorité d'un type quelconque);
(NT) = terme spécifique (relation de subordination d'un type quelconque);
(OT) = antonyme;
(RT) = terme associé (type de relation non spécifié).

Les termes faisant l'objet de renvois de cet ordre sont rangés dans l'ordre suivant:

(BT) – (NT) – (OT) – (RT).

3 Index

La *Terminologie* comprend cinq index alphabétiques: anglais; français; allemand; russe; espagnol.

Figurent à l'index:

Tous les termes contenus dans le vocabulaire, c'est-à-dire non seulement les termes principaux, mais aussi les équivalents;

Tous les éléments du terme jugés significatifs, c'est-à-dire qu'il s'agit d'index par rotation (le texte donné après le mot vedette suivant l'ordre normal des mots).

Autrement dit, dans l'index anglais, par exemple, l'expression "needle-operated punched card" apparaîtra sous les trois formes suivantes:

"card, needle-operated punched"
"needle-operated punched card"
"punched card, needle-operated".

Chaque entrée de l'index comprend le terme et le (ou les) indice(s) correspondant à sa (ou ses) définition(s).

Un index distinct donne les indices de la CDU pour les sujets sur lesquels porte le vocabulaire. Chacun de ces indices renvoie au groupe ou à la notice pertinente dans le corps du vocabulaire.

4 Bibliographie des sources

Cette bibliographie énumère tous les documents dont on a tiré parti directement ou indirectement au cours de l'élaboration du vocabulaire. D'autres sources qui pourraient présenter de l'intérêt pour les utilisateurs ont également été incluses; cependant aucune publication antérieure à 1960 n'a été prise en considération. Les titres sont classés d'après la (ou les) langue(s) de parution.

Einleitung

1. Allgemeines

1.1 Hintergrund

Aufgrund eines Kontraktes zwischen Unesco und FID legte 1962 Anthony Thompson auf der FID-Konferenz in Scheveningen einen ersten Entwurf eines *Vocabularium documentationis* vor. Ein zweiter Entwurf wurde im November 1963 vorgelegt, ein dritter im Juni 1964. Der dritte Entwurf mit ca. 1 200 Benennungen und deren Definitionen in Englisch und Äquivalenten in Französisch, Deutsch, Russisch und Spanisch wurde während der Sitzung des FID-Studienkomitees für Sprachfragen im September 1964 in Scheveningen diskutiert, aber nicht publiziert.

Im November 1970 unternahm die Unesco einen zweiten Anlauf zur Erarbeitung eines *Vocabularium documentationis*. In der Zwischenzeit hatte sich die Situation grundlegend verändert: Eine Reihe von Zusammenstellungen von Definitionen im Bereich der Dokumentation waren publiziert worden (siehe Bibliographie, S. 47); in einer Reihe von Ländern waren Komitees zur Vereinheitlichung und Normung der Terminologie der Information und Dokumentation eingerichtet worden; seit 1969 hatte sich eine Arbeitsgruppe des Technischen Komitees der ISO (ISO/TC 46) bemüht, eine internationale Norm der Terminologie der Information und Dokumentation zu erarbeiten.

1.2 Arbeitsabschnitte

Im Rahmen eines Unesco-Kontrakts wurde 1971 eine vorläufige Version der *Terminology of documentation* zusammengestellt, die ca. 1 200 englische Benennungen mit Definitionen in Englisch sowie französische und deutsche Äquivalente enthielt. Diese vorläufige Version wurde einer großen Zahl von Experten zur Stellungnahme zugeleitet. Ihre Kommentare wurden im Rahmen eines Unesco-Kontrakts 1973 in eine revidierte Version eingearbeitet. Die französischen Äquivalente wurden anderen mehrsprachigen Quellen entnommen und dann von AFNOR überarbeitet. Die deutschen Äquivalente wurden mit dem Komitee Terminologie und Sprachfragen der Deutschen Gesellschaft für Dokumentation diskutiert. Im Rahmen eines Unesco-Kontrakts wurden die russischen Äquivalente von VINITI erarbeitet und ohne Änderung übernommen. Die spanischen Äquivalente wurden von A. Sandoval zusammengestellt, einer Reihe von Experten gesandt und in revidierter Form in die endgültige Version eingearbeitet.

1.3 Ordnungssystem

Weder die DK, noch die Ordnungssysteme der ISO/TC 46 Arbeitsgruppe schienen vollständig für die sachliche Ordnung der Terminologie geeignet zu sein.

Es wurde daher vorgezogen, einen Mittelweg zwischen alphabetischer und detaillierter systematischer Anordnung zu beschreiten, indem die Benennungen pragmatisch in Großgruppen gegliedert, aber innerhalb der Gruppen alphabetisch angeordnet wurden. Dies ermöglicht den Zugriff zu den Benennungen jeweils eines wesentlichen Teilbereichs der Information und Dokumentation. Ein spezifischerer Zugriff zu Begriffsbezeichnungen, wie er bei Verwendung einer sehr detaillierten Klassifikation ermöglicht würde, wurde durch andere Hilfsmittel angestrebt (vgl. Abschnitt 2.6).

Für die Konstituierung der Gruppen waren drei Gesichtspunkte ausschlaggebend: Erstens Benennungen zusammenzuführen, die zu einem bestimmten Bereich des gegebenen Sachgebiets gehören, z.B. Benennungen, die zu Lochkartensystemen gehören; Zweitens Benennungen zusammenführen, die derselben Facette des gegebenen Sachgebiets zugehören, z.B. Benennungen für spezifische Systeme; Drittens sollten nicht zu viele Benennungen zu einer Gruppe zusammengefaßt werden. Deshalb wurde versucht, nicht mehr als ca. 60 Benennungen zu einer Gruppe zusammenzufassen.

Ein Register der Dezimalklassifikation ermöglicht den Zugang durch DK- Zahlen.

1.4 Quellen

Die folgenden Quellen erwiesen sich als große Hilfe bei der Auswahl von Benennungen und Definitionen:
Die 11 Wörterbücher, die Florence Casey für COSATI zusammengefaßt hatte (B7)
Die Arbeit des Subcommittee OC/20/12 (Dokumentations-Terminologie) des Committee OC/20 Dokumentations-Normen der British Standards Institution (B6)
Die Arbeit des Subcommittee 1 (Terminologie der Datenverarbeitung) des ISO Technical Committee 97, Computer und Datenverarbeitung (A10)
Die Arbeit der Working Group 3 (Terminologie) des ISO Technical Committee 46, Dokumentation (A6, A7).
Weiterhin wurden die Quellen, die in Kap. 4 verzeichnet sind, benutzt. Die Hauptquellen für die einzelnen Gruppen der Terminologie waren die folgenden:
  1 Grundlegende Aspekte der Information und Dokumentation
 11 Wissenschaften mit Bedeutung für Information und Dokumentation: B 7
 12 Begriffe: A6, A7, A16, D3, D20, D21 (1)
 13 Grundlegende Elemente der Darstellung: A5, A6, A10 (01, 04), D3, D21 (1)
 14 Sprachelemente: A6, A7, A10 (01, 04), B19, D3, D20, D21 (1)
 15 Sprachtypen: A7, A10 (10), D4, D21 (1)
 16 Darstellung von Wortsammlungen: A6, A7, B19
 17 Kommunikations- und Informationstheorie: A7, B7, D20, D21 (2)
 18 Umsetzung und Codierung: A10 (01, 04), B7
 19 Informationsverbreitung: B6, B7
110 Reprographie und Druck: A4, B6

2 Dokumente
21 Typen von Dokumenten: B6, B7
22 Teile von Dokumenten: B6, B7
3 Aktivitäten in Information und Dokumentation
31 Hauptaktivitäten in Information und Dokumentation: B6, B7
32 Kataloge und Katalogisierung: B6, B7
33 Dateien und Einträge in Dateien: B6, B7
34 Anordnung von Dateien: B6, B7
35 Indexierung und Register: B6, B7
36 Elemente von Dokumentationssprachen: B6, B7, D15
37 Dokumentationssprachen vom Thesaurus-Typ: B6, B7, D15
38 Begriffs-, Bezeichnungs- und Klassenbeziehungen: A6, A7, A16, B7
39 Elemente und Prinzipien von Klassifikationen: A16, B6, B7
310 Notationen und Nummern: B6, B7
311 Klassifikationstypen: B6, B7
312 Speicherung: A10 (18), B6
313 Retrieval: A10, B6, B7
314 Referatendienst und Informationsdienst
315 Bibliographische Dienste: B6, B7, D8
4 Systeme in Information und Dokumentation
41 Systemtypen: A7, B7, B20
42 Elektronische Datenverarbeitung: A10
43 Lochkartensysteme: A7, A17, D19
44 Systemanalyse und -entwurf: A7, B20
45 Systemtest und -bewertung: B20, D5
46 Benutzungs- und Benutzeranalyse: B6, B7
5 Organisationen und Berufe in Information und Dokumentation
51 Organisationen: B6, B7, D7
52 Berufe: B6, B7

1.5 Definitionen

Die Einbringung von Definitionen in die Terminologie brachte einige Schwierigkeiten
mit sich, da:
Viele bestehende Wörterbücher unterschiedliche Definitionen für dieselbe Benennung
    anbieten;
Diese Definitionen sich oft nicht sachlich, sondern nur im Wortlaut unterscheiden;
In einigen der wichtigsten Wörterbücher recht gute Zusammenstellungen von Defini-
    tionen enthalten sind;
Wörterbücher oft Definitionen einer anderen Quelle ohne Quellenangabe übernehmen.
Die folgende Regelung wurde getroffen:
Von den in der Literatur gefundenen Definitionen wurde diejenige ausgewählt, die
    sachlich am richtigsten schien und den klarsten Wortlaut hatte. Nur wenn unter-
    schiedliche Begriffe durch die gleiche Benennung bezeichnet wurden, wurden unter-
    schiedliche Definitionen angenommen.
Für ähnliche Bezeichnungen (z. B. Bezeichnungen für Systeme) wurde versucht, einen
    Standardtext zu entwickeln, in den die Definitionsunterschiede eingesetzt werden
    konnten.
Um größere Genauigkeit und Klarheit zu erreichen, wurde der Wortlaut der Defini-
    tionen wo möglich geändert, um Benennungen einzufügen, die in der Terminologie
    ohnehin definiert worden sind.

Innerhalb jeder Definition ist jede Benennung, die an anderer Stelle in der Terminologie definiert ist, entsprechend gekennzeichnet.
Dieser Regelung konnte natürlich nicht immer konsequent gefolgt werden. Der Benutzer wird eine Reihe von Fällen finden, in denen nach seiner Auffassung Definitionen aus anderen Quellen verständlicher, besser mit anderen verknüpft und systematischer sind. Andererseits wurde nach unserem Wissen bisher kein ähnlicher Versuch auf internationaler Ebene unternommen, ein Wörterbuch auf diese Art und Weise zusammenzustellen. Bis zu einem gewissen Grade kann die hier vorgelegte Terminologie daher als einmalig gelten, von der wir hoffen, daß sie dem Benutzer wirkungsvoller dient, als es traditionelle Definitionssammlungen tun würden.

1.6 Sachgebiete

Die Entwicklung der letzten Jahre machte es notwendig, besonders die folgenden Gebiete zu berücksichtigen:
Linguistische Probleme, besonders wegen der Einführung der elektronischen Datenverarbeitung im Bereich der Information und Dokumentation;
Kommunikationstheorie, wegen der ständig wachsenden Bedeutung der Informationswissenschaften für die praktische Arbeit;
Dokumentationssprachen, da die Entwicklung der computergestützten Informationssysteme neue Probleme in diesem Bereich hervorgebracht hat (z.B. Thesauri);
Systemanalyse, -entwurf und -bewertung, da diese in den letzten Jahren entwickelten Techniken für die praktische Arbeit zunehmend Bedeutung erlangen;
Allgemeine Begriffe der elektronischen Datenverarbeitung, da viele Systeme bereits dieses Hilfsmittel verwenden oder es in Zukunft tun werden.
Dabei muß betont werden, daß die vorgelegte Terminologie kein Ersatz sein kann für Spezialwörterbücher für Bereiche wie elektronische Datenverarbeitung, Linguistik oder Kybernetik.
Sie versucht, den in Information und Dokumentation Tätigen ein Hilfsmittel zu sein, das es ihnen ermöglicht, an der fachlichen Kommunikation in ihrem Bereich sich zu beteiligen und im Gesamtgebiet der Information und Dokumentation zu orientieren.

1.7 Sprachen

Die Zusammenstellung eines Fachwörterbuchs, das gleichzeitig mehrsprachig sein soll, ist keine einfache Aufgabe. Aus der Untersuchung der existierenden Wörterbücher und der wesentlichen Fachliteratur ergab sich, daß eine perfekte Abstimmung von nur zwei Sprachen nicht durchführbar war. Es mußte festgestellt werden, daß viele Benennungen des anglo-amerikanischen Gebrauchs nicht ins Deutsche übersetzt werden konnten und umgekehrt. Die Berücksichtigung anderer Sprachen machte die Situation noch komplizierter.
Es wurde daher beschlossen, Englisch als die Leitsprache zu wählen, da die meisten verfügbaren Quellen in Englisch verfaßt waren.

2   Struktur der Terminologie

2.1 Allgemeine Bemerkungen

Im allgemeinen folgt die Präsentation der Terminologie den folgenden drei Vorbildern:
Dem dritten Entwurf von A. Thompson von 1964;
Der Arbeit von /50/TC 97/SC 1 bezüglich des Wörterbuchs der Datenverarbeitung;
Der Verweisungstechnik von Thesauri.
Um eine Kombination von sachlich geordneter Terminologie und mehrsprachigem Wörterbuch zu erreichen, war es notwendig, einige der wesentlichen Bestandteile der Vorbilder abzuändern und ein eigenes Regelwerk festzulegen.

2.2 Einträge

Ein Eintrag in diese Terminologie besteht aus:
Der Leitbenennung, d.h. der englischen Benennung, die für die alphabetische Einord-
    nung des Eintrags innerhalb der Gruppe ausgewählt wurde;
Englischen Benennungen, die als Synonyme zur Leitbenennung angesehen werden;
Französischen Äquivalenten;
Deutschen Äquivalenten;
Russischen Äquivalenten;
Spanischen Äquivalenten;
Einer oder mehreren Definitionen der Leitbenennung;
So vielen Verweisnummern, als Definitionen im Eintrag vorhanden sind;
Verweisungen auf Benennungen, die in der Definition enthalten sind;
Verweisungen auf Benennungen, die in begrifflicher Beziehung zu der Definition stehen.

2.3 Benennungen

Die folgenden Regeln werden verwendet:
Die englischen und französischen Benennungen wurden in der gleichen Schreibweise aufgeführt, in der sie im Text erscheinen, d.h. ohne Großschreibung.
Die deutschen Benennungen wurden in der gleichen Schreibweise aufgeführt, in der sie im Text erscheinen, d.h. Großbuchstaben am Beginn eines Substantivs.
Nicht alle Schreibweisenvarianten (insbesondere bezüglich der zusammengesetzten Benennungen) wurden aufgeführt.
Die Leitbenennung ist immer im Fettdruck.
Im allgemeinen wurde nicht unterschieden nach Vorzugsbenennungen, zugelassenen oder zurückgewiesenen Benennungen (allerdings gibt die Reihenfolge häufig einen Hinweis auf die mehr persönlichen Präferenzen der Autoren).
Die Benennungen, die nicht in englischer Sprache sind, werden folgendermaßen gekennzeichnet:
    F = Französisch
    D = Deutsch
    R = Russisch
    S = Spanisch.
Ein spezielles Problem entsteht beim Deutschen aufgrund des unterschiedlichen Sprachgebrauchs in Österreich, Schweiz, der Bundesrepublik Deutschland und der Deutschen Demokratischen Republik. In den meisten Fällen wurden diese Unter-

scheidungen nicht berücksichtigt; nur in Fällen, wo Bedeutungen erheblich zwischen der Bundesrepublik Deutschland und der Deutschen Demokratischen Republik variieren, ist dies durch nachgesetzte Symbole angedeutet: (FRG) = vorgezogen in der Bundesrepublik Deutschland; (UDR) = vorgezogen in der Deutschen Demokratischen Republik.

In einigen Fällen konnten nicht alle Äquivalente der Leitbenennung allen Definitionen des Eintrags zugeordnet werden. Hier wurde die für die Benennung zutreffende Definition durch nachgesetzte Nummern gekennzeichnet: (1) = Definition (1) trifft zu; (2) = Definition (2) trifft zu, usw.

2.4 Numerierung

Die folgenden Regeln wurden verwendet:
Jede Definition hat eine eigene Verweisnummer. Die Verweisnummer identifiziert daher nicht den Eintrag, sondern die einzelne Definition innerhalb des Eintrags.

Die Verweisnummer besteht aus drei Teilen: zwei (oder drei) Stellen, die die Gruppe bezeichnen, zu der die definierte Benennung gehört; ein Bindestrich als Separator; zwei Stellen zur Bezeichnung der laufenden Nummer jeder Definition innerhalb einer Gruppe, beginnend mit 01 für die erste Definition.

Die Verweisnummern werden benutzt für: Verweisungen innerhalb der Terminologie; Verweisungen von Registern auf Einträge.

2.5 Definitionen

Es wurde versucht, die Definitionen so weit wie möglich zu vereinheitlichen. Häufig war es möglich, sie dadurch präziser zu gestalten, daß Benennungen verwendet wurden, die an anderer Stelle der Terminologie bereits definiert wurden.

Um den Zugriff zu den in den Definitionen verwendeten Benennungen zu ermöglichen, wurden zwei Festlegungen getroffen:

Benennungen, die in der Definition verwendet und in der gleichen Gruppe definiert sind, stehen zwischen Gänsefüßchen (' '). Auf diese Benennungen wird nicht weiter verwiesen.

Benennungen, die in der Definition verwendet und in einer anderen Gruppe definiert sind, werden kursiv gedruckt.

Benennungen, die in der Terminologie als Substantive definiert und in anderen Definitionen als Adjektiv oder Verb benutzt werden, sind nicht gesondert gekennzeichnet. Klammern in den Definitionen deuten an, daß es sich dabei um weniger wichtige Definitionsbestandteile handelt. Das gleiche gilt für Abkürzungen wie "i.e." (Erläuterungen) und "e.g." (Beispiele).

2.6 Verweisungen auf andere Begriffe

Um dem Benutzer weitere Hilfsmittel zu geben, erschien es angemessen, die Begriffsbeziehungen aufzuzeigen. Diese Verweisungen orientieren sich am allgemeinen Begriffsverständnis und nicht – wie in Thesauri – an den Notwendigkeiten von Indexierung und Retrieval. Verweisungen auf andere Definitionen sind nach folgenden Regeln angegeben:

Die Verweisungs-Kategorie selbst ist durch das Symbol "REF" angezeigt.

Auf das Symbol "REF" folgt die betreffende Leitbenennung und die Verweisnummer der betreffenden Definition.

Hinter jeder Benennung und Verweisnummer erläutern die folgenden Symbole die Begriffsbezeichnung:

(BT) = Oberbegriff (auf nicht weiter spezifizierte Weise übergeordnet);

(NT) = Unterbegriff (auf nicht weiter spezifizierte Weise hierarchisch untergeordnet);

(OT) = entgegengesetzter Begriff (Antonym);

(RT) = verwandter Begriff (keine Spezifizierung der Beziehung).

Die folgende Reihenfolge der Begriffsbeziehungen innerhalb dieser Kategorie wird eingehalten:

(BT) – (NT) – (OT) – (RT).

3 Register

Die Terminologie enthält 5 alphabetische Register: Englisch; Französisch; Deutsch; Russisch; Spanisch.

In jedem Register sind Einträge für:

jede Benennung, die im Hauptteil enthalten ist, d.h. nicht nur Leitbenennungen, sondern auch alle Äquivalente;

jeden Benennungsbestandteil, der für bedeutsam geachtet wurde, d.h. die Register sind rotierte Register (der Text, der dem Registereintrag folgt, ist in natürlicher Wortfolge angegeben).

Dies bedeutet, daß im deutschen Register z.B. die Benennung "Nadellochkarte" erscheint als:

"Karte, Nadelloch-";

"Lochkarte, Nadel-";

"Nadellochkarte".

Jeder Registereintrag besteht aus den Benennungen und den Verweisnummern der Benennung zugeordneten Definitionen.

4 Verzeichnis der Quellen

Das Verzeichnis enthält alle die Dokumente, die direkt oder indirekt bei der Zusammenstellung der Terminologie benutzt wurden. Andere Quellen, die möglicherweise für den Benutzer sinnvoll sein könnten, sind ebenfalls aufgenommen, allerdings wurden keine Quellen aufgenommen, die vor 1960 publiziert worden sind. Die Anordnung richtet sich nach der Sprache bzw. den Sprachen der jeweiligen Quellendokumente.

Введение

1 Общий раздел

1.1 История вопроса

В 1962 г. Антони Томпсон представил Конференции МФД в Швеннингене первый вариант проекта *Vocabularium Documentationis* (словарь по документации), составленный по контракту, заключенному между ЮНЕСКО и МФД. Второй вариант проекта был представлен в ноябре 1963 г. и третий в июне 1974 г. Третий вариант проекта, содержавший около 1200 терминов, с определениями на английском языке и их эквивалентами на немецком, испанском, французском и русском, обсуждался на совещании Комитета МФД по лингвистическим проблемам, проходившем в сентябре 1964 г. в Швеннингене, но он не был опубликован.

В ноябре 1970 г. ЮНЕСКО предприняла вторую попытку подготовить *Vocabularium Documentationis* (словарь по документации). К этому времени положение полностью изменилось. Был опубликован ряд сборников определений в области документации (см. библиографию, приведенную после Введения). В ряде стран были учреждены комитеты по стандартизации терминологии в области информации и документации. Начиная с 1969 года Рабочая группа 46 Технического комитета ИСО занималась выработкой международных терминологических стандартов в области информации и документации.

1.2 Этапы работы

В 1971 г. был составлен по контракту с ЮНЕСКО предварительный вариант «Терминологии в области документации», и в него вошло около 1200 английских терминов с определениями на английском языке, а также их французские и немецкие эквиваленты. Этот предварительный вариант был разослан на отзыв большому числу экспертов в этой области. Полученные замечания были затем включены в терминологию, которая пересматривалась по другому контракту

ЮНЕСКО в 1973 г. Французские эквиваленты, взятые из других многоязычных источников, были скорректированы Французской ассоциацией стандартов. Немецкие эквиваленты обсуждались с Комитетом по терминологии и лингвистическим проблемам Германского общества документации. По контракту с ЮНЕСКО русские эквиваленты были разработаны ВИНИТИ и включены без всяких изменений. Испанские эквиваленты, включенные доктором А. Сандовалом, были разосланы ряду специалистов, замечания которых были учтены в настоящем окончательном варианте.

1.3 Классификация

Ни Универсальная десятичная система классификации, ни классификационные схемы, разработанные Рабочей группы 46 ТК/ИСО, не представлялись полностью удовлетворительными для составления настоящего словаря.

Было, поэтому, решено выбрать нечто среднее между алфавитной системой и подробной предметной классификацией, сгруппировав термины в практических целях в широкие группы и разместив их в алфавитном порядке внутри этих групп. Это дает возможность найти термины по широким подобластям информации и документации. Для того, чтобы дать возможность устанавливать взаимосвязи концепций, что было бы возможно при использовании более подробных схем предметной классификации, использовались другие способы (см. пункт 2.6).

Для составления широких словарных групп наиболее существенными являются три аспекта:

Во-первых, собрать вместе термины, относящиеся к определенному разделу данной тематической области, например, термины, относящиеся к системам перфокарт.

Во-вторых, собрать вместе термины, касающиеся одной и той же стороны данной тематической области, например термины, обозначающие определенные системы.

В-третьих, избегать изобилия терминов в каждой отдельной области. Так было решено, что каждая тематическая область не должна содержать более 60 терминов.

С помощью индекса UDC можно пользоваться нотациями UDC.

1.4 Источники

При выборе терминов и определений оказались полезными следующие источники:

11 словарей, составленных Флоренс Кейзи для COSATI (В 7);

работа подкомитета ОС/20/12 по терминологии в области документации Комитета ОС/20 по стандартам в области документации Британского института стандартов (В 6);

работа подкомитета 1 по Словарю по обработке данных, Технического комитета 97 ИСО «Вычислительные машины и обработка информации» (А 10);

работа Рабочей группы 3 по терминологии Технического комитета 46 ИСО «Документация» (А 6, А 7).

Кроме того были использованы источники, перечисленные в разделе 4 — библиография.

Ниже приводятся основные источники по каждой группе, имеющейся в словаре:

1 Основные аспекты информации и документации.

11 Науки, связанные с информацией и документацией: В 7.

12 Понятия: A 6, A 7, A 16, D 3, D 20, D 21 (1).

13 Основные элементы изложения: A 5, A 6, A 10 (01, 04), D 3, D 21 (1).

14 Элементы языка: A 6, A 7, A 10 (01, O 4), B 19, D 3, D 20, D 21 (1).

15 Типы языков: A 7, A 10 (10), D 4, D 21 (1).

16 Оформление словарей: A 6, A 7, B 19.

17 Теория коммуникации и информации: A 7, B 7, D 20, D 21 (2).

18 Преобразование и кодирование: A 10 (01, 04), B 7.

19 Распространение информации: В 6, В 7.

110 Репрография и печатание: A 4, B 6.

2 Документы.

21 Типы документов: В 6, В 7.

22 Части документов: В 6, В 7.

3 Работа в области информации и документации.

31 Основные виды работ в области информации и документации: В 6, В 7.

32 Каталоги и составление каталогов: В 6, В 7.

33 Картотеки и записи в картотеках: В 6, В 7.

34 Структура картотек: В 6, В 7.

35 Составление указателей и указатели: В 6, В 7.

36 Элементы документационных языков: В 6, В 7, D 15.

37 Дескрипторные языки тезаурусного типа: В 6, В 7, D 15.

38 Взаимоотношения между понятием, термином и классом: A 6, A 7, A 16, B 7.

39 Элементы и принципы классификации: A 16, B 6, B 7.

310 Нотация и номера: В 6, В 7.

311 Типы классификации: В 6, В 7.

312 Хранение: A 10 (18), B 6.

313 Поиск: A 10, B 6, B 7.

314 Службы реферирования и информации.

315 Библиографические службы: В 6, В 7, D 8.

4 Системы в области информации и документации.

41 Типы систем: A 7, B 7, B 20.

42 Электронная обработка данных: A 10.

43 Системы перфокарт: A 7, A 17, D 19.

44 Анализ и проектирование систем: A 7, B 20.

45 Испытание и оценка систем: B 20, D 5.

46 Анализ использования и потребителя: В 6, В 7.

5 Организации и профессии в области информации и документации.

51 Организации: В 6, В 7, D 7.

52 Профессии и специальности: В 6, В 7.

1.5 Определения

Включение определений в словарь представляло определенные трудности потому что:

Многие существующие словари дают различные определения одного и того же понятия.

Эти определения часто различаются не по сути, а по способу выражения.

Существуют очень хорошие компиляции определений, данных в некоторых наиболее значительных словарях.

Словари часто берут определения из каких-либо других источников, неуказывая этот источник.

Было принято следующее решение:

Из различных определений, имеющихся в литературе, выбиралось одно, которое представлялось наиболее правильным по содержанию и наиболее четким по формулировке. Только в тех случаях, когда различные понятия определялись одним термином, включались различные определения.

Для аналогичных терминов (например, термины, определяющие системы), отыскивался стандартный текст, в который можно было бы включить различия в определениях.

Для краткости и четкости формулировки определений в случае необходимости менялись с тем, чтобы они охватывали термины, уже определенные в словаре.

В определении отмечается соответствующим образом каждый термин, которому дано определение в каком-либо другом месте настоящего словаря.

Конечно, эта работа не могла быть осуществлена повсеместно. Читатель может найти ряд моментов, когда, по его мнению, определения, данные в других источниках, изложены более понятно, систематично, лучше согласуются с другими. Но, насколько нам известно, на международном уровне еще никто не пытался решить аналогичную задачу составления такого словаря. В определенной степени настоящий словарь может поэтому рассматриваться как уникальный, и мы надеемся, что читатель найдет его более полезным, чем традиционная компиляция определений.

1.6 Объем

Прогресс, достигнутый в последние годы, привел к необходимости уделить особое внимание следующим вопросам:

Лингвистические проблемы в связи с тем, что электронная обработка данных вторгается в область информации и документации.

Теория коммуникации в связи со все растущим влиянием информационных наук на практическую работу.

Документационные языки в связи с развитием электронных информационных систем, что вызвало возникновение новых проблем в этой области (например, тезаурусы).

Анализ, проектирование и оценка систем, поскольку эти методы, разработанные в последние годы, становятся все более важными для практической работы.

Общие концепции электронной обработки данных, поскольку многие системы теперь используют эти устройства и будут использовать их в будущем.

Необходимо подчеркнуть, что настоящий словарь не заменяет и не может заменить собой существующие словари в специальных областях электронной обработки данных, лингвистики или кибернетики.

Он имеет целью предоставить специалистам в области информации и документации средство, которое даст им возможность включиться в общение на профессиональном уровне между людьми их профессии и поможет им ориентироваться в целом в области информации и документации.

1.7 Языки

Нелегкая задача составить технический и в то же время многоязычный словарь. Анализ существующих словарей и соответствующей литературы позволил понять что совершенная синхронизация даже двух языков невозможна. Было обнаружено, что многие термины англо-американского происхождения не могут быть переведены на немецкий язык и наоборот. Введение других языков сделало проблему еще более сложной.

Было решено поэтому выбрать английский язык как ведущий, потому что большинство имеющихся источников были на английском языке.

2 Структура словаря

2.1 Общие замечания

В целом при составлении словаря авторы следовали трем следующим моделям:
Работа, представленная А. Томпсоном при подготовке третьего варианта проекта в 1964 г.
Работа, проведенная ИСО/ТК 97/SC 1, при подготовке словаря по обработке данных.
Перекрестные ссылки в рамках резаурусов.
Чтобы объединить в одно целое тематический и многоязычный словарь, было необходимо выбрать основные элементы моделей и следовать конкретному набору правил.

2.2 Словарная статья

В каждую словарную статью входят:
Основной термин, например английский термин, взятый в алфавитном порядке статей в рамках одной группы.
Английские термины, которые рассматриваются как синонимы основного термина.
Французские эквиваленты.
Немецкие эквиваленты.
Русские эквиваленты.
Испанские эквиваленты.
Одно или несколько определений основного термина.
Ряд индексов, соответствующих числу определений в статье.
Перекрестные ссылки на термины, использованнье в определениях.
Перекрестные ссылки на термины, связанные с определениями.

2.3 Термины

При составлении словаря использовались следующие правила:
Английские и французские термины приводятся в том правописании, в котором они взяты из текста, т.е. без заглавных букв.
Немецкие термины пишутся так же, как они написаны в тексте, т.е. заглавная буква сохраняется в начале существительных.
Приводятся не все варианты написания (слитное, раздельное или написание через дефис).
Основной термин всегда выделен жирным шрифтом.
В принципе, не делается различия между предпочтительным, допускаемым и

нежелательным термином (но порядок их следования указывает на личное предпочтение автора).

Термины на любом языке, кроме английского, помечены соответствующими символами:

F=французский;

D=немецкий;

R=русский;

S=испанский;

Особая проблема возникает в связи с немецкой частью словаря, поскольку одни и те же термины используются по разному в Австрии, Швейцарии, Федеративной Республике Германии и Германской Демократической Республике. В большинстве случаев не делается никаких различий; только в тех случаях, когда термины имеют существенное различие в Федеративной Республике Германии и Германской Демократической Республике, в круглых скобках после соответствующего термина приводится значок:

(FRG) — чаще используется в Федеративной Республике Германии;

(GDR) — чаще используется в Германской Демократической Республике.

В некоторых случаях эквиваленты к основному термину могут не соответствовать всем определениям, приведенным в статье. В таких случаях определение, которое относится к данному термину, отмечается соответствующим номером, которое дается в круглых скобках после термина:

(1) — см. определение (1);

(2) — см. определение (2) и т. д.

2.4 Индексы

При составлении словаря авторы придерживались следующих правил:

Каждое определение имеет свой собственный индекс. Таким образом, индекс обозначает не всю словарную статью, а только определение, содержащееся внутри такой статьи.

Индекс состоит из трех частей: две (или три) цифры указывают на группу, к которой относится определяемый термин; дефис — в качестве разделителя; две цифры, обозначающие порядковый номер каждого определения в рамках одной группы, начиная с 01 для первого определения.

Индексы используются для: перекрестных ссылок в словаре; ссылок указателей на словарные статьи.

2.5 Определения

Были приняты меры для того, чтобы максимально стандартизировать определения. В некоторых случаях удалось сделать их более краткими за счет использования терминов, которым даны определения в других разделах словаря. Чтобы облегчить поиск терминов, использованных в определениях, было введено два правила:

Термины, использованные в определении и определенные в рамках той же группы, заключаются в кавычки. На термины, выделенные таким образом, дальнейших перекрестных ссылок не делается.

Термины, используемые в определении и определенные в другой группе словаря, выделяются курсивом.

Термины, которые определяются в словаре как существительные и используются в других определениях как прилагательные или глаголы, не подчеркиваются таким образом.

Внутри определений в скобках даются менее важные элементы определения. То же относится к сокращениям таким, как «i.e» (то есть) и «e.g.» (например).

2.6 Перекрестные ссылки на родственные термины, связанные с определениями

Представляется, что читателю было бы полезно дать указание на связи между концепциями. Эти перекрестные ссылки даются в соответствии с общепринятым употреблением, а не так, как в тезаурусах — в соответствии с необходимостью индексирования и поиска. Перекрестные ссылки на другие определения даются в соответствии со следующими правилами:

Сама категория обозначается символом "REF".

После символа "REF" идут основные термины и индекс соответствующего определения.

После каждого термина и индекса вставляются следующие символы для обозначения характера связи:

(BT) — более широкий термин (в определенном смысле выше по иерархии)

(NT) — более узкий термин (в определенном смысле ниже по иерархии)

(OT) — противоположный термин

(RT) — родственный термин (характер связи не уточняется)

Для терминов, на которые даются перекреестные ссылки в рамках данной категории, установлен следующий порядок

(BT) — (NT) — (OT) — (RT).

3 Указатели

Словарь имеет пять алфавитных указателей: английский, французский, немецкий, русский, испанский.

В каждом указателе имеются ссылки на словарные статьи по:

Каждому термину, имеющемуся в словаре, т. е. не только по основному термину, но также по его эквививалентам,

Каждому элементу термина, который считается важным, т. е. указатели являются переменными (текст, следующий за словом, с которого начинается словарная статья, имеет естественный порядок слов).

Это означает, что в английском указателе, например, термин 'needle-operated punched card', будет изложен следующим образом:

card, needle-operated punched

needle-operated punched card

punched card, needle-operated.

Каждая статья указателя содержит термин и индекс(ы), относящиеся к определению(ям) термина.

В отдельном указателе перечисляются номера UDC, которые относятся к темам, охватываемым словарем.

Каждая словарная статья относится к соответствующей группе или статье в основной части словаря.

4 Библиография источников

В библиографию включены все документы, которые прямо или косвенно использовались при подготовке словаря. Сюда также включены другие источники, которые могут оказаться полезными читателю; однако авторами не использовались источники, вышедшие до 1960 года. Источники располагаются в соответствии с языком или языками соответствующего источника.

Introducción

1 Consideraciones generales

1.1 Antecedentes

En 1962, Anthony Thompson presentó a la conferencia de la FID que se celebraba en Scheveningen, un primer anteproyecto de *Vocabularium documentationis*, compilado en virtud de un contrato entre la Unesco y la FID. En noviembre de 1963 se presentó un segundo proyecto, y en junio de 1964 un tercero. Este tercer proyecto, que contenía unos 1 200 términos, con sus definiciones en inglés y sus equivalentes en alemán, español, francés y ruso, fue examinado en la reunión del Comité de Problemas Lingüísticos de la FID –que se celebró en Scheveningen en septiembre de 1964– pero no ha sido publicado.

En noviembre de 1970, la Unesco hizo un segundo intento de preparar un *Vocabularium documentationis*. Para entonces, la situación había cambiado totalmente. Se habían publicado ya varias compilaciones de definiciones en materia de documentación (véase la bibliografía de la p. 47). En varios países se habían creado comités de normalización de la terminología utilizada en la información y la documentación. Desde 1969, un grupo de trabajo del Comité Técnico 46 de la ISO se viene dedicando a establecer unas normas internacionales aplicables a la terminología de la información y la documentación.

1.2 Fases de este trabajo

En 1971 se compiló, con arreglo a un contrato de la Unesco, una versión preliminar de la *Terminología de la documentación*, que contenía unos 1 200 términos ingleses, su definición en este idioma y sus equivalentes en alemán y en francés. Esta versión preliminar fue distribuida a un gran número de expertos en este campo para que formularan las oportunas observaciones y comentarios. Los comentarios y observaciones recibidos fueron incorporados a la terminología, que se procedió a revisar, con arreglo a otro contrato de la Unesco, en 1973. Los equivalentes franceses se tomaron de otras fuentes plurilingües y fueron corregidos por la AFNOR; los equivalentes alemanes fueron examinados conjuntamente con el Comité de Terminología y Problemas Lingüísticos de la Sociedad Alemana de Documentación. Con arreglo a un contrato de la Unesco, la VINITI preparó los equivalentes en ruso, que quedaron incluidos sin modificación alguna. Los equivalentes en español, añadidos por el Dr. A. Sandoval, fueron enviados a diversos especialistas, cuyos comentarios y observaciones han quedado incorporados en esta versión definitiva.

1.3 Clasificación

Ni la Clasificación Decimal Universal ni los planes de clasificación elaborados por el grupo de trabajo del Comité Técnico de la ISO (ISO/TC 46) parecían plenamente adecuados para la presentación del vocabulario.

Se decidió, por ello, adoptar un sistema intermedio entre el orden alfabético y una clasificación detallada, agrupando los términos de un modo pragmático en grandes categorías y colocándolos por orden alfabético en cada una de ellas. De este modo se puede tener acceso a los términos de un subsector general de la información y la documentación. Se buscó por otros medios un acceso más detallado a las relaciones conceptuales, que podía lograrse mediante un plan de clasificación muy pormenorizado (véase el párrafo 2.6).

Tres fueron los criterios essenciales al preparar esas grandes categorías:

En primer lugar, ensamblar unos términos pertenecientes a un aspecto dado de un sector general, por ejemplo, los referentes a los sistemas de tarjetas perforadas.

En segundo lugar, ensamblar los términos correspondientes a una misma faceta de un sector dado, por ejemplo, los que designan sistemas concretos.

En tercer lugar, evitar la inclusión de un número excesivo de términos en una sola categoría. Se decidió, por ello, que no debía haber más de unos 60 términos en cada grupo.

Un índice de la Clasificación Decimal Universal (CDU) permite el acceso a las categorías de este sistema de clasificación.

1.4 Fuentes

Para determinar los términos y las definiciones resultaron de gran utilidad las siguientes fuentes:

Los once vocabularios compilados por Florence Casey para la COSATI (B7).

Los trabajos del Subcomité OC/120/12 *(Documentation Terminology)*, del Comité OC/20, *(Documentation Standard)* de la British Standards Institution (B6).

Los trabajos del Subcomité 1 (Vocabulario de tratamiento de datos), del Comité Técnico 97 (Computadoras y tratamiento de la información) de la ISO (A10).

Los trabajos del Grupo de Trabajo 3 (Terminología) del Comité Técnico 46 de la ISO (Documentación) (16, 17).

Se emplearon además las fuentes enumeradas en la sección 4 de la Bibliografía.

A continuación se indican las fuentes principales de cada una de las categorías del vocabulario:

  1 Aspectos básicos de la información y la documentación
  11 Ciencias relacionadas con la información y la documentación: B7
  12 Conceptos: A6, A7, A16, D3, D20, D21(1)
  13 Elementos básicos de representación: A5, A6, A10 (01, 04), D3, D21(1)

14 Elementos del lenguaje: A6, A7, A10 (01,04), B19, D3, D20, D21(1)
15 Tipos de lenguaje: A7, A10(10), D4, D21(1)
16 Representación de vocabularios: A6, A7, B19
17 Teoría de la comunicación y la información: A7, B7, D20, D21(1)
18 Conversión y codificación: A10 (01,04), B7
19 Difusión de la información: B6, B7
110 Reprografía e impresión: A4, B6
2 Documentos
21 Tipos de documentos: B6, B7
22 Partes de los documentos: B6, B7
3 Actividades de información y documentación
31 Principales actividades de información y documentación: B6, B7
32 Catálogos y catalogación: B6, B7
33 Archivos y asientos de los archivos: B6, B7
34 Estructura de los archivos: B6, B7
35 Índices e indizado: B6, B7
36 Elementos de los lenguajes documentales: B6, B7, D15
37 Lenguajes descriptores de tipo tesauro: B6, B7, D15
38 Relaciones de conceptos, términos y clases: A6, A7, A16, B7
39 Elementos y principios de clasificación: A16, B6, B7
310 Notación y números: B6, B7
311 Tipos de clasificación: B6, B7
312 Almacenamiento y memorias: A10(18), B6
313 Recuperación: A10 (18), B6, B7
314 Resúmenes y servicio de información
315 Servicios bibliográficos: B6, B7, D8
4 Sistemas de información y documentación
41 Tipos de sistemas: A7, B7, B20
42 Tratamiento (procesamiento) electrónico de datos: A10
43 Sistemas de tarjetas perforadas: A7, A17, D19
44 Análisis y diseño de sistemas: A7, B20
45 Evaluación y pruebas de un sistema: B20, D5
46 Aprovechamiento y análisis de usuarios: B6, B7
5 Organizaciones y profesiones del sector de la información y la documentación
51 Organizaciones: B6, B7, D7
52 Profesiones y tipos de ocupaciones: B6, B7

1.5 Definiciones

La inclusión de definiciones en el vocabulario entrañaba ciertas dificultades, ya que:
Muchos vocabularios dan definiciones distintas de un mismo término.
A menudo, estas definiciones no difieren en su contenido, pero sí en su formulación.
Algunos de los vocabularios más importantes contienen unas compilaciones muy buenas de definiciones.
Los vocabularios adoptan con frecuencia definiciones procedentes de otra fuente sin indicar esa procedencia.
Se siguieron los siguientes criterios:
De entre las diversas definiciones existentes en las obras especializadas, se escogió la que parecía más exacta en cuanto a su contenido y más clara en su formulación. Unicamente cuando un mismo término designa varios temas se dan varias definiciones.

En el caso de términos similares (por ejemplo, los que designan sistemas) se buscó un texto uniforme al que puedan añadirse las diferencias de definición.

A efectos de mayor concisión y claridad, se ha modificado – siempre que ha sido posible – la redacción de las definiciones con objeto de incluir los términos definidos ya en el vocabulario.

Dentro de una misma definición, se indica cada uno de los términos definidos en otro lugar de la terminología.

Como es lógico, no fue posible llevar a cabo este trabajo de un modo constante y uniforme. Quien consulte esta obra encontrará quizá varios casos en los que, a su juicio, las definiciones dadas en otras fuentes resultan más inteligibles, están mejor relacionadas entre sí y son más sistemáticas. Pero no nos consta que se haya hecho en el plano internacional ningún intento similar para compilar de este modo un vocabulario. Cabe, pues, considerar en cierta medida que la presente obra constituye un vocabulario único en su género y esperar que resultará más útil que una compilación tradicional de definiciones.

1.6 Alcance

La evolución característica de los últimos años ha obligado a asignar una importancia especial a:

Los problemas lingüísticos, debido a la introducción del tratamiento (procesamiento), electrónico de datos en el sector de la información y la documentación.

La teoría de la comunicación, dada la creciente influencia de las ciencias de la información sobre el trabajo práctico.

Los lenguajes documentales, ya que la aparición de sistemas de información automatizada ha suscitado problemas nuevos a este respecto (como ejemplo, los tesauros).

Las técnicas de evaluación, diseño y análisis de sistemas, porque esas nuevas técnicas, surgidas en los últimos años, están cobrando una importancia cada vez mayor a efectos del trabajo práctico.

Los conceptos generales del tratamiento electrónico de datos, dado que en muchos sistemas se utilizan ya, o se utilizarán en el futuro, estos métodos.

Procede destacar que el presente vocabulario no es, y no puede ser, un sucedáneo de los vocabularios ya existentes en los campos especiales del tratamiento electrónico de datos, la lingüística o la cibernética.

Su finalidad consiste en proporcionar a los especialistas en información y documentación un instrumento que les permita participar en la comunicación técnica de su especialidad, y en ofrecer un medio de orientación en todo el sector de la información y la documentación.

1.7 Idiomas

La compilación de un vocabulario técnico y, al mismo tiempo, de un diccionario plurilingüe no es una tarea fácil. Partiendo del análisis de los vocabularios existentes y de los textos pertinentes, su pudo comprobar que no resultaba factible una armonización perfecta, ni siquiera de dos idiomas. Se observó que muchos términos de uso angloamericano no podían traducirse al alemán, y viceversa. La introducción de otros idiomas complicó aún más la situación.

Se decidió, por ello, escoger el inglés como idioma guía, ya que la mayoría de las fuentes disponibles estaban escritas en ese idioma.

2 Estructura del vocabulario

2.1 Observaciones generales

En general, la presentación del vocabulario se inspira en los tres modelos siguientes:
El trabajo propuesto por A. Thompson al preparar el tercer proyecto en 1964.
El trabajo realizado por el subcomité ISO/TC 97/SC 1 al preparar el vocabulario de tratamiento de datos.
Unos reenvíos recíprocos de los tesauros.
Para llegar a una combinación de vocabulario sistemático y de diccionario plurilingüe, fue necesario adaptar algunos de los elementos esenciales de los modelos y aplicar una serie predeterminada de reglas.

2.2 Asientos

En este vocabulario, un asiento consiste en:
El término principal, esto es, el término inglés escogido para la ordenación alfabética de los asientos en cada categoría;
Los términos ingleses considerados como sinónimos del principal;
Los equivalentes franceses;
Los equivalentes alemanes;
Los equivalentes rusos;
Los equivalentes españoles;
Una o más definiciones del término principal;
Tantos números índices como definiciones haya en el asiento;
Unos reenvíos a términos empleados en la definición;
Unos reenvíos a términos relacionados con la definición.

2.3 Términos

Se han establecido las siguientes reglas:
Los términos ingleses y franceses se presentan con la misma ortografía con la que figuran en un texto, esto es, sin mayúsculas.
Los términos alemanes se ortografían como figuran en un texto, esto es, se utilizan las mayúsculas iniciales en los sustantivos.
No se enumeran todas las variantes ortográficas (compuestos de una sola palabra, entrecortados por un guión o por un espacio en blanco).
Se subraya siempre el término principal.
En general, no se establece distinción alguna entre términos preferidos, tolerados o postergados (pero su orden de sucesión indica las preferencias personales de los autores).
Los términos de un idioma que no sea el inglés llevan los siguientes símbolos:
F = francés
D = alemán
R = ruso
S = español
Se plantea un problema especial en el caso del vocabulario alemán debido a las diferentes modalidades de uso en Austria, Suiza, la República Federal de Alemania y la República Democrática Alemana. En la mayoría de los casos, no se hace distin-

ción alguna; tan sólo cuando el significado difiere considerablemente en la República Federal de Alemania y en la República Democrática Alemana se han añadido unos símbolos entre paréntesis después del término de que se trate:

(FRG) = preferido en la República Federal de Alemania

(GDR) = preferido en la República Democrática Alemana

En ciertas ocasiones, no todas las definiciones enunciadas en el asiento se refieren a los equivalentes del término principal. En tal caso, la definición que se aplica al término viene indicada por el número correspondiente que figura entre paréntesis después del termino:

(1) = se aplica la definición (1)

(2) = se aplica la definición (2), etc.

2.4 Números índices

Se han seguido las siguientes reglas:

Cada definición lleva un número índice propio. Por consiguiente, el número índice no identifica el asiento sino una definición contenida en él.

El número índice tiene tres partes: dos (o tres) cifras, que indican la categoría a la que pertenece el término definido; un guión de separación; otras dos cifras que indican el número de orden de cada definición en una categoría dada, a partir de 01 en el caso de la primera de ellas.

Los números índice se utilizan para: los reenvíos recíprocos dentro del vocabulario; los reenvíos de los índices a los asientos.

2.5 Definiciones

Se ha procurado normalizar al máximo las definiciones. En ciertos casos ha sido posible hacerlas más concisas empleando términos definidos ya en otros puntos del vocabulario. Para facilitar el acceso a los términos utilizados en las definiciones se han aplicado estas dos reglas:

Los términos empleados en la definición y definidos en esa misma categoría están entre comillas. No se hacen otros reenvíos a los términos subrayados de este modo.

Los términos empleados en la definición y definidos en otra categoría del vocabulario están en cursiva.

Los términos definidos en el vocabulario como sustantivos y empleados en otra definición en forma adjetivada o verbal no están señalados en esa forma. Los paréntesis que figuran en las definiciones indican elementos menos importantes de la definición.

Lo mismo cabe decir de abreviaturas tales como "i. a." (explicaciones) y "e. g." (ejemplos).

2.6 Reenvíos a términos relacionados con la definición

Se ha estimado apropiado indicar las relaciones conceptuales para facilitar la consulta del vocabulario. Esos reenvíos han sido establecidos siguiendo el uso general, y no como en los tesauros, según unas necesidades de indizado y localización (recuperación). Se hacen los reenvíos a otras definiciones con arreglo a las siguientes reglas:

Esta clase de reenvíos viene indicada por el símbolo "REF".

El símbolo REF viene seguido de los términos principales y del número índice de la definición asociado.

Después de cada término y de cada número índice se añaden los siguientes símbolos para especificar la relación:

(BT) = término genérico (en cierto sentido, jerárquicamente superior)
(NT) = término específico (en cierto sentido, jerárquicamente subordinado)
(OT) = término opuesto
(RT) = término asociado (no se especifica el tipo de asociación).

Se ha seguido el siguiente orden para los términos a los que reenvía dentro de esta categoría:

(BT – (NT) – (OT) – (RT).

3 Índices

El vocabulario tiene estos cinco índices alfabéticos: inglés, francés, alemán, ruso, español.

En cada índice figuran:

Cada uno de los términos comprendidos en el vocabulario, esto es, no solamente los principales sino también los equivalentes,

Cada elemento del término que se estima significativo, esto es, se trata de índices por rotación (el texto subsiguiente a la palabra inicial figura en el orden natural de las palabras).

Lo cual quiere decir que, en el índice inglés, un término como, por ejemplo "needle-operated punched card" figurará como

"card, needle-operated punched"
"needle operated punched card"
"punched card, needle operated"

Cada asiento del índice consiste en el término correspondiente y el número o números índice asignados a su definición o definiciones.

En otro índice figuran los números de la CDU que están relacionados con los temas comprendidos en el vocabulario. Cada asiento se refiere al asiento o a la categoría pertinente de la parte principal del vocabulario.

4 Bibliografía de fuentes

Se indican en la bibliografía todos los documentos que se utilizaron directa o indirectamente para preparar el vocabulario. También se señalan otras fuentes que pueden resultar de interés para el usuario, no se consultaron, sin embargo, las fuentes anteriores a 1960. Se ha seguido en la bibliografía el orden del idioma o idiomas del documento correspondiente.

Bibliography
Bibliographie
Verzeichnis
Библиография
Bibliografía

A Multilingual sources

A1 W. E. Clason. *Elsevier's dictionary of library science and documentation.* Amsterdam, London, New York, 1973. (English, French, Spanish, Italian, Dutch, German.)

A2 Deutscher Normenausschuss. *Begriffe der Reprographie.* German Standard Draft DIN 19060, Berlin, 1968. (German, English.)

A3 Deutscher Normenausschuss: *Informationsverarbeitung; Begriffe.* German Standard Draft DIN 44300. Berlin, 1968. (German, English.)

A4 *Dictionary of reprography.* German-English, English-German. Frankfurt a.M., 1967.

A5 J. Herbert. *Lexicon of archive terminology.* New York, 1964. (French, English, German, Spanish, Italian, Dutch.)

A6 ISO/TC 37. *Vocabulary of terminology.* ISO-Rec. 1087. Geneva, 1969. (English, French.)

A7 ISO/TC/46/WG 3. *Vocabulary of information and documentation.* Draft for paragraph 1: Basic concepts of related fields. Basic terms for documentation and information. ISO/TC 46/WG 3 (secr.-607) 1067 E/F Rev. and Amend. January 1973. (English, French.)

A8 ISO/TC 46/WG 3. Project for 1.4.3.1. Literary and artistic copyright. ISO/TC 46/WG 3 (France 7) 50 E/F, Paris, April 1971. (English, French.)

A9 ISO/TC 46/WG 3. *Vocabulary of information and documentation.* Draft for point '3' Identification-acquisition treatment of documents and data. ISO/TC 46/GT 3 (France 6) 49 E/F, Paris, February 1971. (English, French.)

A10 ISO/TC 97/SC 1. *Vocabulary of data processing.* (English, French):
01 Fundamental terms. Draft ISO recommendation.
02 Mathematics and logic. ISO/TC 97/SC 1 (Secr. 76) 163 F/E, Paris, July 1970. Draft proposal.
03 Engineering technology. ISO/TC 97/SC 1 (Secr. 91)193 F/E, Paris, October 1970. 2nd working document.
04 Organization of data. Draft ISO recommendation.
05 Representation of data. ISO/TC 97/SC 1 (Secr. 45) 102 F/E, October 1968. Draft proposal.

06 Preparation and handling of data. ISO/TC 97/SC 1 (Secr. 46) 103 F/E Novembre 1968. Draft proposal.

07 Arithmetical and logical operations. ISO/TC 97/SC 1 (Secr. 96) 199 F/E, November 1970; ISO/TC 97/SC 1 (Secr. 77) 164 F/E, Paris, March 1970. Draft proposal.

10 Preparation and formalization of programs. ISO/TC 97/SC 1 (Secr. 97) 200 F/E. Paris, November 1970, ISO/TC 97/SC 1 (Secr. 78) 165 F/E. Draft proposal.

11 Programming techniques. ISO/TC 97/SC 1 (Secr. 98) 201 F/E, Paris, November 1970; ISO/TC 97/SC 1 (Secr. 79) 166 F/E, Paris, April 1970. Draft proposal.

12 Instructions. ISO/TC 97/SC 1 (Secr. 94) 196 F/E Paris, September 1970. Draft proposal.

A10 16 Component units of control, input and output equipment. ISO/TC 97/SC 1 (Secr. 87) 189 F/E, Paris, July 1970, 3rd working document.

17 Component units of arithmetical equipment. ISO/TC 97/SC 1 (USA 24) 174 E, Paris, March 1970, 1st working document.

18 Storage techniques. ISO/TC 97/SC 1 (USA 38) 198 E, Paris, October 1970. 1st working document.

A11 H. Kunze, G. Rückl (Hrsg.). *Lexikon des Bibliothekswesens.* Leipzig 1969. (Russian, German, English, French.)

A12 M. Müllerott. Die Facetten- und Phasenanalyse der Kolen-Klassifikation Ranganathans und ihre Anwendungsmöglichkeit in anderen Klassifikationssystemen. *Nachrichten für Dokumentation,* vol 8, 1957, p. 183-87. (German, English.)

A13 *Russko-anglo-franchizckij terminologizeskij slovar' po informazionnoj teorii i praktike.* Moskwa, 1968. (Russian, English, French.)

A14 SEV (RGW). *Terminologiceskij slovar po nancnoj informaeii.* Moskwa, 1966. (Bulgarian, Hungarian, German, Polish, Romanian, Slovak, Czech.)

A15 Siemens AG. *Data processing vocabulary English-German.* 8. Rd Berlin-München 1968.

A16 A. Thompson. *Vocabularium bibliothecarii.* 2nd ed. Paris, Unesco, 1962. (English, French, German, Spanish, Russian.)

A17 A. Thompson. *Vocabularium Documentationis.* Prov. ed. Den Haag, FID, 1964. (English, French, German, Spanish, Russian.)

A18 L. Trollhann, A. Wittmann. *Fachwörterbuch der Nachrichtenverarbeitung mit Anwendungsgebieten in drei Sprachen.* München-Wien, 1964. (English, French, German.)

A19 Unesco. *Recommendation concerning the international standardization of library statistics.* Adopted by the General Conference at its sixteenth session, Paris, 13 November 1970; Paris, 1971. (English, Spanish, French, Russian.)

A20 A. Wieckowska, H. Pliszsynka: *Bodeczny slovnik bibliothekarza.* Warschau 1961. (Polish, English, French, German, Russian.)

B English sources

B1 American Documentation Institute. *Tutorial glossary of documentation terms.* Compiled by R. C. Evans for the twenty-ninth annual meeting of the institute, 3-7 October 1960, Santa Monica, Calif.

B2 American National Standards Institute. Proposed revision of X3.12 1966. *USA standard vocabulary for information processing.* August 1969.

B3 American National Standards Institute. Standards Committee Z 39 Library Automation. Subcommittee 9 Terminology. *Specialized terminology of information dissemination.* Preliminary draft. 19 March 1971.

B4 D. M. Avedon. *Glossary of terms from microphotography and reproductions made from micro-images.* Annapolis, Md., National Microfilm Ass., 1967.

B5   W. J. Barret. *Glossary of photocopying.* London, 1961.
B6   British Standards Institution. Subcommittee OC/20/12 Documentation Terminology. *Glossary of documentation terms.* Private circulation. Doc. No. 71/80211.
B7   F. Casey. *Compilation of terms in information sciences technology.* Washington, D.C., Federal Council Science and Technology, April 1970. PB 193 346.
B8   P. Fox. *Glossary of terms frequently used in physics and computers.* Cambridge, Mass. 1964.
B9   N. Gardin, F. Lévy. *Documentary lexicon for scientific information.* Marseille, 1967.
B10 A. Gilchrist. Further comments on the terminology of the analysis of library systems. *Aslib proc.,* vol. 20, 1968, p. 408-12.
B11 *Glossary of classification terms.* Indian Standard 2550-1963. New Dehli, ISI, 1963.
B12 *Glossary of fifty definitions-scientific and technical information.* Washington, D.C., Committee on Scientific Information. January 1964.
B13 B. Gaha, J. S. Gosh. Some new terms in documentation and a glossary of acronyms. *Annual of library science and documentation,* vol 14 1967, p. 62-75.
B14 C. E. Harris. *Glossary of microfilm information retrieval terms.* New York, N.Y., Recondale Corp.; rev. ed., White Plains, N.Y., 1964.
B15 *New science communications glossary* (first draft). 14 April 1966.
B16 IBM. *Glossary for information processing.* Rev. ed. White Plains, N.Y., October 1964.
B17 IFIP-ICC. *Vocabulary of information processing.* First English-language edition. 3rd printing 1968.
B18 F. Luther. The language of Lilliput; a thesaurus for uses of microfilm. *Library journal,* vol. 86, 1961, p. 929-32, 2425-30, 3238-41, 3743-46, vol 87, 1962, p. 48-54.
B19 M. Pei. *Glossary of linguistic terminology.* Garden City, N.Y., 1966.
B20 K. Samuelson. Information systems analysis to meet user's goals—a framework of concepts and definitions. In: H. Borko, H. Schur, G. X. Amery, K. Samuelson, *System analysis, an approach to information.* FID/TM tutorial session at the FID Congress in Buenos Aires, 23 September 1970.
B21 H. A. Stolk. *Glossary of documentation terms.* 3rd rev. Neuilly-sur-Seine, AGARD, 1968.
B22 S. R. Taylor. *Glossary of terms frequently used in scientific documentation.* American Institute of Physics, 1962.
B23 P. A. Thomas, E. East. Comments on the terminology of the analysis of library systems and the function of forms therein. *Aslib. Proc.,* vol. 20, 1968, p. 340-4.
B24 D. L. Thompson. *Glossary of STINFO terminology.* Washington, D.C., AFOSR, October 1963. AFOSR 5266.
B25 U.S. Bureau of Budget. *Automatic data processing glossary.* Washington, D.C., 1962.
B26 UNIVAC. *Vocabulary of information processing.* 1968 UDT-1604.
B27 F. S. Wagner. A dictionary of documentation terms, p. 102-19. *American documentation,* vol. 11, 1960.
B28 W. S. Williams. Glossary. In: W. S. Williams, *Principles of automated information retrieval,* p. 431-58. Elmhurst, 1968.

C   **French sources**

C1   Y. Chauvin. Petit dictionnaire de classement. In: Y. Chauvin, *Pratique du classement alphabétique,* p. 9-20, Paris, 1966.

D   German sources

D1   R. Blum, W. Totok, K. H. Wimann, Entwurf einer bibliographischen Terminologie. *Zeitschrift für Bibliothekswesen und Bibliographie*, vol. 12, 1965, p. 224-31.

D2   M. Ciganik. *Der Informationsfonds in Wissenschaft, Technik und Ökonomie*. Berlin, 1967. S. 369-86.

D3   Deutsche Gesellschaft für Dokumentation e.V. Komitee Terminologie und Sprachfragen. *Arbeitsergebnis der 17. Sitzung des Komitees Terminologie und Sprachfragen der DGD vom 14./15. 10. 1970 in Bad Reichenhall*. Berlin, 1970. Mimeo.

D4   Deutsche Gesellschaft für Dokumentation e.V. Komitee Terminologie und Sprachfragen. *Arbeitsergebnis der 18. Sitzung des Komitees Terminologie und Sprachfragen der DGD vom 15.12.1970 in Bonn. Begriffsfeld Sprachtypen*. Berlin, 1971. Mimeo.

D5   Deutsche Gesellschaft für Dokumentation e.V. Komitee Terminologie und Sprachfragen. *Begriffsfeld Effizienz* (Arbeitsergebnis der Komiteesitzung vom 9./10.3.1971). Berlin, 1971. Mimeo. DGD-KTS 71/7.

D6   Deutsche Gesellschaft für Dokumentation e.V. Komitee Terminologie und Sprachfragen: Arbeitsrgebnis der 20. Sitzung des Komitees Terminologie und Sprachfragen der DGD vom 22./23.6.1971 in Bonn. *Begriffsfeld Dokumentbeschreibung*. Berlin, 1971. Mimeo. DGD-KTS 71/12.

D7   Deutsche Gesellschaft für Dokumentation e.V. Komitee Terminologie und Sprachfragen: Arbeitsergebnis des Komitees Terminologie und Sprachfragen der DGD von seiner Sitzung am 22./23.6.1971 in Bonn. *Begriffsfeld Informations- und Dokumentationseinrichtungen*. Berlin, 1971. Mimeo. DGD-KTS 71/13.

D8   Deutsche Gesellschaft für Dokumentation e.V. Komitee Terminologie und Sprachfragen. *Vorschlag Begriffsfeld Dienstleistungen von Informations- und Dokumentationseinrichtungen*. Berlin, 1971. Mimeo. DGD-KTS 71/10.

D9   Deutscher Normenausschuss. *Lochkarten für Zwecke der Dokumentation; Begriffe und Benennungen*. German Standard DIN 1424. Berlin, 1966.

D10 *Fachwörterbuch Begriffe und Sinnbilder der Datenverarbeitung*. Dresden, 1968.

D11 D. Franke. Begriffe und Benennungen im Fachgebiet der Reprographie. *Reprographie*, vol. 7, 1963, no. 3, p. 55-8.

D12 K.-H. Herrlich. *Fachausdrücke zur Handlochkartentechnik*. LID-Schrift 1. Frankfurt a.M., Lehrinstitut für Dokumentation, 1967.

D13 G. Kirschstein, E. Ühlein: *Terminologie der Lochkartentechnik*. Frankfurt a.M., 1962. Nachrichten für Dokumentation, Beiheft Nr. 7.

D14 Komitee Terminologie und Sprachfragen in der DGD. Fachwörterbuch der Dokumentation, Begriffsfeld Schlüsselwort. *Nachrichten für Dokumentation*, vol. 19, 1968, p. 143-4.

D15 Komitee Terminologie und Sprachfragen in der DGD. Fachwörterbuch der Dokumentation Thesaurus-Typen. *Nachrichten für Dokumentation*, vol. 20, 1969, p. 87-8.

D16 G. Schmoll. *Wortschatz der Information und Dokumentation*. 2nd rev. ed. Leipzig, 1971.

D17 C. Schneider. *Taschenlexikon der Datenverarbeitung*. Stuttgart, 1968.

D18 Terminologische Richtlinien für die Benennung von Fachbegriffen auf dem Gebiet der Thesauri. In: *Thesauri für mechanisierte Informations-recherchesystems. Nationales Symposium (Berlin, 5.-6.4.1967)*. Berlin, 1967, p. 27-32. ZMD-Schriftenreihe 16.

D19 E. Ühlein. *Terminologie der Dokumentation*. Frankfurt a.M., 1966. Nachrichten für Dokumentation, Beiheft 13.

D20 G. Wersig. *Information, Kommunikation, Dokumentation*. Berlin-München-Pullach, 1971.

D21 G. Wersig, K.-H. Meyer-Uhlenried. Versuche zur Terminologie in der Dokumentation. *Nachrichten für Dokumentation*. I: Sprache, vol. 20, 1969, p. 116-23; II: Kommunikation und Information, vol. 20, 1969, p. 199-204; III: Dokumentation. Zugleich Bericht des Komitees Terminologie und Sprachfragen, vol. 21, 1970, p. 14-19; IV: Dokumentationssysteme und -verfahren. Mit einem Bericht des Komitees Terminologie und Sprachfragen, vol. 21, 1970, p. 98-103,

Classified vocabulary
Vocabulaire systématique
Terminologie der Dokumentation
Список использованных
Vocabulario sistemático

1 Basic aspects of information and documentation

11 Sciences related to information and documentation

classification research
F   recherches sur les classifications
D   Klassifikationsforschung
R   исследования по классификации
S   investigación sobre las clasificaciones
11-01 That branch of scientific research concerned with the classification of *knowledge* and of the sciences as well as the structures, development and evaluation of *documentary languages*
DEF: 12-24, 15-08
REF: informatics 11-08 (BT), library science 11-12 (BT), taxonomy 11-20 (RT)

communication sciences
F   sciences de la communication
D   Kommunikationswissenschaften
R   науки о коммуникации
S   ciencias de la comunicación
11-02 All sciences concerned with the study of *communication processes* and *systems*
DEF: 17-08, 41-05
REF: communication theory 11-03 (NT), mathematical communication theory 11-14 (NT), semiotics 11-18 (NT), information S. 11-11 (RT)

communication theory
F   théorie de la communication
D   Kommunikationstheorie
R   теория связи
S   teoría de la comunicación
11-03 The scientific discipline concerned with the study of *communication processes* and *systems*
DEF: 17-08, 41-05
REF: communication sciences 11-02 (BT) mathematical communication theory 11-14 (NT)

computational linguistics
F   traitement automatique du langage
D   Computerlinguistik ;
linguistische Datenverarbeitung
R   математическая лингвистика
S   automatización del lenguaje
11-04 The branch of 'linguistics' concerned with the study of the application of *computers* to linguistic problems and the processing of *natural language* by computers
DEF: 42-10, 15-18
REF: linguistics 11-13 (BT), computer science 11-05 (RT)

computer science
F   technologie des ordinateurs
D   Informatik (FRG);
Computerwissenschaft
R   теория математических машин
S   ciencia de la computación
11-05 The science concerned with the techniques of *computer* design and application
DEF: 42-07
REF: computational linguistics 11-04 (NT), cybernetics 11-06 (RT)

cybernetics
F   cybernétique
D   Kybernetik

R кибернетика
S cibernética
11-06 The science concerned with the study of control and *feedback systems*
DEF: 41-08
REF: computer science 11-05 (RT), general systems theory 11-07 (RT)

general systems theory
F théorie générale des systèmes
D allgemeine Systemtheorie
R общая теория систем
S teoría general de los sistemas
11-07 The science concerned with the general study of structures and behaviours of *systems* which may be applicable in different branches of learning
DEF: 41-40
REF: cybernetics 11-06 (RT), taxonomy 11-20 (RT)

informatics
   information science;
   information and documentation science
F science de l'information et de la documentation
D Informations- und Dokumentationswissenschaft (FRG, GDR); Informatik (GDR)
R информатика
S ciencia de la información y de la documentación
11-08 The science concerned with the study of problems connected with processes of *specialized information* and *documentation*
DEF: 17-64, 31-19
REF: information sciences 11-11 (BT), classification research 11-01 (NT), information science 11-09/10 (RT), library science 11-12 (RT)

information science
F science de l'information
D (Informationswissenschaft)
R информатика
S ciencia de la información
11-09 (1) The science concerned with creation, management and exploitation of recordable *knowledge*
DEF: 12-23/24
REF: information sciences 11-11 (BT), informatics 11-08 (RT), library science 11-12 (RT)
11-10 (2) The study of the properties, structure and transmission of *information*, and the development of methods for the useful organization of *data* and *dissemination* of information
DEF: 17-27/29, 17-12, 19-04
REF: information sciences 11-11 (BT), informatics 11-08 (RT)

information sciences
F sciences de l'information
D Informationswissenschaften
R науки об информации
S ciencias de la información
11-11 All sciences concerned with the study of *information processes* and *systems*
DEF: 17-32/33, 41-19/20
REF: informatics 11-08 (NT), information science 11-09/10 (NT), information theory 11-12 (NT), library science 11-12 (NT), communication sciences 11-02 (RT)

library science
F bibliothéconomie
D Bibliothekswissenschaft
R библиотековедение
S biblioteconomía
11-12 The branch of learning concerned with collecting, storing and distributing written or printed *records* by means of *libraries*, and of the management of libraries
DEF: 21-44, 51-25
REF: information sciences 11-11 (BT), classification research 11-01 (NT), informatics 11-08 (RT)

linguistics
F linguistique
D Linguistik; Sprachwissenschaft; allgemeine Sprachwissenschaft
R лингвистика; языкознание
S lingüística
11-13 The science of *natural language*
DEF: 15-18
REF: semiotics 11-18 (BT), computational linguistics 11-04 (NT), semantics 11-17 (RT), syntactics 11-19 (RT)

mathematical communication theory
F théorie mathématique de la communication
D mathematische Kommunikationstheorie
R теория передачи информации
S teoría matemática de la comunicación
11-14 A mathematical discipline dealing with the probabilistic features of the transmission of *data* in the presence of *noise*
DEF: 17-12, 17-47
REF: communication theory 11-03 (BT)

pragmatics
F pragmatique logique
D Pragmatik
R прагматика
S pragmática
11-15 The branch of 'semiotics' concerned with the relation between *signs* and their users
DEF: 13-29
REF: semiotics 11-18 (BT), semantics 11-17 (RT), syntactics 11-19 (RT)

science of science
F   science des sciences
D   Wissenschaftswissenschaft;
     Wissenschaft der Wissenschaft
R   науковедение
S   ciencia de la ciencia
     11-16 A discipline concerned with laws and rules of scientific work and development

semantics
F   sémantique
D   Semantik
R   семантика
S   semántica
     11-17 The branch of 'semiotics' concerned with the relation between *signs* and the *meaning* of signs
     DEF: 13-29, 14-27
     REF: semiotics 11-18 (BT), linguistics 11-13 (RT), pragmatics 11-15 (RT), syntactics 11-19 (RT)

semiotics
F   sémiotique
D   Semiotik; Zeichentheorie
R   семиотика
S   semiótica
     11-18 The science concerned with the study of *signs* and sign *systems*
     DEF: 13-29, 41-37
     REF: communication sciences 11-02 (BT), linguistics 11-13 (NT), pragmatics 11-15 (NT), semantics 11-17 (NT), syntactics 11-19 (NT)

syntactics
F   syntaxe
D   Syntaktik
R   синтактика
S   sintáctica
     11-19 The branch of 'semiotics' concerned with the relations between *signs*
     DEF: 13-29
     REF: semiotics 11-18 (BT), linguistics 11-13 (NT), pragmatics 11-15 (RT), semantics 11-17 (RT)

taxonomy
F   taxonomie
D   Taxonomie; Systemkunde
R   таксономия
S   taxonomía
     11-20 The branch of learning concerned with the study of *natural classifications*
     DEF: 311-16
     REF: classification research 11-01 (RT), general systems theory 11-07 (RT), terminology 11-21 (RT)

terminology
F   terminologie
D   Terminologie ; Terminologiearbeit
R   терминология

S   terminología
     11-21 The discipline concerned with the formation and naming of *concepts*, either in a special *subject field* or in the aggregate of all subject fields
     DEF: 12-05, 12-31
     REF: communication sciences 11-02 (BT), classification research 11-01 (RT), taxonomy 11-20 (RT)

12 Concepts

attribute
F   attribut
D   Attribut
R   свойство; неотъемлемое свойство
S   atributo
     12-01 A 'characteristic' of an 'element'
     REF: characteristic 12-02 (BT)

characteristic
     quality; property
F   caractère; caractéristique; qualité
D   Merkmal; Charakteristikum; Eigenschaft
R   признак; свойство; характеристика
S   característica; cualidad; carácter; propiedad
     12-02 Any of the properties that constitute a 'concept'
     REF: attribute 12-01 (NT), characteristic of origin 12-03 (NT). ch. of purpose 12-04 (NT), equivalent ch. 12-13 (NT), extrinsic ch. 12-16 (NT), generic ch. 12-18 (NT), incidental ch. 12-19 (NT), specific ch. 12-28 (NT)

characteristic of origin
F   caractère d'origine
D   Herkunftsmerkmal
R   источник; происхождение
S   característica de origen
     12-03 A 'characteristic' indicating where, through whom or how an object comes into existence or use, or becomes known
     REF: extrinsic characteristic 12-16 (BT), ch. of purpose 12-04 (RT)

characteristic of purpose
F   caractère de finalité; caractère d'emploi
D   Anwendungsmerkmal
R   назначение; цель
S   característica de finalidad
     12-04 A 'characteristic' indicating the purpose which an object serves
     REF: extrinsic characteristic 12-16 (BT), ch. of origin 12-03 (RT)

concept
     notion
F   notion; concept
D   Begriff
R   понятие

s concepto; noción
12-05 Any unit of thought; a mental *image* formed by generalization
DEF: 110-22
REF: specific concept 12-29 (NT), subordinate c. 12-32 (NT), superordinate c. 12-33 (NT), characteristic 12-02 (RT), definition 12-11 (RT), extension 12-17 (RT), intension 12-20 (RT), subject 12-30 (RT)

conjunction
F conjonction
D Konjunktion
R конъюнкция
S conjunción
12-06 (1) A *relation* formed by the 'logical product' of two entities
DEF: 38-27
REF: conjunction 12-06 (OT)
12-07 (2) The combination of two 'concepts' by building the 'logical product'
REF: conjunction 12-07 (OT)

contextual definition
definition of context
F définition par l'exemple
D Anwendungsdefinition
R контекстуальное определение
s definición por el contexto
12-08 'Definition' by way of an example from actual usage
REF: definition 12-11 (BT), extensional d. 12-15 (RT), intensional d. 12-21 (RT)

disjunction
F disjonction
D Disjunktion ;
Umfangsvereinigung
R дизъюнкция
s disyunción
12-09 (1) A *relation* formed by the 'logical sum' of two entities
DEF: 38-27
REF: disjunction 12-09 (OT)
12-10 (2) The combination of two 'concepts' by building the 'logical sum'
REF: disjunction 12-10

definition
F définition
D Definition; Begriffsbestimmung
R определение понятия
s definición
12-11 Verbal determination of a 'concept' by distinguishing it from other concepts
REF: contextual definition 12-08 (NT), extensional d. 12-15 (NT), intensional d. 12-21 (NT), concept 12-05 (RT)

element
F élément
D Element
R элемент; составная часть

s elemento
12-12 Part of a whole, considered separately
REF: system 41-40 (BT)

equivalent characteristics
F caractères équivalents
D gleichwertige Merkmale; äquivalente Merkmale
R эквивалентные характеристики; равнозначащие характеристики
s características equivalentes
12-13 Different 'characteristics' which may be substituted for each other in a given 'intension' without modifying the 'extension'
REF: characteristic 12-02 (BT), incidental characteristic 12-19 (RT)

extension
denotation
F extension
D Begriffsumfang
R объём (понятия)
s extensión
12-14 The set of all 'elements' which belong to a *class* or 'concept'
DEF: 39-15/16
REF: intension 12-20 (OT), concept 12-05 (RT)

extensional definition
definition by extension
F définition par extension
D Umfangsdefinition
R определение через объём понятия
s definición extensional
12-15 'Definition' by determining the 'extension' of a 'concept'
REF: definition 12-11 (BT), intensional d. 12-21 (OT), contextual d. 12-08 (RT)

extrinsic characteristic
F caractère extrinsèque
D Beziehungsmerkmal
R внешний признак; характеристика отношения
s característica extrínseca
12-16 A 'characteristic' belonging to an object only in its relations to another
REF: characteristic 12-02 (BT), ch. of origin 12-03 (NT), ch. of purpose 12-04 (NT), intrinsic ch. 12-22 (OT)

fact
F
D Sachverhalt ;
Tatsache
R факт
s hecho
12-17 The state of things or *relation* between things which may or may not be expressed, which exists or has existed,

occurs or has occured in reality
DEF: 38-27
REF: knowledge 12-24 (RT), subject 12-30 (RT)

generic characteristic
characteristic of division
caractère générique
F   Unterteilungsmerkmal;
D   generisches Merkmal
R   основание деления понятия
S   característica genérica
12-18 A 'characteristic' of a 'concept' which is used to divide the concept into several 'subordinated concepts'
REF: characteristic 12-02 (BT), incidental ch. 12-19 (RT), specific ch. 12-28 (RT)

incidental characteristic
incidental property
F   caractère incident
D   unwesentliche Eigenschaft
R   несущественный признак
S   característica incidental
12-19 A 'characteristic' of a 'concept' which is not essential for 'definition'
REF: characteristic 12-02 (BT), generic ch. 12-18 (RT)

intension
connotation
F   compréhension
D   Begriffsinhalt
R   содержание (понятия)
S   intensión
12-20 The set of all 'attributes' which constitute a *class* or 'concept'
DEF: 39-15/16
REF: extension 12-14 (OT), concept 12-05 (RT)

intensional definition
definition by intension; definition by genus and species
г   définition spécifique;
définition par compréhension
D   Inhaltsdefinition
R   реальное определение
S   definición intensional
12-21 Definition by determining the 'intension' of a 'concept'
REF: definition 12-11 (BT), extensional d. 12-15 (OT), contextual d. 12-08 (RT), generic characteristic 12-18 (RT)

intrinsic characteristic
F   caractère intrinsèque
D   Eigenmerkmal; inhärentes Merkmal
R   собственный признак;
неотъемлемый признак
S   característica intrínseca
12-22 A 'characteristic' belonging to a 'concept' or an object itself, not its relations to another

REF: characteristic 12-02 (BT), extrinsic ch. 12-16 (OT)

knowledge
F   connaissance
D   Wissen
R   знание; знания
S   conocimiento
12-23 (1) the complete set of 'concepts' and concept relations of an individual
12-24 (2) The complete set of 'concepts' and concept relations realized by humans
REF: fact 12-17 (RT)

logical difference
differentia
F   différence logique
D   logische Differenz; relatives Komplement
R   логическая разность;
отличительное свойство
S   diferencia lógica
12-25 Given two *classes* A and B the logical difference A–B consists of all elements belonging to class A but not to class B
DEF: 39-15/16
REF: logical product 12-26 (OT), l. sum 12-27 (OT)

logical product
intersection
F   produit logique; intersection
D   logisches Produkt; Konjunktion; UND-Verknüpfung; Durchschnitt
R   логическое произведение;
отношение перекрещивания
S   producto lógico
12-26 Given two *classes* A and B, the logical product AB consists of the common part of classes A and B
DEF: 39-15/16
REF: logical difference 12-25 (OT), l. sum 12-27 (OT), disjunction 12-09/10 (RT)

logical sum
F   somme logique
D   logische Summe; ODER-Verknüpfung; Disjunktion; Adjunktion; Vereinigung
R   логическая сумма
S   suma lógica
12-27 Given two *classes* A and B the logical sum A + B consists of all elements belonging to either A or B or both
DEF: 39-15/16
REF: logical difference 12-25 (OT), l. product 12-26 (OT), conjunction 12-06/07 (RT)

specific characteristic
F   caractère spécifique
D   spezifisches Merkmal
R   видовой признак

s   característica específica
12-28 A 'characteristic' which applies only to a 'subordinate concept' but not to the 'superordinate concept'
REF: characteristic 12-02 (BT), generic ch. 12-18 (RT)

specific concept
F   notion spécifique
D   spezifischer Begriff
R   видовое понятие
s   concepto específico
12-29 A 'concept' which is established by subdivision of 'superordinate concepts' and has no significant 'subordinate concepts'
REF: concept 12-05 (BT), subordinate c. 12-32 (RT)

subject
(in documentation)
F   sujet
D   Sachverhalt; Gegenstand
R   предмет; тема
s   tema
12-30 Any 'concept' or concept combination looked at as an entity
REF: fact 12-17 (RT)

subject field
subject area
F   domaine
D   Gegenstandsbereich; Sachbereich; Sachgebiet
R   тематическая область
s   campo temático
12-31 A set of 'concepts' looked at as a unit in human activity
REF: knowledge 12-24 (BT)

subordinate concept
F   notion subordonnée
D   Unterbegriff
R   подчинённое понятие
s   concepto subordinado
12-32 A 'concept' is subordinated to another concept if it has been established by one step of division, i.e. it has one 'specific characteristic' the 'superordinate concept' does not possess
REF: concept 12-05 (BT), superordinate c. 12-33 (OT), specific c. 12-29 (RT), subordination 38-21 (RT)

superordinate concept
F   notion générique
D   Oberbegriff
R   подчиняющее понятие
s   concepto superordinado
12-33 A 'concept' is a superordinate concept if it has several 'subordinate concepts' which are established by one step of division, i.e. it possesses one 'generic characteristic' which the subor-

dinate concept does not possess
REF: concept 12-05 (BT), subordinate c. 12-32 (OT), superordination 38-22 (RT)

system of concepts
F   système des notions
D   Begriffssystem
R   система понятий
s   sistema de conceptos
12-34 A group of 'concepts' related to each other and looked at as a closed set or a *system*
DEF: 41-40
REF: classification scheme 39-20 (RT)

13 Basic elements of representation

alphabet
F   alphabet
D   Alphabet
R   алфавит
s   alfabeto
13-01 (1) A finite ordered set of 'signs' used to represent the sounds of a spoken *language*
DEF: 15-13
REF: subalphabet 13-32 (NT), character set 13-12 (RT)
13-02 (2) An ordered set of all the 'letters' and 'special characters' used in a *language* to build words
DEF: 15-13/14, 14-55/56
REF: subalphabet 13-32 (NT), character set 13-12 (RT)

alphabetic character set
F   jeu de caractères alphabétiques
D   alphabetischer Zeichenvorrat
R   буквенный алфавит
s   juego de caracteres alfabéticos; conjunto de caracteres alfabéticos
13-03 A 'character set' that contains 'letters' and may contain 'control characters', 'special characters', and the 'space character', but not 'digits'
REF: character set 13-12 (BT), alphanumeric ch. s. 13-04 (RT), numeric ch. s. 13-26 (RT)

alphanumeric character set
F   jeu de caractères alphanumériques
D   alphanumerischer Zeichenvorrat
R   буквенно-цифровой алфавит
s   juego de caracteres alfanuméricos; conjunto de caracteres alfanuméricos
13-04 A 'character set' that contains both 'letters' and 'digits' and may contain 'control characters', 'special characters' and the 'space character'

REF: character set 13-12 (BT), alphabetic ch. s. 13-03 (RT), numeric ch. s. 13-26 (RT)

arbitrary sign
     natural sign
F   signe naturel; signe arbitraire
D   Anzeichen; natürliches Zeichen
R   произвольный знак
S   signo natural; signo arbitrario
     13-05 A 'sign' that is interpreted by the connexion of cause and effect
     REF: sign 13-29 (BT), conventional s. 13-16 (OT)

binary digit
     bit
F   chiffre binaire
D   Bit; Binärzeichen
R   бит; двоичная единица информации
S   dígito binario; punto magnetizado
     13-06 One of the elements of a 'character set' containing only two 'digits', usually 0 and 1
     REF: digit 13-18 (BT), binary element 13-07 (RT)

binary element
F   élément binaire; binon
D   Binärelement
R   бинарный элемент
S   elemento binario
     13-07 A constituent element of *data* that may take either of two values or states
     DEF: 17-12
     REF: binary digit 13-06 (RT), discrete representation 13-19 (RT)

blank
F   blanc; espace
D   Leerstelle
R   пробел
S   espacio; blanco
     13-08 A part of a *data medium* in which no 'characters' (1) are recorded
     DEF: 17-13
     REF: space character 13-31 (RT)

byte
F   multiplet
D   Byte
R   байт
S   bait
     13-09 A *string* of 'binary digits' operated upon as a unit and usually shorter than a *computer word*, and capable of storing one 'character'
     DEF: 14-10/11

character
F   caractère
D   Zeichen; Schriftzeichen (2)

R   знак; символ
S   carácter
     13-10 (1) (in data processing) A member of a set of *elements* upon which agreement has been reached and that is used for the organization, control or representation of *data*
     DEF: 12-12, 17-12
     REF: sign 13-30 (BT), check character 13-14 (NT), diacritical marks 13-17 (NT), digit 13-18 (NT), graphic ch. 13-21 (NT), letter 13-23 (NT), space ch. 13-21 (NT), special ch. 13-32 (NT), alphabet 13-02 (RT), set 13-12 (RT), discrete representation 13-19 (RT)
     13-11 (2) The smallest *element* that can be isolated in a given *language* for graphic recording of expressions of that language
     DEF: 12-12, 15-13/14
     REF: sign 13-30 (BT), diacritical marks 13-17 (NT), digit 13-18 (NT), graphic character 13-21 (NT), letter 13-23 (NT), special ch. 13-32 (NT), alphabet 13-01 (RT), set 13-12 (RT)

character set
F   jeu de caractères
D   Zeichenvorrat
R   алфавит
S   juego de caracteres; conjunto de caracteres
     13-12 A finite set of different 'characters' (1) upon which agreement has been reached and that is considered complete for some purpose
     REF: alphabetic character set 13-03 (NT), alphanumeric ch. s. 13-04 (NT), character subset 13-13 (NT), numeric ch. s. 13-26 (NT) alphabet 13-01/02 (RT)

character subset
F   jeu partiel (de caractères); sous-ensemble de caractères
D   Teil eines Zeichenvorrats; Teilmenge eines Zeichenvorrats
R   подалфавит
S   subconjunto de caracteres
     13-13 A selection of 'characters' (1) from a 'character set' used for a specific purpose
     REF: character set 13-12 (BT), subalphabet 13-33 (RT)

check character
F   caractère de contrôle
D   Prüfzeichen
R   контрольный знак
S   carácter de comprobación; carácter de verificación
     13-14 A 'character' (1) used for the purpose of performing a *check*, e.g. check bit, check digit

DEF: 42-08
REF: character 13-10 (BT), parity bit 42-33 (NT)

control character
    control symbol
F   caractère de commande
D   Steuerzeichen
R   управляющий знак; знак управления
S   carácter de control
13-15 A 'character' (1) whose occurrence in a particular context initiates, modifies, or stops a *control* operation, i.e. an action that affects the recording, processing, transmission or interpretation of *data*
DEF: 44-06, 17-12
REF: character 13-10 (RT)

conventional sign
F   signe conventionnel
D   konventionalisiertes Zeichen
R   условный знак
S   signo convencional
13-16 A 'sign' to be interpreted by known conventions
REF: sign 13-29/30 (BT)

diacritical mark
    diacritics
F   signe diacritique
D   diakritisches Zeichen
R   диакритические знаки
S   signo diacrítico
13-17 A 'mark' added to a 'letter', to indicate a phonetic or semantic value different from that of the unmarked letter
REF: character set 13-10/11 (BT), mark 13-24 (BT)

digit
    numeric character
F   chiffre
D   Ziffer
R   цифра
S   dígito
13-18 A 'graphic character' that represents an integer
REF: graphic character 13-21 (BT), binary digit 13-06 (NT), letter 13-23 (OT), special character 13-32 (OT), space character 13-31 (OT)

discrete representation
F   représentation discrète
D   diskrete Darstellung
R   дискретное представление
S   representación discreta
13-19 A representation of *data* by 'characters', each character or a group of characters designating one or a number of alternatives
DEF: 17-12
REF: binary element 13-07 (RT), character set 13-10 (RT)

form
F   forme
D   Zeichenform; Form
R   физическое представление (знака)
S   forma
13-20 (1) The perceptible manifestation of a 'sign'
REF: meaning 14-27 (OT)

graphic character
F   caractère graphique
D   graphisches Zeichen; Schreibzeichen
R   графический знак
S   carácter gráfico
13-21 A 'character', other than a 'control character' that is normally represented by a graphic symbol, i.e. produced by a process such as hand-writing, drawing or printing
REF: character 13-10/11 (BT), sign 13-30 (BT), digit 13-18 (NT), letter 13-23 (NT), space ch. 13-31 (NT), special character 13-32 (NT)

identifier
F   identificateur
D   Identifikator
R   опознавательный символ
S   identificador
13-22 A 'symbol' whose purpose is to identify, indicate or name a body of *data*
DEF: 17-12
REF: sign 13-30 (BT), mark 13-24 (NT)

letter
F   lettre
D   Buchstabe
R   буква
S   letra
13-23 A 'graphic character' that, when used alone or combined with others, represents in a written *language*, one or more sound elements of a spoken language (excluding 'diacritical marks' used alone and 'punctuation marks')
DEF: 15-13/14
DEF: graphic character 13-21 (BT), digit 13-18 (OT), space character 13-31 (OT), special character 13-32 (OT)

mark
F   marque
D   Kennzeichnung; Kennzeichen; Markierung
R   метка; отметка
S   marca
13-24 A 'symbol' used to signify or indicate an event in time or space
REF: identifier 13-22 (BT)

mnemonic symbol
F   symbole mnémonique
D   mnemotechnisches Zeichen; mnemotechnisches Symbol

R   мнемонический знак;
    мнемонический символ
S   símbolo mnemotécnico
    13-25 A 'symbol' chosen to assist the
    human memory
    REF: sign 13-30 (BT)

numeric character set
F   jeu de caractères numériques
D   numerischer Zeichenvorrat
R   цифровой алфавит
S   juego de caracteres numéricos,
    conjunto de caracteres numéricos
    13-26 A 'character set' that contain 'di-
    gitis' and may contains 'control charac-
    ters, special characters', and the 'space
    character', but not 'letters'
    REF: character set 13-12 (BT), alphabetic
    ch. s. 13-03 (RT), alphanumeric ch. s.
    13-04 (RT)

phoneme
F   phonème
D   Phonem
R   фонема
S   fonema
    13-27 Any distinctive phonic *element* of a
    given *language*
    DEF: 12-22, 15-13
    REF: character 13-11 (BT), graphic
    character 13-21 (OT)

punctuation marks
F   signe de ponctuation
D   Interpunktionszeichen
R   знаки препинания
S   signos de punctuación
    13-28 'Special characters' used for the
    representation of the grammatical struc-
    ture of compounds, phrases and sen-
    tences
    REF: special character 13-32 (BT)

sign
    symbol
F   signe
D   Zeichen
R   знак; символ
S   signo
    13-29 (1) A manifestation of phenomena
    which may be interpreted as a representa-
    tion of *concepts*
    DEF: 12-05
    REF: arbitrary sign 13-05 (NT), conven-
    tional s. 13-16 (NT)
    13-30 (2) (in linguistics) An *element* of a
    system which makes use of distinctive
    contrasting relations between different
    elements to express a *concept*
    DEF: 12-22, 41-40, 12-05

space character
F   caractère espace
D   Leerzeichen; Zwischenraum

R   пробельный знак
S   carácter de espacio
    13-31 A 'graphic character' that is
    usually represented by a 'blank' in a
    series of graphical symbols
    REF: graphic character 13-21 (BT), digit
    13-18 (OT) letter 13-23 (OT), special ch.
    13-32 (OT), blank 13-08 (RT)

special character
F   caractère spécial
D   Sonderzeichen
R   специальный знак
S   carácter especial
    13-32 A 'graphic character' in a 'character
    set' that is not a 'letter', not a 'digit', and
    not a 'space character'
    REF: graphic character 13-21 (BT), punc-
    tuation marks 13-28 (NT), letter 13-23
    (OT), space ch. 13-31 (OT), diacritical
    marks 13-17 (RT)

subalphabet
F   sous-ensemble d'un alphabet
D   Teil eines Alphabets;
    Teilmenge eines Alphabets
R   подалфавит
S   subalfabeto; subconjunto de alfabeto
    13-33 The subset of an 'alphabet' that is
    used for specific purposes
    REF: alphabet 13-01/02 (BT), character
    subset 13-13 (RT)

symbol
    13-34 See 13-30 (2)

14 Elements of language

acronym
F   mot en forme de sigle; sigle
D   Akronym
R   аббревиатура; акроним
S   sigla
    14-01 A pronounceable abbreviation of a
    'compound', 'name' or 'phrase' used as
    one 'word' (1), often composed of the
    initial *letters* or 'syllables' of the items
    abbreviated
    DEF: 13-23
    REF: term 14-01 (BT)

affix
    bound form
F   affixe
D   Affix
R   аффикс
S   afijo
    14-02 A 'morpheme' which has distinct
    'meaning' only when it is attached
    (prefixed, suffixed or infixed) to a 'word',
    to produce 'derivatives', inflectional forms
    or the basis of part or all of a paradigm

REF: morpheme 14-28 (BT), infix 14-24 (NT) prefix 14-38 (NT), suffix 14-46 (NT), root 14-41 (OT)

ambiguity
equivocality
F ambiguïté
D Mehrdeutigkeit; Uneindeutigkeit
R многозначность; неоднозначность
S ambigüedad
14-03 The quality of a 'term' having several 'meanings' which may be taken for one another even within a 'context'
REF: homonym 14-22 (RT), plurivalent term 14-35 (RT), polyseme 14-36 (RT)

block
F bloc
D Block
R блок (слов, знаков или цифр)
S bloque
14-04 (1) A group of 'computer words' considered as a unit by virtue of their being stored in successive *storage locations*
DEF: 312-33
14-05 (2) A 'string' of *records*, a string of 'words, a character string' or a 'binary' element 'string' formed for technical or logical reasons to be treated as an entity
DEF: 24-43

character string
F chaînes de caractères
D Zeichenkette; Zeichenfolge
R цепочка знаков
S cadena de caracteres
14-06 A 'string' consisting solely of *characters* (1)
DEF: 13-10
REF: string 14-45 (BT), block 14-04 (RT)

class name
class term
F nom de classe
D Gattungsname
R название класса
S nombre de clase
14-07 A 'word' (1) or a 'phrase' used to denote an individual *class* of beings or objects
DEF: 39-15/16
REF: name 14-29 (BT), term 14-52 (BT), proper n. 14-39 (OT), class heading 36-03 (RT)

complex term
word combination
F terme complexe
D Wortverbindung
R сложный термин
S término complejo
14-08 A 'term' containing several 'mor-

phemes' expressing more than merely syntactical relations
REF: term 14-52 (BT), compound 14-09 (RT)

compound
F mot composé
D zusammengesetztes Wort; Wortzusammensetzung; Kompositum
R составное слово; составной термин
S compuesto
14-09 A 'term' formed two or more 'words' (1) or 'roots'
REF: term 14-52 (BT), complex term 14-08 (RT), phrase 14-34 (RT)

computer word
machine word
F mot-machine
D Computerwort; Maschinenwort
R машинное слово
S palabra de computadora
14-10 (1) A 'character string' or a *binary element* 'string' that is stored in one 'storage location' and capable of being treated as a unit
DEF: 312-33
REF: character string 14-06 (BT), word 14-56 (RT)
14-11 (2) A 'character string' or a *binary element* 'string' of a standard number of *characters* which a *digital computer* regularly handles in each transfer
DEF: 13-07, 13-10/11, 42-16
REF: character string 14-06 (BT), halfword 14-20 (NT), word 14-56 (RT)

connotative meaning
F signification associative
D konnotative Bedeutung; Konnotation
R дополнительное значение; коннотативное значение
S connotación
14-12 The *concepts* assigned to *signs* in addition to the 'conventional meaning'
DEF: 12-05, 13-29
REF: meaning 14-27 (BT), conventional m. 14-14 (OT)

context
F contexte
D Kontext (eines Terminus)
R контекст
S contexto
14-13 The *text* surrounding a 'term', or the situation in which the term is used
DEF: 22-22
REF: contextual definition (RT)

conventional meaning
denotative meaning
F signification conventionnelle
D konventionalisierte Bedeutung; denotative Bedeutung; Denotation

R основное (собственное) значение; денотативное значение
S significado convencional
14-14 The concepts assigned to signs by conventions
DEF: 12-05, 13-29
REF: meaning 14-27 (BT), connotative m. 14-12 (OT)

deprecated term
F terme déconseillé
D nicht zugelassene Benennung
R нерекомендуемый термин
S término prohibido
14-15 A term which should be avoided, according to a standard
REF: term 14-52 (BT), permitted t. 14-33 (OT), preferred t. 14-37 (OT, non-descriptor 37-15 (RT)

derivate
derivative; derivative word; derived word
F dérivé
D abgeleitetes Wort; Ableitung
R производное слово
S derivado
14-16 An 'orthographic word' in which one of the components is an 'affix'
REF: orthographic word 14-31 (BT), root-word 14-52 (OT)

dictionary word
F mot dictionnaire
D lexikalisches Wort; lexikographisches Wort
R словарная форма слова
S forma diccionárica de la palabra
14-17 The single form of a 'word' (1) or 'term' used in standard dictionaries to represent all potential *forms* and all 'meanings'
DEF: 13-20
REF: term 14-52 (BT), word 14-55 (BT), lexeme 14-25 (RT)

general term
F terme général
D Allgemeinwort
R общеупотребительное слово; общий термин
S término general
14-18 A 'term' forming part of the *common language* and being used in many *technical languages* with identical 'meaning'
DEF: 15-05, 15-29
REF: term 14-52 (BT)

grammar
F grammaire
D Grammatik
R грамматика
S gramática
14-19 The complete set of rules governing the *forms* and structures of 'words' (1)

(morphology) and their customary arrangement in 'phrases' and 'sentences (syntax)'
DEF: 13-20
REF: syntax 14-50 (NT), vocabulary 16-15 (OT)

half-word
F demi-mot
D Halbwort
R полуслово
S semí-palabra
14-20 A 'character string' or *binary element* 'string' comprising half a 'computer word' (2) and being capable of being addressed as a unit
DEF: 13-07
REF: computer word 14-11 (BT)

homograph
F homographe
D Homograph
R омограф
S homógrafo
14-21 A 'homonym' having one graphic *form*
DEF: 13-20
REF: homonym 14-22 (BT), homophone 14-23 (OT)

homonym
F homonyme
D Homonym
R омоним
S homónimo
14-22 A 'term' having the same *form* but different 'meaning' than another term
DEF: 13-20
REF: plurivalent term 14-35 (BT), homograph 14-21 (NT), homophone 14-23 (NT) synonym 14-49 (OT), polyseme 14-36 (RT)

homophone
F homophone
D Homophon
R омофон
S homófono
14-23 A 'homonym' having the same phonic *form*
DEF: 13-20
REF: homonym 14-22 (BT), homograph 14-21 (OT)

infix
F infixe
D Infix
R инфикс
S infijo
14-24 An 'affix' inserted within the 'word' (1)
REF: affix 14-02 (BT), prefix 14-38 (RT), suffix 14-46 (RT)

lexeme
    lexical moneme
F   lexème
D   Lexem
R   лексема
S   lexema
    14-25 A 'word' (1) or 'root' that is an item of *vocabulary* abstracted from 'sentence' words
    DEF: 16-16
    REF: root 14-41 (BT), word 14-55 (BT), dictionary word 14-17 (RT)

lexical meaning
F   sens lexical
D   lexikalische Bedeutung
R   лексическое значение
S   significado léxico
    14-26 The 'meaning' of a 'term' included in a *vocabulary* as it is used within the vocabulary
    DEF: 16-16
    REF: meaning 14-27 (BT), conventional m. 14-14 (RT)

meaning
    sense; significance
F   signification; sens
D   Bedeutung; Sinn
R   значение; смысл
S   significado
    14-27 The *concepts* assigned to *signs*
    DEF: 12-05, 13-29
    REF: connotative meaning 14-12 (NT), conventional m. 14-14 (NT), lexical m. 14-26 (NT), transferred m. 14-53 (NT), form 13-20 (OT), information 17-29 (RT)

morpheme
F   morphème
D   Morphem
R   морфема
S   morfema
    14-28 Any indivisible constituent of a 'word' (1) or of a 'term'
    REF: word 14-55 (BT), affix 14-02 (NT), root 14-41 (NT), semanteme 14-43 (RT)

name
F   nom
D   Name; Bezeichnung
R   название; имя; наименование
S   nombre
    14-29 A 'word' (1) or a 'phrase' to denote a specific being or object, i.e. to identify one of a general *class* of items
    DEF: 39-15/16
    REF: phrase 14-34 (BT), word 14-55 (BT), class name 14-07 (NT), proper n. 14-39 (NT)

numeric word
F   mot numérique

D   numerisches Wort
R   цифровое слово
S   palabra numérica
    14-30 A 'word' (1, 2) consisting of *digits*, possible *space characters* and *special characters*
    DEF: 13-18, 13-30, 13-31
    REF: word 14-55/56 (BT)

orthographic word
    written word
F   mot écrit; mot orthographique
D   orthographisches Wort; geschriebenes Wort
R   письменное слово
S   palabra escrita; palabra ortográfica
    14-31 A written 'word' (1) which is marked off by empty spaces before and after it
    REF: word 14-55 (BT)

paradigm
F   paradigme
D   Paradigma
R   парадигма
S   paradigma
    14-32 The complete set of all the various *forms* of a 'word' (1) made by attaching 'affixes'
    DEF: 13-20
    REF: dictionary word 14-17 (OT)

permitted term
    tolerated term
F   terme autorisé
D   zugelassene Benennung
R   допустимый термин; разрешённый термин
S   término permitido
    14-33 A 'term' the use of which, as a 'synonym' or a 'quasi-synonym' of a 'preferred term' is admitted, according to a standard
    REF: term 14-52 (BT), deprecated t. 14-15 (OT), preferred t. 14-37 (OT)

phrase
    word group
F   locution; groupe de mots
D   Wortgruppe
R   сочетание; выражение; оборот; фразеологическая единица
S   frase
    14-34 A chain of 'words' (1) grammatically connected and having a unitary 'meaning'
    REF: word 14-55 (OT), sentence 14-44 (RT) term 14-52 (RT)

plurivalent term
F   terme polysémique
D   mehrdeutige Benennung
R   многозначный термин
S   término plurivalente; término polisémico

14-35 A 'term' having two or more meanings, i.e. being either a 'homonym' or a 'polyseme'
REF: term 14-52 (BT), homonym 14-22 (NT), polyseme 14-36 (NT), ambiguity 14-03 (RT)

polyseme
F   polysème
D   Polysem
R   многозначное слово; полисемантическое слово
S   polisema
14-36 A 'term' having two or more interdependent overlapping or connected 'meanings'
REF: plurivalent term 14-35 (BT), homonym 14-22 (RT)

preferred term
F   terme préféré
D   Vorzugsbenennung; Vorzugsbezeichnung
R   предпочтительный термин; рекомендуемый термин
S   término preferido
14-37 (1) A 'term' the use of which is preferred according to a *standard*
DEF: 21-58
REF: term 14-52 (BT), deprecated t. 14-15 (OT), permitted t. 14-33 (OT), descriptor 37-05 (RT)

prefix
F   préfixe
D   Präfix
R   префикс
S   prefijo
14-38 An 'affix' which precedes the 'root' of a 'word' (1) immediately or before another prefix
REF: affix 14-02 (BT), infix 14-24 (RT), suffix 14-46 (RT)

proper name
F   nom propre
D   Eigenname
R   собственное имя
S   nombre propio
14-39 A 'word' (1) or 'phrase' used to denote an individual entity
REF: name 14-29 (BT), class n. 14-07 (OT), identifier 13-22 (RT)

quasi-synonym
near-synonym
F   quasi-synonyme
D   Quasi-Synonym
R   квазисиноним; относительный синоним
S   casi-sinónimo
14-40 A 'term' having a different *form* but a similar 'meaning' to at least one other term and which may for some specific purposes be considered a 'synonym' to the other terms
DEF: 13-20
REF: term 14-52 (BT), synonym 14-49 (RT), equivalence relation 38-16 (RT)

root
word root; stem
F   racine; radical
D   Wurzel; Wortwurzel; Stamm; Wortstamm
R   корень; корневая основа
S   raíz
14-41 A meaningful 'morpheme' recurring with affixes or replacives in grammatically different *forms*
DEF: 13-20
REF: morpheme 14-28 (BT), affix 14-02 (OT)

root-word
morpheme-word
F   mot-racine
D   Stammwort; Wurzelwort
R   корневое слово; первичное слово
S   palabra raíz
14-42 An 'orthographic word' constituted by a single meaningful 'morpheme', i.e. a 'root'
REF: orthographic word 14-31 (BT), derivative 14-16 (OT)

semanteme
F   sémantème
D   Semantem
R   семантема
S   semantema
14-43 The smallest, irreducible element or unit of 'meaning'
REF: concept 12-04 (RT)

sentence
F   proposition; phrase
D   Satz
R   предложение
S   frase
14-44 A 'string' of 'words' (1) grammatically and syntactically arranged to constitute a grammatically complete unit of 'meaning'

string
F   chaîne
D   Kette; Folge
R   цепочка; последовательность; ряд
S   cadena; serie
14-45 A linear sequence of entities
REF: character string 14-06 (NT)

suffix
F   suffixe
D   Suffix
R   суффикс

s   sufijo
14-46 An 'affix' which follows the 'root' of a 'word' (1) immediately or after another suffix
REF: affix 14-02 (BT), infix 14-24 (RT), prefix 14-38 (RT)

syllable
F   syllabe
D   Silbe
R   слог
s   sílaba
14-47 (1) A group of *phonemes* representing a complete articulation or complex of articulations, and constituting the unit of 'word' formation
DEF: 13-27
REF: word 14-55 (BT)
14-48 (2) A 'character string' or *binary element* 'string' in a 'word' (2)
DEF: 13-07
REF: word 14-56 (BT)

synonym
F   synonyme
D   Synonym
R   синоним
s   sinónimo
14-49 A 'term' having a different *form* but exactly or nearly the same 'meaning' as another term
DEF: 13-20
REF: term 14-52 (BT), homonym 14-22 (OT), quasi-synonym 14-40 (RT), equivalence relation 38-16 (RT)

syntax
F   syntaxe
D   Syntax
R   синтаксис
s   sintaxis
14-50 The rules governing the construction of statements or 'sentences' in *language*
DEF: 15-13/14
REF: grammar 14-19 (BT)

technical term
F   terme technique
D   Fachausdruck; Fachwort; Fachbenennung; Fachbezeichnung; Fachterminus
R   технический термин
s   término técnico
14-51 A 'term' of a *technical language*
DEF: 15-29
REF: term 14-52 (BT)

term
F   terme
D   Terminus; Ausdruck; Bezeichnung; Benennung
R   термин; название
s   término

14-52 A 'word' (1) or 'phrase' used to denote a *concept*
DEF: 12-05
REF: class name 14-07 (NT), complex term 14-08 (NT), compound 14-09 (NT), deprecated t. 14-15 (NT), dictionary word 14-17 (NT), general t. 14-18 (NT), homonym 14-22 (NT), permitted t. 14-33 (NT), plurivalent t. 14-35 (NT), polyseme 14-36 (NT), preferred t. 14-37 (NT), quasi-synonym 14-40 (NT), synonym 14-49 (NT), transferred t. 14-54 (NT), technical t. 14-51 (NT), name 14-29 heading 36-08 (RT), descriptor 36-05/06 (RT)

transferred meaning
F   glissement sémantique
D   übertragene Bedeutung
R   переносное значение
s   sentido traslaticio
14-53 The 'meaning' of a 'term' which has been changed, e.g. by specialization, metaphor or metonymy
REF: meaning 14-27 (BT)

transferred term
F   terme transféré
D   übertragene Benennung
R   термин с переносным значением
s   término transferido
14-54 A 'term' used with 'transferred meaning'
REF: term: 14-52 (NT)

word
F   mot
D   Wort
R   слово
s   palabra
14-55 (1) The smallest entity in a *language* which can convey a specific 'meaning' by itself
DEF: 13-07
REF: dictionary word 14-17 (NT), lexeme 14-25 (NT), orthographic w. 14-31 (NT), root-word 14-42 (NT), name 14-29 (RT), paradigm 14-32 (RT), term 14-52 (RT)
14-56 (2) A 'character string' or a *binary element* 'string' that is convenient for some purposes to consider as an entity
DEF: 13-07
REF: computer word 14-10/11 (RT)

word family
F   famille de mots
D   Wortfamilie
R   парадигма; совокупность словоформ
s   familia de palabras
14-57 The complete set of 'derivates' from one and the same 'root' and the 'compounds' containing the root

15 Types of languages

algorithmic language
F   langage algorithmique
D   algorithmische Sprache
R   алгоритмический язык
S   lenguaje algorítmico
     15-01 An 'artificial language' designed for expressing algorithms
     REF: artificial language 15-02 (BT) programming l. 15-22 (RT)

artificial language
F   langage artificiel
D   künstliche Sprache
R   искусственный язык
S   lenguaje artificial
     15-02 A constructed 'language' based on a set of prescribed rules that are established prior to its use
     REF: language 15-13/14 (BT), algorithmic l. 15-01 (NT), documentary l. 15-08 (NT), programming l. 15-22 (NT), natural l. 15-18 (OT), technical l. 15-29 (RT)

assembly language
     symbolic programming language
F   langage d'assemblage
D   symbolische Programmiersprache; Assembler-Sprache
R   компилирующий язык
S   lenguaje de ensamblaje; lenguaje de compaginación
     15-03 A 'machine-oriented language', which may contain some macro-*instructions* facility and whose instructions are otherwise usually in one-to-one correspondence with *computer instructions*
     DEF: 42-33, 42-11
     REF: machine-oriented language 15-16 (BT), machine l. 15-15 (OT), assembler 42-04 (RT)

command language
F   command langage
D   Befehlssprache
R   язык команд
S   lenguaje de instrucciones
     15-04 A 'source language' (2) consisting primarily of procedural operators, each capable of involving a function to be executed
     REF: source language 15-25 (BT)

common language
     everyday language; colloquial language
F   langage commun
D   Gemeinsprache; Umgangssprache
R   общеупотребительный язык
S   lenguaje coloquial; lenguaje común
     15-05 The language system within a

'natural language' used by all people for everyday *communication*
DEF: 17-04
REF: natural language 15-18 (BT), jargon 15-12 (NT), specialized l. 15-26 (OT), technical l. 15-27 (OT), common machine l. 15-06 (RT), dialect 15-09 (RT)

common machine language
F   langage machine
D   einheitliche Maschinensprache
R   единый машинный язык
S   lenguaje común de máquinas
     15-06 A 'machine language' which is common to a group of *computers* and associated equipment
     DEF: 42-10
     REF: machine language 15-15 (BT), common l. 15-05 (RT)

descriptor language
F   langage de descripteurs
D   Deskriptorsprache; Deskriptorensprache
R   дескрипторный язык
S   lenguaje de descriptores
     15-07 A 'documentary language' using *descriptors* (2) taken from 'natural language'
     DEF: 36-06
     REF: documentary language 15-08 (BT), indexing l. 15-10 (RT), retrieval l. 15-23 (RT), thesaurus 37-22 (RT)

documentary language
     documentation language; information storage and retrieval language; information language
F   langage documentaire
D   Dokumentationssprache
R   информационно-поисковый язык; информационный язык
S   lenguaje para la documentación
     15-08 An 'artificial language' used by *documentation systems* for purposes of *indexing, storage* and *retrieval*
     DEF: 41-13, 31-21, 312-28, 312-32
     REF: artificial language 15-02 (BT), descriptor l. 15-07 (NT), indexing l. 15-10 (NT), retrieval l. 15-23 (NT), thesaurus 37-22 (NT), classification 311-05 (NT), semantic code 18-24 (NT)

dialect
F   dialecte
D   Dialekt
R   диалект
S   dialecto
     15-09 The subset of a 'natural language' peculiar to a district, community or class
     REF: natural language 15-18 (BT) specialized language 15-26 (OT), tech-

nical language 15-27 (OT), common language 15-05 (RT)

indexing language

F   langage d'indexation
D   Indexierungssprache
R   язык индексирования; информационно-поисковый язык
S   lenguaje para indizar
15-10 An 'artificial language' used by *documentation systems* for purposes of *indexing. Quasi-synonym* to *documentary language*
DEF: 41-13, 31-21, 14-40
REF: documentary language 15-08 (BT), retrieval l. 15-23 (BT), descriptor l. 15-07 (RT)

input language

F   langage d'entrée
D   Eingabesprache
R   входной язык
S   lenguaje de entrada; lenguaje de alimentación
15-11 An 'artificial' or 'natural language' used as *input* to a *dynamic system* converting *data* or *languages*
DEF: 17-34, 41-14, 17-12
REF: language 15-13 (BT), output l. 15-20 (OT), source l. 15-24/25 (RT)

jargon

    common technical language
F   jargon technique
D   Fachumgangssprache; Jargon
R   жаргон; профессиональный язык
S   lenguaje técnico común
15-12 The 'common language' in a specific field of *knowledge*
DEF: 12-24
REF: common language 15-05 (BT), technical language 15-29 (BT)

language

F   langage; langue
D   Sprache
R   язык
S   lenguaje
15-13 (1) A *system* of *signs*, for *communication*, usually consisting of *vocabulary* and rules *(grammar)*
DEF: 41-40, 13-29, 17-04, 16-15, 14-19
REF: artificial language 15-02 (NT), input l. 15-11 (NT), metalanguage 15-17 (NT), natural l. 15-18 (NT), object l. 15-19 (NT), output l. 15-20 (NT), source l. 15-24/25 (NT), target l. 15-27/28 (NT), technical l. 15-29 (NT)
15-14 (2) A set of *signs*, conventions and rules, the signs possibly represented by *symbols*, that is used for conveying *information* (1, 3) (in data processing)

DEF: 13-29, 13-34, 17-27/29
REF: like 15-13

machine language

    computer language; machine code
F   langage-machine
D   Maschinensprache; Maschinencode
R   машинный язык
S   lenguaje de máquina
15-15 An 'artificial language' for direct addressing of basic technical operations of a *computer*
DEF: 42-10
REF: artificial language 15-02 (BT), machine-oriented l. 15-16 (RT)

machine-oriented language

    computer-oriented language
F   langage lié au calculateur
D   maschinenorientierte Sprache; maschinenorientierte Programmiersprache
R   машиноориентированный язык
S   lenguaje orientado a la máquina
15-16 A 'programming language' designed for interpretation and use by a machine without *translation* into the 'machine language'
DEF: 18-26
REF: programming language 15-22 (BT), assembly l. 15-03 (NT), procedure-orientated l. (15-21 (OT)

metalanguage

F   métalangage; métalangue
D   Metasprache
R   метаязык
S   metalenguaje
15-17 A 'language' used to describe another language ('the object language')
REF: language 15-13/14 (BT), object l. 15-19 (OT)

natural language

F   langage naturel
D   natürliche Sprache
R   естественный язык
S   lenguaje natural
15-18 A 'language' which has evolved and whose rules reflect current usage without being explicitly prescribed
REF: language 15-13/14 (BT), common l. 15-05 (NT), dialect 15-09 (NT), specialized l. 15-26 (NT), artificial l. 15-02 (OT)

object language

F   langage résultant; langage-objet
D   Objektsprache
R   язык-объект
S   lenguaje objeto
15-19 A 'language' (1, 2) used to describe

knowledge being described by another language, the 'metalanguage'
REF: language 15-13/14 (BT), meta-language 15-17 (OT)

output language
F   langage de sortie
D   Ausgabesprache
R   выходной язык
S   lenguaje de salida
   15-20 An 'artificial' or 'natural language' produced as the *output* of a *dynamic system* converting *data* or 'languages'
   DEF: 17-49, 41-14, 17-12
   REF: language 15-13 (BT), input l. 15-11 (OT), target l. 15-27/28 (RT)

procedure-oriented language
   procedural language; problem-oriented language
F   langage adapté aux procédures
D   problemorientierte Programmiersprache
R   проблемно-ориентированный язык
S   lenguaje de procedimientos
   15-21 A 'programming language' designed for the convenient expression of procedures used in the solution of a wide *class* of problems
   DEF: 39-15/16
   REF: programming language 15-22 (BT), machine-oriented l. 15-16 (OT), compiler 42-09 (RT)

programming language
   program language
F   langage de programmation
D   Programmiersprache; Programmsprache
R   язык программирования
S   lenguaje de programación
   15-22 An 'artificial language' used to prepare *computer programs*
   DEF: 42-13
   REF: artificial language 15-02 (BT), machine-oriented l. 15-16 (NT), procedure-oriented l. 15-21 (NT), machine l. 15-15 (O), algorithmic l. 15-01 (RT)

retrieval language
   information retrieval language
F   langage de recherche documentaire
D   Recherchesprache; Informationsrecherchesprache; Retrievalsprache
R   информационно-поисковый язык
S   lenguage de recuperación
   15-23 An 'artificial language' used by 'documentation systems' for the purpose of 'retrieval'. Quasi-synonym to 'documentary language'
   DEF: 42-12, 313-31, 14-40
   REF: documentary language 15-08 (BT), indexing l. 15-10 (OT), descriptor l. 15-07 (RT)

source language
F   langage d'origine
   langue d'origine; langage source
D   Quellensprache
R   входной язык; исходный язык; язык-источник
S   lenguaje original; lenguaje fuente
   15-24 (1) The 'input language' to a *translation* process
   DEF: 18-26
   REF: language 15-13/14 (BT), target l. 15-27 (OT)
   15-25 (2) The 'language' (2) from which *statements* are translated in *programming*
   DEF: 42-45, 42-37
   REF: target language 15-28 (OT)

specialized language
   special language
F   langage spécialisé
D   Sondersprache
R   жаргон
S   lenguaje especializado
   15-26 A 'language' used for specific purposes by a particular social group
   REF: natural language 15-13/14 (BT), common l. 15-05 (OT), technical l. 15-29 (RT)

target language
F   langue cible; langage résultant
D   Zielsprache
R   выходной язык
S   lenguaje objeto
   15-27 (1) The 'output language' of a given *translation* process
   DEF: 18-26
   REF: language 15-13/14 (BT), source l. 15-24 (OT)
   15-28 (2) The 'language' into which *statements* are translated in *programming*
   DEF: 42-45, 42-37
   REF: source language 15-25 (OT)

technical language
F   langage technique
D   Fachsprache
R   профессиональный язык
S   lenguaje técnico
   15-29 A 'language' based on a 'natural language' but designed to reduce *ambiguities* for the purpose of assisting *communication* in a specific field of *knowledge* (2)
   DEF: 14-03, 17-04, 12-24
   REF: language 15-13/14 (BT), common l. 15-05 (OT), specialized l. 15-26 (RT)

16 Representation of vocabularies

automatic dictionary
machine dictionary;
mechanical dictionary
F dictionnaire en machine;
dictionnaire automatisé
D (Maschinenwörterbuch)
R автоматический словарь;
словарь для машинного перевода
S diccionario automatizado para
traducciones
16-01 A 'dictionary' stored in an automatic *translating* machine which will
provide a *word* by word substitution from
one *language* into another
DEF: 18-26, 14-55/56, 15-13/14
REF: bilingual dictionary 16-02 (BT),
automatic translation 18-03 (RT), root
d. 16-11 (RT)

bilingual dictionary
F dictionnaire bilingue
D zweisprachiges Wörterbuch
R двуязычный словарь
S diccionario bilingüe
16-02 A dictionary listing the 'words'
of one *natural language* and giving the
equivalents in another natural language
DEF: 14-55, 15-18
REF: dictionary 16-03 (BT), polyglot d.
16-10 (RT)

dictionary
F dictionnaire
D Wörterbuch
R словарь
S diccionario
16-03 An *alphabetically ordered* 'vocabulary' (2) of a *language*
DEF: 34-08, 15-18
REF: automatic dictionary 16-01 (NT),
bilingual d. 16-02 (NT), etymological d.
16-05 (NT), polyglot d. 16-10 (NT),
root d. 16-11 (NT), special d. 16-12 (NT),
glossary 16-06 (RT), lexicon 16-07 (RT),
terminology (16-13 (RT), vocabulary
16-16 (RT)

encyclopaedia
F encyclopédie
D Enzyklopädie; enzyklopädisches
Wörterbuch; Konversationslexikon
R энциклопедия
S enciclopedia
16-04 An alphabetical or systematically
arranged listing of *terms* and *names*
containing as much *information* as
possible about the covered *subject field*
DEF: 14-52, 14-29, 17-27, 12-31

etymological dictionary
F dictionnaire étymologique
D etymologisches Wörterbuch
R этимологический словарь
S diccionario etimológico
16-05 A 'dictionary' giving in addition
to the *meanings* of the *words* their
derivations
DEF: 14-27, 14-55
REF: dictionary 16-03 (BT)

glossary
explanatory dictionary
F glossaire
D Glossar; Definitionswörterbuch
R толковый словарь; глоссарий
S glosario
16-06 A 'vocabulary' (1, 2) not necessarily
in *alphabetic order*, with *definitions or
explanations* for all terms
DEF: 34-03, 12-11
REF: dictionary 16-03 (RT), lexicon
16-07 (RT), terminology 16-13 (RT),
vocabulary 16-15/16 (RT)

lexicon
F lexique
D Lexikon; Wörterbuch
R словарь; лексикон
S léxico
16-07 An alphabetically arranged listing
of the total stock of linguistic *signs* (*words*
or *morphemes* or both) in a given *natural
language*
DEF: 13-29, 14-55, 14-28, 15-18

linguistic thesaurus
F thesaurus linguistique
D linguistischer Thesaurus; Wortschatz
R тезаурус естественного языка
S tesauro lingüístico
16-08 A 'vocabulary' (2) of a given
natural language ordered systematically
and showing *concept relations* between
the *terms*
DEF: 15-18, 38-13, 14-52
REF: vocabulary 16-16 (BT), thesaurus
32-22 (RT)

nomenclature
F nomenclature
D Nomenklatur
R номенклатура
S nomenclatura
16-09 An organized set of *names* or
class names used in a specific *subject
field*
DEF: 14-29, 14-07
REF: classification 311-05 (RT)

polyglot dictionary
multilingual dictionary
F dictionnaire multilingue

D mehrsprachiges Wörterbuch
R многоязычный словарь
S diccionario multilingüe;
diccionario políglota
16-10 A 'dictionary' listing the *words* of one *natural language* and giving the equivalents in more than one other natural language
DEF: 14-55, 15-18
REF: dictionary 16-03 (BT), bilingual d. 16-02 (RT)

root dictionary
stem dictionary
F dictionnaire de racines
D Wortstammwörterbuch
R словарь основ
S diccionario de raíces
16-11 'A dictionary' of a *natural language* listing only the *roots*
DEF: 15-18, 14-41
REF: dictionary 16-03 (BT), automatic d. 16-01 (RT)

special dictionary
subject dictionary
F dictionnaire spécialisé
D Fachwörterbuch
R отраслевой словарь
S diccionario especializado;
diccionario técnico
16-12 A 'vocabulary' (2) in one or more *languages* concerning a specific *subject field*
DEF: 15-13, 12-31
REF: dictionary 16-03 (BT), glossary 16-06 (RT), vocabulary 16-16 (RT)

terminology
F terminologie (sens courant)
D Terminologie; Terminologiesammlung
R терминологический словарь
S terminología
16-13 (2) An organized set of *technical terms* whose *meanings* have been explained or defined.
DEF: 14-51, 14-27
REF: dictionary 16-03 (RT), lexicon 16-07 (RT), glossary 16-06 (RT), vocabulary 16-15/16 (RT)

term list
F liste des termes
D Benennungsliste
R терминологический словник
S lista de términos
16-14 A list of *terms* in *alphabetic order*, collected for some specific purpose
DEF: 14-52, 34-03
REF: authority list 35-04 (RT), word l. 16-17 (RT), descriptor association l. 37-06 (RT)

vocabulary
F vocabulaire

D Vokabular
R словарь (1); лексикон (1);
терминологический словарь (2)
S vocabulario
16-15 (1) The set of *terms* used in a *language*
DEF: 14-52, 15-13/14
REF: grammar 14-19 (OT), lexicon 16-07 (RT)
16-16 (2) An organized set of *terms* in one or more *languages*, whose *meanings* have been explained or defined, mostly concerned with one *specialized language* or *technical language*
DEF: 14-52, 13-15/14, 14-34, 15-26, 15-29
REF: linguistic thesaurus 16-08 (NT), dictionary 16-03 (RT), glossary 16-06 (RT), lexicon 16-07 (RT), terminology 16-13 (RT)

word list
F liste de mots;
liste orthographique
D Wortliste
R словник
S lista de palabras
16-17 A list of *orthographic words* usually in alphabetical order
DEF: 14-31
REF: authority list 35-04 (RT), term l. 16-14 (RT)

17 Information and communication theory

analog data
F données analogiques
D Analogdaten
R аналоговые данные
S datos analógicos
17-01 Representation of 'data' by means of continuously variable physical quantities
REF: data 17-12 (BT), discrete d. 17-20 (OT)

automatic data processing
automatic information processing
F traitement automatique de l'information;
traitement automatique de données
D automatische Datenverarbeitung;
automatische Informationsverarbeitung
R автоматизированная обработка данных; автоматизированная обработка информации
S tratamiento automático de datos
17-02 'Data processing' largely performed by automatic means
REF: data processing 17-15 (BT), electronic d. p. 17-21 (NT)

channel
F voie
D Kanal; Übertragungskanal
R канал связи
S canal
17-03 That part of a *communication system*' that connects 'message source' with the 'message sink'; mathematically this part can be characterized by the set of conditional probabilities of all the 'messages' (1) at the message sink, given all the messages at the message source
DEF: 41-05
REF: communication channel 17-05 (NT)

communication
F communication
D Kommunikation
R связь; коммуникация
S comunicación
17-04 The transfer of 'meaning' by means of 'transmission of signals'
DEF: 14-27
REF: communication process 17-08 (RT), information 17-30 (RT), direct c. 17-19 (RT), group c. 17-24 (NT), human c. 17-25 (NT), indirect c. 17-26 (NT), interposed c. 17-37 (NT), man-machine c. 17-39 (NT), mass c. 17-40 (NT), scientific c. 17-59 (NT), specialized c. 17-61 (NT), technological c. 17-66 (NT), data transmission 17-17 (RT)

communication channel
F voie de communication
D Kommunikationskanal
R канал связи
S canal de comunicación
17-05 The path along which 'communication processes' take place, including 'transmitters, communication media, etc.
REF: channel 17-03 (BT)

communication medium
F moyen de communication
D Kommunikationsmittel
R средство связи
S medio de comunicación
17-06 (1) A 'data medium' (1, 2) transmitting 'data' during a 'communication process'
REF: data medium 17-13/14 (BT)
17-07 (2) A physical apparatus or an organization intervening in a 'communication channel'
REF: mass media 19-07 (NT)

communication process
F processus de communication
D Kommunikationsprozeß
R процесс связи
S proceso de comunicación
17-08 The process of producing, transmitting and processing a 'message' (1, 2)
REF: transmission 17-67 (BT), communication 17-04 (RT), information 17-30 (RT), information process 17-32 (RT), information p. 17-33 (NT)

communicator
F communicateur
D Kommunikator
R передатчик
S trasmisor
17-09 A *system* which *encodes* and emits *signs* intended to be *decoded*
DEF: 18-17, 18-14
REF: recipient 17-53 (OT), transmitter 17-68 (RT), message source 17-44 (RT)

content
F contenu; signifié
D Inhalt
R содержание (сообщения)
S contenido
17-10 The *meaning* that may be assigned to a 'message' (1, 2)
DEF: 14-27

content analysis
F analyse de contenu
D Inhaltsanalyse
R анализ содержания
S análisis del contenido
17-11 The analysis of the objective 'content' of 'messages' (1, 2)

data
F données
D Daten
R данные
S datos
17-12 A representation by *signs* of *facts*, *concepts* or *instructions* in a formalized manner suitable for 'communication' interpretation or processing by humans or by *automatic* means
DEF: 13-29/30, 12-17, 12-05, 42-05
REF: analog data 17-01 (NT), digital d. 17-18 (NT), discrete d. 17-20 (NT), numeric d. 17-48 (NT), raw d. 17-51 (NT), statistical d. 17-65 (NT), information 17-28 (RT)

data medium
  medium
F support d'information;
  support de données
D Datenträger
R носитель данных;
  носитель информации
S soporte de datos
17-13 (1) The material object in or on which a specific physical variable may represent 'data'

REF: communication 17-06 (NT), document 21-18 (NT)
17-14 (2) The physical quantity which may be varied to represent 'data'
REF: communication medium 17-06 (NT)

data processing
    information processing
F   traitement de l'information;
    traitement de données
D   Datenverarbeitung;
    Informationsverarbeitung
R   обработка данных;
    обработка информации
S   tratamiento de datos;
    procesamiento de datos
17-15 The execution of a systematic sequence of operations upon 'data'
REF: automatic data processing 17-02 (NT), data reduction 17-16 (NT), data transmission 17-17 (NT), integrated d. p. 17-36 (NT)

data reduction
F   réduction de données
D   Datenreduktion
R   преобразование данных;
    обработка данных
S   reducción de datos
17-16 The transformation of a set of 'raw data' into a more useful form according to a given standard or for some specific purposes
REF: data processing 17-15 (BT)

data transmission
F   transmission de l'information;
    transmission de données
D   Datentransmission; Datenübertragung
R   передача данных
S   trasmisión de datos
17-17 The 'transmission' of 'signals' representing 'data'
REF: data processing 17-15 (BT), transmission 17-62 (BT), communication 17-04 (RT)

digital data
F   données numériques
D   Digitaldaten;
    digital dargestellte Daten
R   цифровые данные
S   datos digitales
17-18 'Data' represented by *digits*
DEF: 13-18
REF: discrete data 17-20 (BT), numeric d. 17-48 (RT)

direct communication
    face-to-face communication
F   communication directe
D   direkte Kommunikation
R   прямая связь
S   comunicación directa

17-19 'Communication' where the 'message' (2) immediately reaches the 'recipient'
REF: communication 17-04 (BT), indirect c. 17-26 (OT), interpersonal c. 17-37 (RT)

discrete data
F   données discrètes
D   diskrete Daten
R   дискретные данные
S   datos discretos
17-20 'Data' represented by distinct elements, such as *characters* or physical quantities only having distinct values
DEF: 13-10/11
REF: data 17-12 (BT), digital d. 17-18 (NT), analog d. 17-01 (OT), numeric d. 17-48 (NT), statistical d. 17-64 (NT)

electronic data processing
F   traitement électronique de l'information
D   elektronische Datenverarbeitung
R   электронная обработка данных
S   tratamiento electrónico de datos;
    procesamiento electrónico de datos
17-21 'Data processing' largely performed by electronic devices
REF: automatic data processing 17-02 (BT)

entropy
F   entropie
D   Entropie
R   энтропия
S   entropía
17-22 The degree of disorganization in an assembly of 'information' (2) or 'data'

feedback
F   rétroaction
D   Rückkopplung
R   обратная связь
S   retroalimentación
17-23 Use of the 'output' (1) or the effects of the output as 'input' (1) to influence the *state of the system*
DEF: 41-36

group communication
F   communication en groupe
D   Gruppenkommunikation
R   внутригрупповая связь
S   comunicación en grupo
17-24 'Communication' within a social group, following the group standards
REF: communication 17-04 (BT), interpersonal c. 17-34 (OT), mass c. 17-40 (OT), invisible college 19-09 (RT)

human communication
F   communication humaine
D   Humankommunikation;
    menschliche Kommunikation
R   связь между людьми

S   comunicación humana
17-25 'Communication' between humans
REF: communication 17-04 (BT), group
c. 17-24 (NT), interpersonal c. 17-37
(NT), mass c. 17-40 (NT), scientific
c. 17-58 (NT), technological c. 17-66
(NT), man-machine c. 17-39 (OT)

indirect communication
F   communication indirecte
D   indirekte Kommunikation
R   непрямая связь
S   comunicación indirecta
17-26 'Communication' where the 'messages' (2) do not reach the 'recipient' immediately in the original form, because of
the intervention of 'communication media' (2)
REF: communication 17-04 (BT), direct c.
17-19 (OT)

information
knowledge (1, 2); data (2); meaning (3);
information process (4)
F   information; renseignement (1, 2);
processus d'information (4)
D   Information; Wissen (1); Daten (2);
Informationen (2); Bedeutung (3);
Informationstätigkeit (4)
R   информация (1, 2); данные (2);
сообщение (2); информирование (4)
S   información
17-27 (1) *Facts* being communicated
DEF: 12-17
REF: recorded information 17-54 (NT),
scientific i. 17-60 (NT), specialized i. 17-
62 (NT)
17-28 (2) A 'message' used to represent
a *fact* or *concept* by the unity of a 'data
medium' and its *meaning*
DEF: 12-17, 12-05, 14-27
REF: machine-sensible information 17-38
(NT), scientific i. 17-60 (NT), specialized
i. 17-62 (NT), recorded i. 17-54 (RT)
17-29 (3) (in data processing) The *meaning*
that a human assigns to 'data' by means
of the conventions used in their representation
DEF: 14-27
17-30 (4) The process of communication
facts or *concepts* in order to increase *knowledge*
DEF: 12-17, 12-05, 12-23/24
REF: scientific information 17-59 (NT),
specialized i. 17-63 (NT), communication
17-04 (RT), process 17-32/33 (RT), communication process 17-08 (RT)
17-31 (5) The increase of *knowledge* by
'communication'
DEF: 12-23/24
REF: specialized information 17-64 (NT)

information process
F   processus d'information

D   Informationsprozeß; Information
R   информационный процесс
S   proceso informativo
17-32 (1) The process of communicating
'information' (1, 2)
REF: communication process 17-08 (RT),
information 17-30 (RT)
17-33 (2) The process of effecting 'information' (5)
REF: communication process 17-08 (BT)

input
F   entrée
D   Input; Eingabe
R   ввод
S   entrada (de un sistema); alimentación
(de un sistema)
17-34 (1) Anything coming from the
environment of a system into the *system*
DEF: 41-16, 41-40
REF: output 17-49 (OT)
17-35 (2) Every change the *environment*
causes in the *system*
DEF: 41-16, 41-40
REF: output 17-50 (OT)

integrated data processing
F   traitement unifié des données;
traitement intégré des données
D   integrierte Datenverarbeitung;
integrierte Informationsverarbeitung
R   интегральная обработка данных
S   integración de datos
17-36 'Data processing' in which the co-
ordination of 'data' acquisition and other
stages of data processing are combined in
a coherent *data processing system*
DEF: 31-03, 41-09
REF: data processing 17-15 (BT)

interpersonal communication
F   communication humaine
D   interpersonelle Kommunikation
R   личная связь; личные контакты
S   comunicación interpersonal
17-37 'Communication' between two
humans
REF: human communication 17-25 (BT),
direct c. 17-19 (RT)

machine-sensible information
F   données directement utilisables
par la machine
D   maschinenlesbare Daten
R   машиночитаемая информация;
информация в машиночитаемой форме
S   información computable
17-38 'Data or information' (2) in a form
which can be read by a specific machine
REF: data 17-12 (BT), information 17-28
(BT)

man-machine communication
F   communication homme-machine

D   Mensch-Maschine-Kommunikation
    ergonomische Kommunikation
R   связь "человек-машина"
S   comunicación hombre-máquina
    17-39 'Communication' between humans
    and machines, i.e. the 'transmission' of
    'data' and 'instructions' to machines to
    perform 'automatic data processing'
    DEF: 42-24
    REF: communication 17-04 (BT),
    human c. 17-25 (OT)

mass communication
F   communication de masse
D   Massenkommunikation; Publizistik
R   массовое информирование;
    распространение информации
    с помощьюмассовых средств
S   comunicación de masas
    17-40 The simultaneous public *dissemi-
    nation* of 'information (1. 2)' to the largest
    possible number of 'recipients'
    DEF: 19-04
    REF: indirect communication 17-26 (BT),
    human c. 17-25 (BT), group c. 17-24 (OT),
    direct c. 17-19 (OT)

measure of information
F   mesure de l'information
D   Informationsgehalt
R   мера информации
S   medida de la información
    17-41 A function of the frequency of
    occurrence of a specified event from a set
    of possible events, conventionally taken
    as a measure of the relative value of
    intelligence conveyed by this occurrence.
    REF: redundancy 17-56 (RT)

message
F   message
D   Nachricht; Aussage; Mitteilung
R   сообщение
S   mensaje
    17-42 (1) An ordered sequence of
    characters, intended to convey 'informa-
    tion' (3)
    DEF: 13-10/11
    17-43 (2) A set of *signs* emitted by a
    'communicator' or received by a 'reci-
    pient'
    DEF: 13-29

message source
F   source de messages
D   Nachrichtenquelle
R   источник сообщений
S   fuente de mensajes
    17-44 That part of a *communication sys-
    tem* wherein 'messages' (1) are considered
    to be originated
    DEF: 41-05
    REF: message sink 17-45 (OT), communi-
    cator 17-09 (RT), transmitter 17-68 (RT)

message sink
F   collecteur de messages
D   Nachrichtensenke
R   приёмник сообщений
S   colector de mensajes
    17-45 That part of a *communication
    system* wherein 'messages' (1) are con-
    sidered to be received
    DEF: 41-05
    REF: message source 17-44 (OT), receiver
    17-52 (RT), recipient 17-53 (RT)

noise
F   bruit
D   Rauschen; Störung
R   шум; помехи
S   ruido
    17-46 (1) Any disturbance of a 'mes-
    sage' (2) after emission and before
    reception
    17-47 (2) Any disturbance of a 'mes-
    sage (1, 2) caused by the physical
    characteristics of the 'channel'

numeric data
F   données numériques
D   numerische Daten
R   числовые данные
S   datos numéricos
    17-48 'Data' represented by numerals
    and some *special characters*
    DEF: 13-32
    REF: discrete data 17-20 (BT), statistical
    d. 17-65 (NT), digital d. 17-18 (RT)

output
F   sortie
D   Ausgabe; Output
R   вывод; выход; выдача
S   salida (de un sistema)
    17-49 (1) Anything going from a *system*
    to its *environment*
    DEF: 41-40, 41-16
    REF: input 17-35 (OT)
    17-50 (2) Every change of the *environ-
    ment of a system* caused by the *system*
    DEF: 41-16, 41-40
    REF: input 17-36 (OT)

raw data
F   données brutes
D   Rohdaten; unbearbeitete Daten
R   необработанные данные
S   datos brutos
    17-51 'Data' upon which no 'data
    processing' has taken place
    REF: data 17-12 (BT), statistical d. 17-64
    (OT)

receiver
F   récepteur
D   Empfänger
R   приёмник

S receptor
17-52 An apparatus or organ which receives 'signals' from a 'transmitter' and reconverts them into 'messages' (1) for a 'message sink'
REF: transmitter 17-68 (OT), message sink 17-45 (RT), recipient 17-53 (RT)

recipient
F destinataire
D Rezipient
R получатель (информации); приёмник
S destinatario
17-53 A *system* which receives and *decodes (1) signs*
DEF: 41-40, 18-15, 13-29
REF: communicator 17-09 (OT), message sink 17-45 (RT), receiver 17-52 (RT)

recorded information
F information enregistrée
D aufgezeichnete Information
R записанная информация; зафиксированная информация
S información registrada
17-54 'Information' (1) fixed in or on a 'data medium' (1)
REF: information 17-27 (BT), information 17-28 (RT)

redundancy
F redondance
D Redundanz
R избыточность; избыточность сообщения
S redundancia
17-55 (1) In general, any part of a 'message' (1, 2) that is not necessarily needed for correct *decoding (1)* of the message in ideal conditions, e.g. without 'noise' (1, 2)
DEF: 18-14
17-56 (2) In information theory deliberate repetition in a 'message' (1) in order to lessen the possibility of *error*
DEF: 42-19
REF: measure of information 17-41 (RT)

signal
F signal
D Signal
R сигнал
S señal
17-57 A time-dependent value attached to a physical phenomenon and conveying 'data'

scientific communication
F communication scientifique
D wissenschaftliche Kommunikation
R научная коммуникация
S comunicación de datos científicos
17-58 'Specialized communication' in the field of science

REF: specialized communication 17-61 (BT), scientific information 17-59 (RT), technological c. 17-66 (RT)

scientific information
F information scientifique
D wissenschaftliche Informationen (1); wissenschaftliche Daten (1); wissenschaftliche Informationstätigkeit (2); wissenschaftliche Information
R научная информация
S información científica
17-59 (1) 'Information' (4) by 'scientific communication'
REF: information 17-30 (OT), specialized i. 17-63 (RT)
17-60 (2) 'Information' (1, 2) restricted to 'scientific communication'
REF: information 17-27/28 (BT), specialized i. 17-62 (RT)

specialized communication
F communication spécialisée
D fachliche Kommunikation
R распространение специализированной информации
S comunicación especializada
17-61 'Human communication' in a specific field of *knowledge (2)*
DEF: 12-24
REF: human communication 17-25 (BT), scientific c. 17-58 (NT), technological c. 17-66 (NT), specialized information 17-63 (RT), information transfer 19-06 (RT)

specialized information
F information spécialisée
D fachliche Informationen (1); Fachinformationen (1); Fachinformation (2, 3); fachliche Informationstätigkeit (2)
R специализированная информация; отраслевая информация
S información especializada
17-62 (1) 'Information' (1, 2) recognized to be useful in a specific field of *knowledge*
DEF: 12-24
REF: information 17-27/28 (BT), scientific i. 17-60 (RT)
17-63 (2) 'Information' (4) in a specific field of *knowledge*
DEF: 12-24
REF: information 17-30 (BT), scientific i. 17-59 (RT), specialized communication 17-62 (RT), information transfer 19-06 (RT)
17-64 (3) 'Information' (5) effected by 'specialized communication'
REF: information 17-31 (BT)

statistical data
F données statistiques

D   statistische Daten
R   статистические данные
S   datos estadísticos
17-65 'Data' produced from 'raw data' by 'data processing' using statistical procedures
REF: numeric data 17-48 (BT), raw d. 17-51 (OT)

technological communication
F   communication technique
D   technische Kommunikation; Kommunikation im Bereich der Technik
R   распространение специализированной технической информации
S   comunicación tecnológica
17-66 'Specialized communication' in a technical field
REF: specialized communication 17-61 (BT), scientific c. 17-58 (RT)

transmission
F   transmission
D   Transmission; Übermittlung; Übertragung
R   передача
S   transmisión
17-67 Action of conveying between two points, either directly or indirectly, by physical means or by 'signal', an object, *document*, picture or sound, or 'information' (1, 2, 3) of any nature
DEF: 21-18
REF: communication process 17-08 (NT), information 17-30 (NT), information process 17-31 (NT)

transmitter
emitter
F   émetteur
D   Sender
R   передатчик
S   emisor
17-68 An apparatus or organ which produces for 'transmission signals' representing 'messages' (1) from a 'message source'
REF: receiver 17-52 (OT), communicator 17-09 (RT), message source 17-44 (RT)

18 Conversion and coding

alphabetic code
F   code alphabétique
D   alphabetischer Code; alphabetischer Schlüssel; Alpha-Code
R   алфавитный код; буквенный код
S   código alfabético
18-01 A 'code' (2) whose 'code set' consists only of *letters* and associated *special characters*
DEF: 13-23, 13-32

REF: code 18-06 (BT), alphanumeric c. 18-02 (RT), binary c. 18-04 (RT), numeric c. 18-22 (RT)

alphanumeric code
F   code alphanumérique
D   alphanumerischer Code; alphanumerischer Schlüssel
R   алфавитно-цифровой код; буквенно-цифровой код
S   código alfanumérico
18-02 A 'code' (2) whose 'code set' consists of *letters*, *digits* and associated *special characters*
DEF: 13-23, 13-18, 13-32
REF: code 18-06 (BT), alphabetic c. 18-01 (RT), binary c. 18-04 (RT), numeric c. 18-22 (RT)

automatic translation
mechanical translation; machine translation
F   traduction automatique
D   maschinelle Übersetzung; automatische Übersetzung; maschinelle Sprachübersetzung
R   автоматический перевод; машинный перевод
S   traducción mecánica; traducción automatizada
18-03 'Translation' performed by *automatic* means
DEF: 42-05
REF: translation 18-26 (BT), automatic dictionary 16-01 (RT)

binary code
F   code binaire
D   Binärcode; binärer Code
R   двоичный код
S   código binario
18-04 A 'code' (2) whose 'code set' makes use of exactly two distinct *characters*, usually 0 and 1
DEF: 13-11
REF: code 18-06 (BT), alphabetic c. 18-01 (RT), alphanumeric c. 18-02 (RT), numeric c. 18-22 (RT)

code
coding scheme (2)
F   code
D   Code; Schlüssel (2)
R   код
S   código
18-05 (1) A set of rules specifying the manner in which 'data transformations' may be carried out
REF: translation 18-26 (NT), transliteration 18-28 (NT), transcription 18-27 (NT)
18-06 (2) A set of rules enabling the representation of *data* in a discrete form

DEF: 17-12
REF: alphabetic code 18-01 (NT), alphanumeric c. 18-02 (NT), binary c. 18-04 (NT), direct c. 18-16 (NT), error-checking c. 18-19 (NT), numeric c. 18-22 (NT), data c. 18-12 (OT), triangular c. 43-26 (NT), punch tape c. 43-19 (NT)
18-07 (3) A set of rules for the transformation of a *language* into another language
DEF: 15-13/14
REF: translation 18-26 (NT)

code element
code representation; code value; code (deprecated in this sense)
F élément de code; combinaison de code
D Code-Element; Codierungselement
R кодовый элемент
S elemento de codificación
18-08 The representation of an item of *data* established by a 'code' (2) or the representation of a *character* established by a 'coded character set'
DEF: 17-12, 13-11
REF: code set 18-09 (BT)

code set
code (deprecated in this sense); data code (deprecated in this sense
F jeu d'éléments de code; jeu de représentations
D Codiervorrat
R алфавит кода
S lista código
18-09 The complete set of 'code elements' defined by a 'code' (2) or by a 'coded character set'
REF: code element 18-08 (NT), coded character set 18-11 (NT)

coding
F codage; codification
D Codierung
R кодирование
S codificación
18-10 'Data transformation' or representation applying a 'code' (1, 2)
REF: data transformation 18-13 (BT), decoding 18-15 (NT), encoding 18-18 (NT), fixed field coding 18-20 (NT), generic c. 18-21 (NT), random c. 18-23 (NT), superimposed c. 18-25 (NT), combination c. 43-04 (NT), double row c. 43-05 (NT), translation 18-26 (RT)

coded character set
code
F jeu de caractères codés
D Code-Tabelle; codierter Zeichenvorrat
R таблица кодирования
S juego de caracteres codificados
18-11 A set of unambiguous rules that

establish a *character set* and the one-to-one relationship between the *characters* of the set and their coded representations ('code elements')
DEF: 13-12, 13-11
REF: character set 13-12 (BT), code s. 18-09 (BT)

data code
F code de données
D Datencode
R цифровой код; код для данных
S código de datos
18-12 A set of rules and conventions according to which the *signals* representing *data* should be formed, transmitted, received and processed (in telecommunications)
DEF: 17-57, 17-12
REF: code 18-06 (OT)

data transformation
data conversion
F conversion de données
D Datenumsetzung; Konvertierung
R преобразование данных; преобразование информации
S conversión de datos
18-13 The changing of *data* from one form of representation to another, according to specific rules without changing significantly the *meaning* of the data
DEF: 17-12, 14-27
REF: coding 18-10 (NT), transcription 18-27 (NT), transliteration 18-28 (NT) translation 18-26 (RT)

decoding
F décodage
D Decodierung; Entschlüsselung (2)
R декодирование
S descodificación
18-14 (1) The assignment of *concepts* to *signs* to reconstruct *meaning*
DEF: 12-05, 13-29, 14-27
REF: encoding 18-17 (OT)
18-15 (2) Application of a 'code' (1, 2) to reverse some previous 'encoding' (2)
REF: coding 18-10 (BT), encoding 18-18 (OT)

direct code
F code direct
D Direktschlüssel
R прямой код
S código directo
18-16 A 'code' (1, 2) which represents one subject by one *mark* (in *punched cards*: one hole)
DEF: 13-24, 43-20
REF: code 18-05/06 (BT), superimposed c. 18-25 (OT)

encoding
F   encodage
D   Encodierung; Verschlüsselung (2)
R   кодирование
S   codificación
18-17 (1) The assignment of *signs* to *concepts* to obtain a representation
DEF: 13-29, 12-05
REF: decoding 18-14 (OT)
18-18 (2) Application of a 'code' (1, 2) such that a subsequent 'decoding' (2) is possible
REF: coding 18-10 (BT), decoding 18-15 (OT)

error-checking code
     error-detecting code; self-checking code
F   code détecteur d'erreurs
D   Fehlerprüfcode; Fehlererkennungscode
R   код с обнаружением ошибок
S   código detector de errores
18-19 A 'code' (2) in which each acceptable expression conforms to specific rules of construction so that if certain *errors* occur in an expression the resulting expression will not conform to the rules of construction and thus the presence of errors is detected
DEF: 42-19
REF: code 18-06 (BT)

fixed field coding
F   codage à zone fixe; codage en zone fixe
D   Festfeldverschlüsselung
R   кодирование по фиксированной схеме кодовых полей
S   codificación en campo fijo
18-20 The use of a dedicated part of a coding field for particular classes or groups of coded *data*
DEF: 17-12
REF: punched-card field 43-21 (RT)

generic coding
F   codage générique
D   generische Verschlüsselung; generische Codierung
R   кодирование с отражением иерархических отношений
S   codificación genérica
18-21 Use of a 'code' (2) that indicates *hierarchical relations* in the resulting coded representations
DEF: 38-19
REF: coding 18-10 (BT), classification schedule 39-19 (RT), notation 310-22 (RT)

numeric code
F   code numérique
D   numerischer Code; Schlüssel
R   цифровой код
S   código numérico
18-22 A 'code' (2) whose 'code set'

consists only of *digits* and associated *special characters*
DEF: 13-18, 13-32
REF: code 18-06 (BT), alphabetic c. 18-01 (RT), alphanumeric c. 18-02 (RT), binary c. 18-04 (RT)

random coding
F   codage aléatoire
D   aleatorische Codierung
R   произвольное кодирование; случайное кодирование
S   codificación aleatoria; codificación al azar
18-23 The selection of a set of 'code elements' to represent a *character* in such a manner that the probability of choice of any one set of code elements is equal to the probability of any other set
DEF: 13-11
REF: coding 18-06 (BT)

semantic code
F   code sémantique
D   semantischer Code
R   семантический код
S   código semántico
18-24 A *documentary language* leading to coded *index terms* reflecting the relationships between the *subjects* encoded
DEF: 15-08, 36-10
REF: documentary language 15-08 (BT), relational indexing 35-33 (RT), faceted classification 311-11 (RT)

superimposed coding
F   codage surimposé
D   Überlagerungscode; Überlagerungscodierung
R   суперпозиционное кодирование
S   codificación superpuesta
18-25 The use of 'code elements' as elements in more than one coded *character* or *word*, thereby making possible the entry of more characters or words than there are elements in a given coding field
DEF: 13-10/11, 14-55
REF: coding 18-10 (BT), direct code 18-16 (OT)

translation
F   traduction
D   Übersetzung
R   перевод
S   traducción
18-26 Conversion from one *language* into another language, usually *natural languages*
DEF: 15-13, 15-18
REF: code 18-07 (BT), coding 18-10 (RT), data transformation 18-13 (RT)

transcription
F transcription
D Transkription; Umschriftung
R транскрипция; транскрибирование
S transcripción
18-27 The representation of the *phonemes* of one *language* by the *alphabet* of another language
DEF: 13-27, 15-13, 13-02
REF: data transformation 18-12 (BT), transliteration 18-28 (RT)

transliteration
F translittération
D Transliteration
R транслитерация; транслитерирование
S transliteración
18-28 The representation of the *characters* of one *alphabet* by those of another
DEF: 13-10, 13-02
REF: data transformation 18-13 (BT), transcription 18-27 (RT)

19 Dissemination of information

active dissemination
F diffusion de l'information
D aktive Informationsverbreitung; Aktivinformation
R активное распространение
S difusión activa de la información; diseminación activa de la información
19-01 'Dissemination' of *primary* or *secondary documents* without having been requested for each specific *document* disseminated
DEF: 21-41, 21-50, 21-18
REF: dissemination 19-04 (BT), automatic 19-02 (NT), selective of information 314-25 (RT)

automatic dissemination
F diffusion automatique d'information
D automatische Informationsverbreitung
R автоматическое распространение
S difusión automatizada de la información; diseminación automatizada de la información
19-02 'Active dissemination' to selected addressees, carried out by clerical or *automatic* means, in accordance with pre-planned rules, and involving the matching of pre-determined selection criteria with prerecorded indications of potential customer interest
DEF: 42-05
REF: active dissemination 19-01 (BT), selective of information 314-25 (RT)

copyright
F droit d'auteur
D Urheberrecht; Copyright
R авторское право
S derechos de autor; copyright
19-03 The exclusive right to reproduce and 'disseminate' a literary, dramatic, musical or artistic work in any material form and to perform the work in public

dissemination
dissemination of information
F diffusion de l'information
D Informationsverbreitung
R распространение
S difusión de la información; diseminación de la información
19-04 The supply of *information* or *records* from a storage point to persons or organizations
DEF: 17-27/28, 21-44
REF: active dissemination 19-01 (NT), distribution 19-05 (NT), publication 19-13 (NT)

distribution
F distribution
D Distribution; Verteilung; Austeilung
R распределение (информации)
S distribución
19-05 The act of 'disseminating' items of *information* when presented in form of *records*
DEF: 17-27/28, 21-44
REF: dissemination 19-04 (BT), primary d. 19-11 (NT), secondary d. 19-15 (NT), prepublication 19-10 (NT)

information transfer
F transfert de l'information
D Informationstransfer
R передача информации
S transferencia de la información
19-06 The whole set of processes involved in the *transmission* of *information* from its originator to other persons
DEF: 17-67, 17-27
REF: specialized information 17-63 (RT), specialized communication 17-61 (RT), invisible college 19-09 (RT)

mass media
mass communication media
F mass media; moyens de communication de masse
D Massenkommunikationsmittel; Massenmedien
R средства массового информирования
S medios de comunicación de masas
19-07 (1) The organizational and technical means realizing the process of *mass communication*
DEF: 17-40
REF: publication 19-13 (RT)

19-08 (2) *Messages* or *documents* produced for *mass communication*, e.g. *newspapers*, magazines, broadcasts, etc.
DEF: 17-43, 21-18, 17-40, 21-30
REF: publication 19-14 (RT)

invisible college
F   collège invisible
D   "invisible College"
R   "незримый коллектив"
S   colegio invisible
19-09 An informal group of individuals exchanging *information* in a specific field of common interest
DEF: 17-27
REF: information transfer 19-06 (RT), group communication 17-24 (RT)

prepublication
F   prépublication
D   Vorveröffentlichung
R   предварительное издание
S   prepublicación; publicación previa
19-10 'Distribution' of small *editions* of scientific or technical *documents* prior to 'publication (2)' in regularly issued *serials*
DEF: 21-20, 21-18, 21-52
REF: distribution 19-05 (BT)

primary distribution
F   distribution primaire
D   Eigenvertrieb; Vorabvertrieb
R   первичное распространение (копий документа автором или издателем)
S   distribución primaria
19-11 'Distribution' of 'copies' of a *document* using a distribution list by source organization or individual
DEF: 110-05, 21-18
REF: distribution 19-05 (BT), secondary d. 19-15 (OT)

primary publication
F   publication primaire
D   Erstveröffentlichung; Primärveröffentlichung
R   первичное опубликование
S   publicación primaria
19-12 'Publication (1)' of *records* of *knowledge* for the first time
DEF: 21-44, 12-23/24
REF: publication 19-13 (BT), secondary p. 19-16 (OT)

publication
F   publication
D   Publikation; Veröffentlichung
R   опубликование (1); публикация (2)
S   publicación
19-13 The act of 'disseminating information' to a public
DEF: 17-27/28
REF: dissemination 19-04 (BT), primary p. 19-12 (NT), secondary, p. 19-16 (NT),

mass media 19-07 (RT), publishing 31-27 (RT)
19-14 (2) A *document* 'distributed' to a public
DEF: 21-18
REF: manuscript 21-26 (OT), document (RT), mass media 19-07 (RT)

secondary distribution
F   distribution secondaire
D   Vertrieb; Fremdvertrieb
R   вторичное распространение (копий документа)
S   distribución secundaria
19-15 Supplying or selling *copies* of *documents* by other than the source *publisher*
DEF: 110-05, 21-18, 52-20
REF: distribution 19-05 (BT), primary d. 19-11 (OT)

secondary publication
F   publication secondaire
D   Sekundärpublikation
R   повторное опубликование
S   publicación secundaria
19-16 'Publication (1)' of *records* of *knowledge* which have been published before
DEF: 21-44, 12-24
REF: publication 19-13 (BT), primary p. 19-12 (OT)

110 Reprography and printing

blue print
    cyanotype copy
F   bleu
D   Blaupause; Eisenblaudruck
R   синька
S   copia heliográfica
110-01 A 'copy' produced by a wet process using iron (ferroprussiate) salt and showing white lines on blue ground
REF: contact copy 110-03 (DT), diazo print 110-07 (RT), master print 110-27 (RT), master print 110-27 (RT), direct copy 110-09 (BT)

chip
F   image de titre
D   codierte Mikrofilmkarte
R   дискретный микрофильмовый носитель информации
110-02 A unit of 'microfilm' containing a 'microimage' and coded identification
REF: microfilm 110-31 (BT)

contact copy
F   copie par contact
D   Kontaktkopie
R   контактная копия;
     контактный отпечаток
S   copia de contacto
110-03 A 'copy' produced by holding a sheet of sensitized material in form and even contact with the original *document* or photographic 'negative'
DEF: 21-18
REF: copy 110-05 (BT), blue print 110-01 (NT), diazo print 110-07 (NT), direct c. 110-09 (NT), reflex c. 110-50 (NT), microform 110-34 (OT), diazo-copy 110-06 (RT), photocopy 110-43 (RT)

convenience copy
F   exemplaire de travail
D   Gebrauchskopie
R   рабочая копия
S   copia de prueba
110-04 A 'copy' made quickly and economically, which is not necessarily of the highest standard of quality or permanence
REF: copy 110-05 (BT)

copy
F   copie
D   Kopie; Abzug
R   копия
S   copia
110-05 A fascimile 'reproduction' of an 'original'
REF: reproduction 110-51 (BT), contact copy 110-03 (NT), convenience c. 110-04 (NT), duplicate 110-14 (NT), intermediate 110-23 (NT), master c. 110-26 (NT), master print 110-27 (NT), opaque c. 110-39 (NT), optical c. 110-40 (NT), photocopy 110-43 (NT), original 110-41 (OT), microcopy 110-29 (RT)

diazo-copy
     diazo process; dyeline; diazo copying
F   diazocopie
D   Diazokopie; Lichtpausverfahren
R   диазокопирование; светокопирование
S   diazocopia; copia diazoica
110-06 A reprographic process using diazo compounds for reproducing from transparent 'originals'
REF: dry process 110-11 (BT), semidry process 110-54 (NT), electrostatic process 110-18 (OT), gelatine dye transfer process 110-21 (OT), silver halide process 110-56 (OT), thermography 110-60 (OT), contact copy 110-03 (RT), direct copy 110-09 (RT)

diazo print
     white print; dye-line copy
F   diazocopie; héliographie

D   Lichtpause; Diazokopie; Trockenpause
R   диазотипная копия; светокопия
S   diazocopia; heliografía
110-07 A transmission print which can be produced on diazo material
REF: contact copy 110-03 (BT), direct copy 110-09 (BT), blue print 110-01 (RT), master p. 110-27 (RT)

diffusion transfer process
     chemical transfer process
F   copie par transfert
D   Diffusionsverfahren
R   диффузионное копирование
S   copia por transferencia
110-08 Copying process through transfer of non-exposed soluble silver components of the 'negative' by diffusion to create a 'positive image' in various, nonsensitive materials
REF: dry process 110-11 (OT)

direct copy
F   copie directe
D   Direktkopie
R   прямое изображение (результат прямого копирования)
S   copia directa
110-09 A 'contact copy' produced by the direct method, in which the light or heat passes through the 'original' directly on the surface of the sensitized material
REF: contact copy 110-03 (BT), blue print 110-01 (NT), diazo print 110-07 (NT), reflex c. 110-50 (OT)

direct positive
     self-positive
F   positif direct
D   Direktpositiv
R   прямое позитивное изображение
S   positivo directo
110-10 A 'positive' produced by the direct positive process in which a 'positive image' from a positive 'original' is produced without the intermediate use of a 'negative'
REF: positive 110-45 (BT)

dry process
F   procédé à sec
D   Trockenentwicklung
R   сухой способ (фотокопирования)
S   procedimiento en seco
110-11 A processing method does not use chemical solutions
REF: diazo-copy 110-06 (NT), gelatine dye transfer process 110-21 (NT), thermography 110-60 (NT), diffusion transfer 110-08 (OT), electrostatic 110-18 (RT), reversal p. 110-53 (OT)

duo method
F   méthode duo

D   Duo-Methode
R   микрофильмирование дуометодом
S   método duo
110-12 A microfilming method by which in two successive passes the one and the other half of the 'microfilm' width is exposed
REF: duplex method 110-13 (OT), simplex m. 110-57 (OT)

duplex method
F   méthode duplex
D   Duplex-Methode
R   микрофильмирование дуплекс-методом
S   método duplex
110-13 A method of microfilming whereby both sides of a *document* are simultaneously photographed side by side on the same film
DEF: 21-18
REF: duo method 110-12 (OT), simplex m. 110-57 (OT)

duplicate
added copy; identical copy; multiple copy
F   double
D   Duplikat
R   дублет; копия
S   duplicado
110-14 An exact 'copy' of the 'original' which can be used in the same way or in place of the original
REF: copy 110-05 (BT), original 110-41 (RT)

enlargement
blow-up; projection print
F   agrandissement
D   Vergrößerung
R   увеличенная копия
S   amplificación; ampliación
110-15 An 'optical copy' with a larger scale than the 'original'
REF: optical copy 110-40 (BT), microfilm print 110-32 (NT), reduction 110-48 (OT)

enlargement ratio
enlargement factor
F   échelle d'agrandissement
D   Vergrößerungsfaktor
R   коэффициент увеличения; кратность увеличения
S   factor de ampliación
110-16 An expression of the number of times a 'reproduction' or 'image' is larger in linear dimensions than the image from which it was made
REF: reduction factor 110-49 (OT)

enlarger-printer
F   copieur-agrandisseur
D   Vergrößerungsdruckgerät

R   копировальный аппарат с увеличителем
S   amplificador-impresor
110-17 An optical device for producing 'images' larger than those on the 'intermediate' from which the 'enlargement' is made and incorporating processing facilities for the rapid production of hard 'copy'
REF: microfilm reader 110-33 (RT), reader-printer 310-47 (RT)

electrostatic process
electrophotography; electrostatic photography; xerography
F   procédé électrostatique; photographie électrostatique; xérographie
D   Elektrophotographie; elektrostatische Photographie; Elektrokopierverfahren; elektrostatisches Kopierverfahren; Elektrofotografie; elektrostatische Fotografie; Xerographie
R   электростатическое копирование; электрофотография; ксерография
S   xerografía
110-18 The formation of an 'image' by the effect of light on an electrically charged photoconductive surface
REF: diazo-copy 110-06 (OT), diffusion transfer process 110-08 (OT), gelatine dye transfer p. 110-21 (OT), silver halide p. 110-56 (OT), thermography 110-60 (OT), dry p. 110-11 (RT)

flat-bed camera
planetary camera; step-and-repeat camera; stepwise-operated camera
F   appareil de prise de vues statique
D   Schrittkamera; Schrittschaltkamera
R   микрофильмирующий аппарат покадровой (шаговой) съёмки
S   tomavistas estático
110-19 A 'microfilm' camera in which the 'original' and the film are stationary during exposure
REF: flow camera 110-20 (OT)

flow camera
rotary camera
F   appareil de prise de vues dynamique
D   Durchlaufkamera
R   микрофильмирующий аппарат непрерывной съёмки; щелевой микрофильмирующий аппарат
S   tomavistas dinámico
110-20 A 'microfilm' camera for photographing single sheet *documents* in which the exposure is made while the 'original' and the film are moving in synchronization

DEF: 21-18
REF: flat-bed c. 110-19 (OT)

gelatine dye transfer process
F   gélatinographie
D
R   желатинография
S   transporte con gelatina
    110-21 A range of processes in which photographically produced dye 'images' are physically transferred from a light sensitive matrix to the receiving sheet
    REF: diazo-copy 110-06 (OT), diffusion transfer process 110-08 (OT), electrostatic p. 110-18 (OT), silver halide p. 110-56 (OT), thermography 110-60 (OT)

image
F   image
D   Abbildung; Bild
R   изображение
S   imagen
    110-22 The 'reproduction' of the subject-matter being reproduced
    REF: micro-image 110-36 (NT), negative 110-37 (NT), positive 110-45 (NT), reproduction 110-51 (RT)

intermediate
    intermediate copy; intermediate master
F   copie intermédiaire
D   Zwischenoriginal; Zwischenkopie
R   промежуточная копия
S   copia intermedia
    110-23 A 'copy' of an 'original' in the form essential to the process being used from which further copies can be made
    REF: copy 110-05 (BT), master copy 110-26 (RT)

letterpress printing
    relief printing; typographical printing
F   impression typographique
D   Hochdruck
R   высокая печать; типографическая печать
S   tipografía
    110-24 A printing process in which the printed 'image' is obtained by the transfer of ink from raised type or from halftone or line blocks
    REF: planographic printing 110-44 (OT)

lithographic printing
    lithography; chemical printing
F   impression lithographique
D   Lithographie
R   литография; литографская печать
S   litografía
    110-25 The 'planographic printing' process where the non-image areas of the printing plate are made water-receptive and the image areas are made water-repellent

REF: planographic printing 110-44 (BT), offset p. 310-38 (NT)

master copy
F   copie originale
D   Mutterkopie; Stammkopie
R   оригинал; матрица (при копировании)
S   copia maestra; copia matriz
    110-26 A 'copy' of a *document*, or in some processes the 'original' itself, from which further copies can be made
    DEF: 21-18
    REF: copy 110-05 (RT), intermediate 110-23 (RT), original 110-41 (RT), master print 110-27 (RT)

master print
F   matrice
D   Mutterpause
R   (прозрачная копия для защиты оригинала при копировании)
S   matriz
    110-27 A transparent 'copy' serving to protect the 'original' or first copy, for successive reprinting
    REF: copy 110-05 (BT), blue print 110-01 (RT), diazo p. 110-07 (RT), master copy 110-26 (RT)

microcard
    micro-opaque; microprint
F   microcarte
D   Mikrokarte
R   микрокарта; эпимикрокарта
S   microtarjeta
    110-28 'Microimages' arranged in a similar manner to those of a 'microfiche' but printed on paper
    REF: microcopy 110-29 (BT), opaque copy 110-39 (BT), microfiche 110-30 (RT)

microcopy
    microrecord; miniature
F   microcopie; microphotocopie
D   Mikrokopie
R   микрокопия
S   microcopia
    110-29 A 'reduction' of an 'original' legible by optimal means only
    REF: microform 110-34 (BT), reduction 110-48 (BT), optical copy 110-40 (OT), microcard 110-28 (NT), microfiche 110-30 (NT), microfilm 110-31 (NT)

microfiche
    transparent microsheet; sheet microfilm
F   microfiche
D   Microfiche; Mikroplanfilm
R   диамикрокарта
S   microficha
    110-30 Sheetfilm on which 'micro-images' are arranged in series along

side each other in a uniform pattern, with a legible title on the top
REF: microcopy 110-29 (BT), microfilm 110-31 (OT), microcard 110-28 (RT)

microfilm
F   microfilm
D   Mikrofilm; Mikrorollfilm
R   микрофильм
S   micropelícula; microfilm
110-31 The unexposed or processed film used in microcopying
REF: microcopy 110-29 (BT), microfiche 110-30 (OT)

microfilm print
     re-enlargement
F   agrandissement de microfilm
D   Rückvergrößerung; Mikrofilmrückvergrößerung
R   увеличенный оттиск с микрофильма
S   ampliación de micropelícula sobre papel
110-32 A 'reproduction' made from 'microfilm' normally on paper and of an enlarged size
REF: enlargement 110-15 (BT), reproduction 110-51 (BT)

microfilm reader
     reader
F   lecteur de microfilm
D   Mikrofilmlesegerät
R   читальный аппарат
S   lector de micropelículas
110-33 A projection device for showing a readable 'image' of a 'microcopy' on a screen or other suitable surface which may be either opaque or translucent
REF: enlarger-printer 110-17 (RT), reader-printer 110-47 (RT)

microform
F   microforme
D   Mikroform
R   микроформа
S   microforma
110-34 Any miniaturized form containing 'micro-images'
REF: reproduction 110-51 (BT), microcopy 110-29 (NT), semimicroform 110-55 (NT), reduction 110-48 (RT)

micrography
     micrographics
F   microcopie
D   Mikrographie
R   микрография
S   microcopiado
110-35 The whole set of techniques connected with 'microcopying'
REF: reprography 110-52 (RT)

micro-image
F   micro-image; microvue

D   Mikrobild
R   микроизображение
S   microimagen
110-36 An 'image' obtained by means of an optical device so reduced by comparison with the 'original' that it is too small to be read by the unaided eye
REF: image 110-22 (BT)

negative
F   négatif
D   Negativ
R   негатив
S   negativo
110-37 A photographic 'image' with tonal values reversed in relation or complementary to the 'original'
REF: image 110-22 (BT), positive 110-45 (OT)

offset printing
     offset litho printing; offset lithography; offset process
F   impression offset; procédé offset
D   Offsetdruck
R   офсет; офсетная печать
S   offset
110-38 A 'lithographic printing' process in which the 'image' is transferred to the 'copy' material via an 'intermediate' surface, e.g. a rubber blanket
REF: lithographic printing 110-25 (BT)

opaque copy
F   copie opaque
D   opake Kopie; Aufsichtkopie
R   копия на непрозрачной основе
S   copia opaca
110-39 A 'copy' on opaque or non-transparent material
REF: copy 110-05 (BT), microcard 110-28 (NT)

optical copy
     lens copying; optical print
F   copie optique
D   optische Kopie
R   оптическое изображение
S   copia óptica
110-40 A 'copy' produced via a lens or other optical devices
REF: copy 110-05 (BT), enlargement 110-15 (NT), reduction 110-48 (NT)

original
F   original
D   Original; Vorlage
R   оригинал
S   original
110-41 The *document* to be copied
DEF: 21-18
REF: copy 110-05 (OT), reproduction 110-51 (OT)

photosetting
    photocomposition
F   photocomposition
D   Fotosatz; Photosatz; Lichtsatz
R   фотонабор
S   fotocomposición
    110-42 The process for composing text matter directly on to photographic or other light-sensitive material.

photocopy
    photoduplicate; photoprint
F   photocopie
D   Fotokopie; Photokopie
R   фотокопия
S   fotocopia
    110-43 A 'copy' produced on or via sensitized material by the action of light or other radiation
    REF: copy 110-05 (BT), electrostatic process 110-18 (RT), gelatine dye transfer process 110-21 (RT), thermography 110-60 (RT)

planographic printing
    flat-bed printing
F   impression à plat
D   Flachdruck
R   плоская печать
S   impresión plana
    110-44 Printing processes in which the printing master has virtually level surface with the 'image' neither appreciably raised above nor etched below the surface
    REF: lithographic printing 110-25 (NT), letterpress p. 110-24 (OT), process camera 110-46 (RT)

positive
F   positif
D   Positiv
R   позитив
S   positivo
    110-45 A photographic 'image' with tonal or colour values as in the 'original'
    REF: image 110-22 (BT), negative 110-37 (OT)

process camera
F
D   Reproduktionskamera
R   репродукционный фотоаппарат
S
    110-46 A camera for the production of photographic 'intermediates' required for creating an 'image' on the printing master
    REF: planographic printing 110-44 (RT)

reader-printer
F   appareil de lecture - agrandisseur
D   Lese- und Rückvergrößerungsgerät
R   читально-копировальный аппарат

S   aparato de lectura e impresión
    110-47 A 'microfilm reader' with additional built-in facilities for producing rapidly an eye-legible 'copy'
    REF: enlarger-printer 110-17 (RT), reader-printer 110-33 (RT)

reduction
F   réduction
D   Verkleinerung
R   уменьшенная копия
S   reducción
    110-48 An 'optical copy' the scale of which is reduced with regard to the 'original'
    REF: optical copy 110-40 (BT), microcopy 110-29 (NT), enlargement 110-15 (OT), microform 110-24 (RT)

reduction ratio
    reduction factor
F   échelle de réduction
D   Verkleinerungsfaktor
R   коэффициент уменьшения; кратность уменьшения
S   factor de reducción
    110-49 An expression of a number of times a 'reproduction' or 'image' is smaller in linear dimensions than the image from which it is made
    REF: enlargement ratio 110-16 (OT)

reflex copy
    reflex print
F   copie par réflexion
D   Reflexkopie
R   копия, полученная методом рефлексного копирования
S   copia por reflexión
    110-50 A 'contact copy' made by the reflex method, in which the light or heat passes through the reverse of the sensitized material and is then reflected upon the surface of the 'original' back to the surface of the sensitized material
    REF: contact copy 110-03 (BT), direct c. 110-09 (OT)

reproduction
F   reproduction
D   Reproduktion
R   репродукция
S   reproducción
    110-51 A facsimile 'copy' or similar generation from a subject
    REF: copy 110-05 (NT), microform 110-34 (NT), original 110-41 (OT)

reprography
F   reprographie
D   Reprographie
R   репрография
S   reprografía

110-52 The whole set of copying and micro-copying processes using any form of radiation, all duplicating and office printing processes including ancillary operations connected with such processes
REF: micrography 110-35 (RT)

reversal process
F   procédé par inversion
D   Umkehrentwicklung
R   проявление с обращением
S   procedimiento por inversión
110-53 The conversion of a 'negative' to a positive by chemical means in one operation
REF: dry process 110-11 (OT), diffusion transfer p. 110-08 (RT)

semi-dry process
F   procédé demi-sec; procédé demi-humide
D   Halbfeuchtentwicklung
R   полусухой способ (фотокопирования)
S   procedimiento semi-seco
110-54 A 'diazo-copy' process in which the diazo compound is contained in the base and the coupler in a separate liquid developer
REF: diazo-copy 110-06 (BT)

semimicroform
F   semi-microforme
D   Semimikroform
R   (микроформа' которую можно читать без помощи сильных оптических средств)
S   semimicroforma
110-55 A 'microform' still readable without strong optical aid
REF: microform 110-34 (BT)

silver halide process
F   procédé aux halogénures d'argent
D   Silberhalogenidentwicklung
R   фотокопирование с применением галиодо-сребряных материалов
S   procedimiento a base de haluros de plata
110-56 A range of photocopying processes in which a latent 'image' is formed by the action of light or other radiation on silver-halide sensitized materials, the image being made visible and stable by subsequent processing
REF: diazo-copy 110-06 (OT), electrostatic process 110-18 (OT), gelatine dye transfer p. 110-21 (OT), thermography 110-60 (OT), diffusion transfer p. 110-08 (RT)

simplex method
F   simplex
D   Simplexmethode
R   (метод микрофильмирования документов с расположением кадров на плёнке в один ряд)
S   método simplex
110-57 A microcopying method using the width of the 'microfilm' for one set of 'image' only
REF: duo method 110-12 (OT), duplex m. 110-13 (OT)

spirit duplicating
hectograph process;
hectographic printing;
hectography
F   hectographie
D   Hektografieren; Hektographie
R   гектография; гектографическая печать
S   hectografía
110-58 A method of producing multiple 'copies' from a specially prepared master having a reversed 'image' prepared with a special wax-based carbon paper containing a spirit soluble dye
REF: stencil duplicating 110-59 (OT)

stencil duplicating
stencil printing
F   duplication par stencil
D   Durchdruck
R   трафаретная печать
S   duplicación mimeográfica
110-59 Duplicating from a specially prepared master having an 'image' formed by perforation of a continuous ink-impervious coating which is supported by a strong but permeable base
REF: spirit duplicating 110-58 (OT)

thermography
thermic copying; heat copying
F   thermocopie
D   Wärmekopierverfahren
R   термография
S   termocopiado
110-60 A range of photocopying processes which rely on heat for the formation of the 'image'
REF: dry process 110-11 (BT), diazo-copy 110-06 (OT), diffusion transfer process 110-08 (OT), electrostatic process 110-18 (OT), gelatine dye transfer process 110-21 (OT)

2 Documents

21 Types of documents

abridged document
abridgement; epitome
F   document abrégé
D   gekürztes Dokument
R   конспект; сжатое изложение
S   documento abreviado
21-01 A shortened version of a work, retaining the essential character and theme of the original
REF: document 21-18 (BT)

advance copy
F   exemplaire précédant la mise en vente; spécimen
D   Vorausexemplar; Signalexemplar
R   сигнальный экземпляр
S   ejemplar anticipado
21-02 A *copy* of a *publication* sent out before publication date for review, notice, or other purposes
DEF: 110-05, 19-14
REF: preprint 21-40 (RT)

almanac
F   almanach
D   Almanach
R   альманах; календарь
S   almanaque
21-03 An annual *publication* usually containing a calendar and other accompanying *information*, e.g. astronomical *data*
DEF: 19-14, 17-27, 17-12
REF: periodical 21-38 (BT), annals 21-04/05 (RT), annual 21-05 (RT), annual report 21-06 (RT), yearbook 21-65 (RT)

annals
F   annales
D   Annalen
R   анналы; летопись; ежегодник
S   anales
21-04 (1) A periodical *publication* recording events of a year, 'transactions' of an organization or progress in a special field
DEF: 19-14
REF: periodical 21-38 (BT), almanac 21-03 (RT), annual 21-06 (RT), annual report 21-07 (RT), proceedings 21-42, (RT), yearbook 21-65 (RT)
21-05 (2) Earlier, a 'record' of events arranged in chronological order
REF: almanac 21-03 (RT), annual 21-06 (RT), annual report 21-07 (RT), yearbook 21-65 (RT)

annual
F   annuaire
D   Jahrbuch
R   ежегодник
S   anuario
21-06 A 'serial' which appears once a year, containing material particularly relevant to the year in which it is issued
REF: serial 21-52 (BT), almanac 21-03 (RT), annals 21-04/05 (RT), annual report 21-06 (RT), yearbook 21-65 (RT)

annual report
F   rapport annuel
D   Jahresbericht
R   годовой отчёт
S   informe anual
21-07 A 'report' issued each year
REF: serial 21-52 (BT), report 21-46/47 (BT), final r. 21-23 (OT), almanac 21-03 (RT), annual 21-06 (RT), interim r. 21-22 (RT), project r. 21-43 (RT), technical r. 21-55 (RT), yearbook 21-65 (RT)

anthology
F   anthologie
D   Anthologie
R   антология
S   antología
21-08 A collection of works of various *authors* or of one author selected for a specific purpose or under specific aspects
DEF: 52-03
REF: monograph 21-29 (BT), monograph 21-28 (OT), composite work 21-14 (RT), memorial volume 21-27 (RT), omnibus volume 21-32 (RT)

book
F   livre
D   Buch
R   книга
S   libro
21-09 A larger number of sheets of paper with writing or printing on them bound together at one edge, usually between prospective covers and being published as an entity
REF: publication 19-14 (BT), document 21-18 (BT), paperback 21-36 (NT), pocket book 21-39 (NT), textbook 21-60 (NT), broadsheet 21-10 (OT), broadside 21-11 (OT), pamphlet 21-33 (OT), leaflet 21-25 (OT), periodical 21-38 (OT), monograph 21-29 (RT), volume 21-62 (RT)

broadsheet
F   feuille volante
D   Einblattdruck

R   лисотовое издание (с печатью
    на обеих сторонах листа)
S   hoja suelta
    21-10 A *publication* consisting usually of
    a single sheet bearing matter printed on
    both sides of the sheet
    DEF: 19-14
    REF: publication 19-14 (BT), book 21-09
    (OT), broadside 21-11 (OT), pamphlet
    21-33 (OT), leaflet 21-25 (OT), periodical
    21-38 (OT)

broadside
    leaflet
F   impression au recto seulement
D   Flugblatt
R   листовое издание (с печатью на одной
    стороне листа); плакат; афиша
S   hoja impresa por un solo lado
    21-11 A *publication* consisting usually of
    a single sheet bearing matter printed as a
    single page, on one side only of the sheet
    DEF: 19-14
    REF: publication 19-14 (BT), book 21-09
    (OT), broadside 21-10 (OT), pamphlet
    21-33, (OT), leaflet 21-25 (OT), periodical
    21-38 (OT)

bulletin
F   bulletin
D   Bulletin
R   бюллетень
S   boletín
    21-12 A *publication*, usually a 'serial',
    containing official or authoritative topical
    information
    DEF: 19-14
    REF: serial 21-51 (BT), newspaper 21-30
    (RT), journal 21-24 (RT), newsletter 21-
    31 (RT)

compendium
    compend; outline
F   précis
D   Kompendium; Grundriß; Leitfaden;
    Abriß
R   конспект; сжатое изложение
S   compendio
    21-13 A work containing the compre-
    hensive treatment of the essentials of a
    subject
    REF: monograph 21-28 (BT), encyclo-
    paedia 16-04 (RT), textbook 21-60 (RT),
    reference work 21-24 (RT)

composite work
    composite book; collective work
F   œuvre collective
D   Sammelwerk
R   коллективное произведение
S   obra colectiva
    21-14 A treatise on a single subject pro-
    duced through the collaboration of two
    or more *authors*, the contribution of each

forming a distinct section or part of the
complete work
DEF: 52-03
REF: monograph 21-28 (BT), memorial
volume 21-27 (OT), anthology 21-08
(RT), omnibus volume 21-32 (RT)

conference paper
F   communication
D   Vortrag; Tagungsbeitrag
R   доклад
S   ponencia; comunicación
    21-15 A 'paper' read at or prepared for a
    conference, meeting, etc.
    REF: paper 21-35 (BT)

digest
F   abrégé
D   Abriß; Überblick
R   дайджест
S   compendio
    21-16 A *publication* consisting of *sum-
    maries* of *information* on a single topic or
    on a number of related topics
    DEF: 19-14, 314-29, 17-28
    REF: publication 19-14 (BT), summary
    314-29 (RT)

directory
F   répertoire
D   Verzeichnis; Adreßbuch
R   справочник; адресная книга
S   directorio
    21-17
    A list of persons or organizations system-
    atically or alphabetically arranged giving
    some *information* about the single units,
    usually at least the addresses
    DEF: 17-28
    REF: reference work 21-24 (BT)

document
F   document
D   Dokument
R   документ
S   documento
    21-18 A unit consisting of a *data medium*,
    the *data* recorded on it and the *meaning*
    assigned to the data
    REF: 17-13, 17-12, 14-27
    REF: data medium 17-13 (BT), publication
    19-14 (NT), other NTs refer to sections
    21, 314, 315, record 21-44 (RT)

documentation
F   documentation
D   Dokumentation
R   документация; подборка документов
S   documentación
    21-19 (1) A set of 'documents' which may
    include *references* and similar materials
    collected for a specific purpose
    DEF: 22-17
    REF: section 314

edition
F   édition
D   Auflage; Ausgabe
R   издание
S   edición
21-20 All those *copies* of a 'document' produced from one unchanged type whether by direct contact or photographic methods
DEF: 110-05

final report
F   rapport final
D   Schlußbericht; Abschlußbericht
R   завершающий отчёт;
     заключительный отчёт
S   informe final
21-21 A 'project report' giving the final conclusions of the whole project
REF: project report 21-43 (BT)

form
    blank form
F   formulaire
D   Formular; Vordruck
R   бланк; формуляр
S   forma; machote; esqueleto
21-22 (2) A *data medium* carrying a format for the recording of *data*
DEF: 17-13, 17-12
REF: data medium 17-13 (BT)

interim report
F   rapport provisoire; rapport intermédiaire
D   vorläufiger Bericht; Zwischenbericht
R   предварительный отчёт
S   informe provisional
21-23 A 'project report' surveying the state of the project at a time where the project is still going on
REF: project report 21-43 (BT), final r. 21-21 (OT), annual r. 21-07 (RT), technical r. 21-59 (RT)

journal
F   bulletin d'information
D   Fachzeitschrift
R   журнал
S   revista
21-24 A 'periodical' issued by an institution, corporation or learned society, containing current news and reports of activities and work in a particular field
REF: periodical 21-38 (BT), newspaper 21-30 (OT), bulletin 21-12 (RT), newsletter 21-31 (RT)

leaflet
    folded leaflet
F   dépliant
D   Faltblatt; gefaltete Drucksache
R   листовка; книга-раскладка
S   hoja plegada

21-25 A *publication* of from two to four pages printed on a small sheet, folded once but not stitched or bound
DEF: 19-14
REF: publication 19-14 (BT), book 21-09 (OT), broadsheet 21-10 (OT), broadside 21-11 (OT), pamphlet 21-33 (OT)

manuscript
F   manuscrit
D   Manuskript
R   рукопись
S   manuscrito
21-26 The handwritten or typescript *copy* of an *author's* work before it is printed
DEF: 110-05, 52-03
REF: publication 19-14 (OT)

memorial volume
    commemorative volume
F   mélanges
D   Festschrift; Gedenkschrift
R   мемориальный том
S   volumen conmemorativo
21-27 A complimentary or memorial *publication* in the form of a collection of essays, addresses, or biographical, bibliographical, scientific, and other contributions, often embodying the results of research issued in honour of a person or an organization, usually on the occasion of an anniversary celebration
DEF: 19-14

monograph
F   monographie
D   Monographie
R   монография
S   monografía
21-28 (1) A treatise on a single *subject*
DEF: 12-30
REF: anthology 21-08 (OT), memorial volume 21-27 (OT), periodical 21-38 (OT), omnibus volume 21-32 (OT), serial 21-52 (OT), composite work 21-14 (NT), report 21-46/47 (NT), book 21-09 (RT), volume 21-62 (RT)
21-29 (2) In *cataloging*, any *publication* which is not 'serial'
DEF: 31-09, 19-14
REF: publication 19-14 (BT), anthology 21-08 (NT), memorial volume 21-27 (NT), monograph 21-28 (NT), omnibus volume 21-32 (NT), serial 21-52 (OT)

newspaper
    daily newspaper
F   journal; quotidien; gazette
D   Zeitung; Tageszeitung
R   газета
S   periódico; diario
21-30 A 'periodical' published mostly daily, usually being not restricted in its

contents to a *subject field*, and containing actual *information*
DEF: 17-10, 12-31, 17-27/28
REF: periodical 21-38 (BT), journal 21-24 (OT), bulletin 21-12 (RT), newsletter 21-31 (RT)

newsletter
F   bulletin de liaison
D   Mitgliederinformationen; Newsletter; Rundschreiben; Rundbrief; Informationsblatt
R   информационный бюллетень
S   boletín de información
21-31 A 'periodical' usually published by an organization containing current *information* of interest to its members
DEF: 17-27/28
REF: periodical 21-38 (BT), bulletin 21-12 (RT), journal 21-24 (RT), newspaper 21-30 (RT)

omnibus volume
F   recueil; recueil de morceaux choisis
D   Sammelband; Sammelwerk
R   сборный том
S   antología
21-32 A compilation of several independent treatises by one or more *authors* on different *subjects*, the treatises often having being published before, the compilation published as a 'volume' (1)
DEF: 52-03, 12-30
REF: monograph 21-29 (BT), monograph 21-28 (OT), anthology 21-08 (RT), composite work 21-14 (RT), memorial volume 21-27 (RT)

pamphlet
   brochure
F   brochure
D   Broschüre
R   брошюра
S   folleto
21-33 A short printed work, consisting of only a few leaves, usually stitched or sewn
REF: document 21-18 (BT), book 21-09 (OT), broadside 21-10 (OT), leaflet 21-25 (OT)

pamphlet volume
F   recueil
D   Sammelband (kleiner Schriften); Mischband
R   искусственный сборник; конволют (составленный из брошюр)
S   compilación miscelánea
21-34 A 'volume' (1) consisting of a number of short *publications* bound together with or without a supplementary title page or *contents list*
DEF: 19-14, 22-06
REF: volume 21-62 (BT)

paper
F   document de travail
D   Schriftstück; Diskussionspapier; Arbeitspapier; Vorlage
R   статья; доклад; сообщение
S   ponencia; comunicación
21-35 A work of informational nature written for reading before a group or being discussed by a group
REF: document 21-18 (BT), conference paper 21-15 (NT), preprint 21-41 (RT), reprint 21-49 (RT)

paperback
F   livre broché
D   Paperback
R   книга в бумажной обложке
S   publicación en rustica; publicación en pasta blanda
21-36 A 'book' issued by a *publisher* in a limp casing
DEF: 52-20
REF: book 21-09 (BT), pocket book 21-39 (RT)

patent
F   brevet
D   Patent
R   патент
S   patente
21-37 A 'document' containing an invention granted by government with the monopoly right to produce, use, sell or get profit from the invention for a certain number of years
REF: document 21-18 (BT)

periodical
   serial (U.S.A.)
F   périodique
D   Periodikum; Zeitschrift
R   периодическое издание
S   publicación periódica; revista
21-38 A *publication* issued at regular intervals, each issue normally being numbered consecutively with no predetermined termination of publication, usually having a variety of *contents* and contributors
DEF: 19-14, 17-10
REF: publication 19-14 (BT), serial 21-52 (BT), almanac 21-03 (NT), annals 21-04/05 (NT), annual 21-06 (NT), annual report 21-07 (NT), journal 21-24 (NT), newspaper 21-30 (NT), newsletter 21-31 (NT), yearbook 21-65 (NT), book 21-09 (OT), broadsheet 21-10 (OT), broadside 21-11 (OT), bulletin 21-12 (RT)

pocket book
F   livre de poche
D   Taschenbuch
R   карманная книга
S   libro de bolsillo

21-39 A 'book' of a small format to be carried in a pocket
REF: book 21-09 (BT), paperback 21-36 (RT)

preprint
F   publication préliminaire
D   Vorabdruck
R   препринт
S   publicación preliminar
21-40 A *copy* of a 'paper' issued prior to formal *publication* or presentation
DEF: 110-05, 19-13
REF: reprint 21-49 (OT), advance copy 21-02 (RT)

primary document
F   document primaire
D   Primärdokument
R   первичный документ
S   documento primario
21-41 An original 'document' which is not the result of a *documentation* process
DEF: 31-19
REF: document 21-18 (BT), secondary d. 21-50 (OT), source d. 21-55 (RT)

proceedings
    transactions
F   comptes rendus; actes; travaux
D   Kongreßberichte; Konferenzberichte; Tagungsberichte; Sitzungsberichte; Verhandlungen; Abhandlungen
R   труды (конференции); протоколы; учёные записки
S   actas
21-42 A *publication* or 'series' containing the texts of 'conference papers' communicated orally to a conference, society or institution and generally also reporting or transcribing discussions arising from the papers and business transacted in connexion with them
DEF: 19-14
REF: publication 19-14 (BT), series 21-53 (RT)

project report
    advances; progress report
F   rapport de recherche; mise au point
D   Projektbericht; Fortschrittsbericht
R   научно-технический отчёт
S   informe de trabajos en curso; informe de investigaciones en desarrollo
21-43 A 'report' (1) surveying the work that has been done in a research or development project or during a particular stage of it
REF: report 21-46 (BT), interim r. 21-23 (NT), final r. 21-21 (NT), annual r. 21-07 (RT), technical r. 21-59 (RT)

record
F   enregistrement
D   Aufzeichnung
R   запись
S   registro
21-44 A collection of related items of *data* treated as a unit and fixed on a *data medium*
DEF: 17-12, 17-13
REF: document 21-18 (RT)

reference work
F   ouvrage de référence
D   Nachschlagewerk
R   справочник; справочное издание
S   obra de consulta
21-45 A printed collection of *data* or *information* published as a 'document' and intended to be used for reference
DEF: 17-05, 17-27/28
REF: document 21-18 (BT), encyclopaedia 16-04 (NT), dictionary 16-03 (NT), compendium 21-13 (RT), textbook 21-60 (RT)

report
F   rapport
D   Bericht; Forschungsbericht (1); Studie; Report
R   отчёт
S   informe
21-46 (1) A 'document' containing the findings of an investigation or study by an individual or group and usually including recommendations
REF: document 21-19 (BT), project report 21-42 (NT), technical r. 21-56 (NT), annual r. 21-07 (RT)
21-47 (2) A 'document' containing an account of the activities of a body over a particular period
REF: document 21-18 (BT), annual report 21-07 (NT), project r. 21-43 (NT), technical r. 21-59 (NT)

reprint
F   réimpression; tirage spécial (2)
D   Nachdruck (1); Sonderdruck (2)
R   дополнительный тираж (1); стереотипное издание (1); отдельный оттиск (2)
S   reimpresión; sobretiro
21-48 (1) All those *copies* of an edition reproduced at an interval after the original printing of the 'edition'
DEF: 110-05
21-49 (2) A *copy* of a 'paper' published in a 'serial' or 'book'-like *publication*, usually supplied or sold to the *author* or other requester by the *publisher*
DEF: 110-05, 19-14, 52-03, 52-20
REF: copy 110-05 (BT), preprint 21-40 (OT), separate 21-51 (RT)

secondary document
F document secondaire
D Sekundärdokument
R вторичный документ
S documento secundario
21-50 A 'document' containing *data* or *information* about 'primary documents'
DEF: 17-12, 17-28
REF: document 21-18 (BT), primary d. 21-41 (OT), to (NT) ref. to sections 314, 315

separate
   offprint
F tiré à part
D Separatum; Sonderabdruck
R отдельный оттиск
S separata; tirada aparte
21-51 A 'reprint' or special *copy* of an article *chapter* or other part of a larger *publication*
DEF: 110-05, 22-04, 19-14
REF: copy 110-05 (BT), preprint 21-40 (OT), reprint 21-49 (RT)

serial
F publication en série
D Serie; Serienwerk; Fortsetzungswerk
R продолжающееся издание
S publicación seriada; folletón
21-52 (1) A *publication* issued in separate and successive parts usually in a uniform *format* with constant *title* and intended to be continued indefinitely
DEF: 19-14, 22-12, 22-23
REF: publication 19-14 (BT), bulletin 21-12 (NT), periodical 21-38 (NT), series 21-54 (NT), book 21-09 (OT)
21-53 (2) A long story published in instalments

series
F suite
D Reihe; Reihenwerk
R серия
S serie
21-54 A 'serial' (1) in which each part is usually characterized by a distinctive *title* in addition to the constant *series title* and of which the parts are published at irregular intervals
DEF: 22-23, 22-18
REF: serial 21-52 (BT), periodical 21-38 (OT), proceedings 21-42 (RT)

source document
   original document
F document original
D Originaldokument; Quelle (2); Quellendokument
R первичный документ (1); документальный источник (2)
S documento original
21-55 (1) The original 'document' in which are recorded the details of a transaction, scientific investigation, etc.
REF: document 21-18 (BT), primary d. 21-41 (RT)
21-56 (2) A 'document' from which *data* is extracted
DEF: 17-12
REF: document 21-18 (BT), source material 21-57 (RT)

source material
   original sources; primary sources
F sources originales
D Quellenmaterial; Originalmaterial; Originalquellen
R первоисточники
S fuentes originales; fuentes primarias
21-57 Fundamental authoritative material relating to a subject, used in the preparation of other written work
REF: document 21-18 (RT), record 21-44 (RT), source document 21-56 (RT)

standard
F norme
D Norm
R стандарт
S normas
21-58 The result of a particular standardization effort, approved by a recognized authority in form of a 'document' containing a set of conditions to be fulfilled

technical report
   research report;
   research and development report
F rapport technique
D Forschungsbericht; Entwicklungsbericht
R научно-исследовательский отчёт; технический отчёт
S informe técnico
21-59 A 'report' concerning the results of a scientific investigation or a technical development, test or evaluation
REF: report 21-46/47 (BT), annual r. 21-07 (RT), final r. 21-21 (RT), interim r. 21-23 (RT), project r. 21-43 (RT)

textbook
F manuel
D Lehrbuch
R учебник
S libro de texto; manual
21-60 A 'book' designed for teaching
REF: book 21-09 (BT), compendium 21-13 (RT), reference work 21-45 (RT)

thesis
F thèse
D Hochschulschrift; universitäre Prüfungsarbeit

R   диссертация; диссертационная работа
S   tesis
21-61 A statement of investigation of research, presenting the *author's* findings and any conclusions reached submitted by the author in support of his candidature for a higher degree or professional qualification or other award
DEF: 52-03
REF: monograph 21-28 (BT), report 21-46 (RT), technical report 21-59 (RT)

volume
F   volume (1); tome (2)
D   Band; Jahrgang (2)
R   том (1); сводный том (2)
S   volumen; tomo
21-62 (1) A collection of written or printed sheets bound together so as to form a 'book'
REF: pamphlet volume 21-34 (NT), book 21-09 (RT), monograph 21-62 (RT)
21-63 (2) The complete set of issues of a 'periodical' issued in a *publication* period looked at as an entity, usually a year
DEF: 19-13
21-64 (3) Main division of a work which may be published as a 'volume' (2)

yearbook
F   annuaire
D   Jahrbuch
R   ежегодник
S   anuario
21-65 An annual 'volume' (1) of current *information* in descriptive and/or statistical form, sometimes limited to a special field
DEF: 17-28
REF: periodical 21-38 (BT), almanac 21-03 (RT), annals 21-04/05 (RT), annual 21-06 (RT), annual report 21-07 (RT)

22 Parts of documents

appendix
F   appendice
D   Anhang
R   приложение
S   apéndice
22-01 Additional matter included at the end of a *document* supplementary to the main 'text' (1)
DEF: 21-18
REF: text 22-22 (BT), foreword 22-11 (OT), introduction 22-14 (OT), text 22-21 (OT)

bibliographical strip
    contents strip
F   manchette bibliographique

D   Inhaltsfahne
R   (вкладка в журнале с библиографическими описаниями отдельных статей)
S   tira bibliográfica
22-02 A strip at the beginning of the issue of a *journal* containing the *bibliographic description* of the single items in a form convenient for the purposes of *documentation*
DEF: 21-24, 31-07, 31-19
REF: contents list 22-06 (RT), contents page 22-07 (RT)

caption
    heading; head
F   rubrique; en-tête
D   Überschrift
R   заголовок; рубрика
S   encabezado
22-03 The *words, phrases* or *sentence* heading a 'chapter' of a *document* or another single part of a document as an article, etc.
DEF: 14-55, 14-34, 14-44, 21-18
REF: title 22-23 (RT)

chapter
F   chapitre
D   Kapitel; Abschnitt
R   глава
S   capítulo
22-04 A division of a *book* or treatise, usually marked by a number and 'caption'
DEF: 21-08
REF: text 22-21 (BT), paragraph 22-16 (NT)

citation (U.S.A.)
    quotation (Brit.)
F   citation
D   Zitat; Literaturangabe
R   ссылка; отсыкла к источнику
S   cita; referencia
22-05 A note of reference to a work from which a passage is quoted or to some *source material* as authority for a statement or proposition
DEF: 21-57
REF: reference 22-17 (RT)

contents list
    table of contents
F   table des matières; sommaire
D   Inhaltsverzeichnis
R   оглавление; содержание
S   tabla de materias; índice; sumario
22-06 A listing of the 'chapters' or parts of a *document* in the order they are presented by the document
DEF: 21-18
REF: bibliographical strip 22-02 (RT), contents page 22-07

contents page
contents sheet
F page de sommaire
D Inhaltsblatt; Dokumentationsblatt
R страница с оглавлением
S sumario
22-07 A page at the beginning of the issue of a *journal* containing the *bibliographic description* and *abstracts* of the main items of the issue
DEF: 21-24, 31-07, 314-01
REF: bibliographical strip 22-02 (RT), contents list 22-05 (RT)

cover
F couverture
D Umschlag; Deckel
R обложка
S cubierta
22-08 The exterior of a *document* including front page, back page and back
DEF: 21-18
REF: text 22-21/22 (OT)

cover title
F titre de couverture
D Umschlagtitel; Aussentitel
R обложечное заглавие
S título exterior; título de cubierta
22-09 The 'title' of a *document* as it reads on the front 'cover'
DEF: 21-18
REF: title 22-23 (BT)

figure
F figure
D Abbildung
R иллюстрация
S figura; ilustración
22-10 A schematic representation, graphical or as a table, placed in a *document* to illustrate the 'text' (2)
DEF: 21-18
REF: table 22-20 (NT), text 22-22 (OT)

foreword
preface
F avant-propos; préface
D Vorwort
R предисловие
S prefacio; prólogo
22-11 Some introductory notes to a document, either by the *author* or someone else, to explain some basic features of the following 'text' (1)
DEF: 52-03
REF: text 22-22 (BT), appendix 22-01 (OT), introduction 22-14 (RT)

format
F format
D Format; Aufmachung (1)

R оформление (внешний вид) книги (1); формат (2)
S formato
22-12 (1) The general form of a *publication* with particular reference to composition, layout, size and general appearance
DEF: 19-14
22-13 (2) The shape and size of the *publication* resulting from adopting a particular paper size
DEF: 19-14

introduction
F introduction
D Einleitung
R введение; вступление
S introducción
22-14 Statements introducing a *document*, either by the *author* or another person, so as to show the general frame of reference of the document, etc.
DEF: 21-18, 52-03
REF: text 22-22 (BT), appendix 22-01 (OT), foreword 22-11 (RT)

main title
F titre principal
D Haupttitel
R основное заглавие
S título principal
22-15 The part of the 'title' which precedes the 'subtitle'
REF: title 22-23 (BT), subtitle 22-19 (OT)

paragraph
F alinéa
D Absatz; Abschnitt
R обзац
S párrafo
22-16 A short passage of a written or printed discourse, beginning on a new and usually indented line
REF: chapter 22-04 (BT)

reference
F référence
D Literaturhinweis; Literaturnachweis; Literaturverweis; Verweisung
R ссылка; библиографическое примечание
S referencia bibliográfica; cita bibliográfica
22-17 A 'citation' referring to a *document* or passage
DEF: 21-18
REF: citation 22-05 (RT)

series title
F titre de collection
D Serientitel; Reihentitel
R серийное заглавие; заглавие серии
S título de serie; título de colección
22-18 The 'title' of a *serial* or *series*

DEF: 21-52, 21-54
REF: title 22-23 (BT)

subtitle
secondary title
F   sous-titre
D   Untertitel
R   подзаголовок
S   subtítulo
22-19 The subordinate and explanatory part of a 'title' following the 'main title', distinguished by a *special character*, e.g. colon, full stop or hyphen.
DEF: 13-32
REF: title 22-23 (BT), main title 22-15 (OT)

table
F   tableau
D   Tabelle
R   таблица
S   cuadro; tabla
22-20 A representation of any kind of *data*, in parallel columns and/or rows
DEF: 17-12
REF: figure 22-10 (BT)

text
F   texte
D   Text; Hauptteil (1)
R   текст; основной текст
S   texto
22-21 (1) The main body of *words* in a *document*, excluding preliminaries, 'appendixes', *indexes*, etc.

DEF: 14-55, 21-18, 35-22
REF: text 22-22 (BT), chapter 22-04 (NT), appendix 22-01 (OT), foreword 22-11 (OT), introduction 22-14 (OT)
22-22 (2) The part of a *document* in which *information* is presented in literal rather than graphical form
DEF: 21-18, 17-28
REF: text 22-21 (NT), figure 22-10 (OT)

title
full title
F   titre
D   Titel
R   заглавие; полное заглавие
S   título
22-23 The distinguishing *name* of a *document* or work including any alternative title, 'subtitle' or associative description
DEF: 14-29, 21-18
REF: cover title 22-09 (NT), main t. 22-15 (NT), series t. 22-18 (NT), subtitle 22-19 (NT), caption 22-03 (RT)

title page
F   page de titre
D   Titelblatt
R   титульный лист
S   página de título; portada
22-24 The second page in a *book* containing the comprehensive *bibliographic description*
DEF: 21-09, 31-07

3   The activities in information and documentation

31 Main activities in the field of information and documentation

(excluded is retrieval, ref. to section 313)

abstracting
F   analyse
D   Referieren; Erstellen von Kurzreferaten
R   реферирование
S   elaboración de extractos o resúmenes
31-01 The act of preparing *abstracts*
DEF: 314-01
REF: document analysis 31-15 (BT), automatic abstracting 31-04 (NT)

accession
F   enregistrement des acquisitions
D   Akzession; Zugangsregistrierung
R   регистрация новых поступлений
S   registro de adquisiciones
31-02 To register acquisitions of *library* materials, usually in the order in which they are added to a *collection*
DEF: 51-25, 312-05
REF: acquisition 31-03 (RT), accession number 310-01 (RT)

acquisition
F   acquisitions à titre onéreux
D   Acquisition; Erwerb; Erwerbung
R   комплектование (фонда)
S   adquisición

31-03 The process of identifying a desired item verifying a need, selecting a proper source and ordering. May include order follow-up, receiving and paying
REF: accession 31-02 (RT)

automatic abstracting
auto-abstracting; machine abstracting
F   préparation automatique des résumés
D   machinelles Referieren;
automatisches Referieren
R   автоматическое реферирование
S   elaboración automatizada de extractos o resúmenes
31-04 Preparing *abstracts* by *automatic means*, usually by extracting *sentences* from the original *text* automatically, which seem to indicate the *content* of the *document*
DEF: 314-01, 42-05, 14-44, 22-22, 17-10, 21-18
REF: abstracting 31-01 (BT), mechanized documentation 31-26 (RT)

automatic classification
mechanized classification
F   classification automatique
D   automatische Klassifizierung; maschinelle Klassifizierung
R   автоматическое классифицирование
S   clasificación automatizada
31-05 'Classifying' (2) by *automatic* means, i.e. assigning *notations* of a *classification system* or *schedule* automatically according to a foregoing automatic 'document analysis'
DEF: 42-05, 310-23, 39-21, 39-20
REF: classifying 31-12 (OT), automatic indexing 31-06 (BT), mechanized documentation 31-26 (RT)

automatic indexing
machine indexing
F   indexation automatique
D   maschinelle Indexierung; automatische Indexierung
R   автоматическое индексирование
S   indizado automatizado
31-06 'Indexing' by *automatic* means, i.e. selecting *keywords* out of the *document*, or 'automatic classification'
DEF: 42-05, 36-12, 21-18
REF: indexing 31-21 (BT), automatic classification 31-05 (NT), mechanized documentation 31-26 (RT)

bibliographic description
F   description bibliographique
D   bibliographische Beschreibung
R   библиографическое описание
S   descripción bibliográfica
31-07 Description of a *document* using only bibliographical categories, as *author*, *title*, *publisher*, etc.

DEF: 21-18, 52-03, 22-23, 52-20
REF: document description 31-16 (BT), descriptive cataloguing 32-18 (RT)

bibliographical unit
F   unité bibliographique
D   bibliographische Einheit
R   библиографическая единица
S   unidad bibliográfica
31-08 The unit to which a 'bibliographical description' is assigned
REF: documentary unit 31-18 (RT)

cataloguing
cataloging
F   catalogage; catalographie
D   Katalogisierung
R   каталогизация
S   catalogación
31-09 The process of compiling a *catalogue* or constructing *entries* for insertion into the catalogue
DEF: 32-08, 33-08
REF: centralized cataloguing 32-14 (NT), collective c. 32-17 (NT), co-operative c. 32-18 (NT), descriptive c. 32-19 (NT), prenatal c. 32-22 (NT), selective c. 32-23 (NT), subject c. 32-29 (NT), document description 31-16 (RT)

circulation work
loans work
F   prêt
D   Ausleihbetrieb; Ausleihe
R   работа на абонементе
S   servicio de préstamo
31-10 Lending to *library users* the *documents* requested
DEF: 51-25, 46-30, 21-18
REF: interlibrary loan 31-23 (RT)

classifying
classification; classing (2)
F   classification (1); indexation (2)
D   Klassifizieren; Klassieren (2); Klassifikationserstellung (1)
R   разработка классификации (1); классифицирование (2)
S   clasificación
31-11 (1) The act of preparing a *classification*
DEF: 311-05
REF: facet analysis 39-35 (RT)
31-12 (2) The act of 'indexing' with a *classification schedule*
DEF: 39-19
REF: indexing 31-21 (BT), automatic classification 31-05 (NT)

clerical operations
F   traitement
D   (Büroarbeiten); Routinearbeiten
R   (вспомогательные технические операции)

S   operaciones de rutina
31-13 Denoted routines of observation, identification and manipulation of marked material objects according to some protocol involving only observation on the marks, including those belonging and accessible to the observing device
REF: collating 34-06 (NT), sorting 34-21 (NT), storage 312-28 (NT), access 313-01 (NT)

data documentation
   fact documentation;
   direct documentation
F   fourniture de données
D   Datendokumentation;
   direkte Dokumentation
R   фактографическое информирование
S   suministro de datos
31-14 'Documentation' providing the *user* with *data* about *facts*
DEF: 46-30, 17-12, 12-17
REF: documentation 31-19 (BT), literature d. 31-25 (OT)

document analysis
   contents analysis
F   analyse de document
D   Dokumentenanalyse;
   dokumentarische Inhaltsanalyse
R   информационный анализ документов
S   análisis de documentos
31-15 The analysis of the subject *contents* of *documents* with the aim to select all the *characteristics* according to which the document should be able to be found in *retrieval*
DEF: 17-10, 21-18, 12-02, 313-31
REF: abstracting 31-01 (NT), indexing 31-21 (NT), contents analysis 17-11 (RT)

document description
F   description de document
D   Dokumentbeschreibung;
   Dokumentationseinheit
R   описание документа;
   поисковый образ документа
S   descripción de documentos
31-16 Description of a *document* containing all the *data* about a document that seem to be of value in a specific *documentation system*, usually including 'bibliographic description' and subject description coming from 'document analysis, abstracting' and 'indexing'
DEF: 21-18, 17-12, 41-13
REF: bibliographic description 31-07(NT), documentary unit 31-17 (RT)

documentary unit
F   unité documentaire
D   Dokumentationseinheit (1);
   dokumentarische Bezugseinheit (2)
R   единица документальной

информации (1);
единичный документ (2)
S   unidad documental
31-17 (1) The set of *data* or the physical unit containing the 'document description';
DEF: 17-12
REF: document description 31-16 (RT)
31-18 (2) The *document* or object to which a 'document description' or an equivalent is assigned
DEF: 21-18
REF: bibliographical unit 31-08 (RT)

documentation
F   documentation
D   Dokumentation
R   документационная деятельность
S   documentación
31-19 (2) The continuous and systematic processing of *documents* or *data*, including e.g. location, identification, 'acquisition', analysis, *storage, retrieval*, circulation and preservation for the *specialized information* of *users*
DEF: 21-18, 17-12, 312-28, 313-31, 17-63, 46-30
REF: data documentation 31-14 (NT), literature d. 31-25 (NT), information handling 31-22 (RT), librarianship 31-24 (RT)

file maintenance
   updating; file updating
F   mise à jour des fichiers;
   mise à jour des collections
D   Weiterführung; Fortschreibung
R   ведение информационного массива;
   обновление информационного массива
S   actualización de registros
31-20 The activity of keeping a *file* up to date by adding, changing or deleting items
DEF: 33-11

indexing
F   indexage; indexation
D   Indexierung (GFR); Indizierung (GDR)
R   индексирование
S   indizado
31-21 Assignment of *index terms* to *documents* or objects with the aim to be able later on to retrieve the documents or objects according to the selected *concepts* designated by the index terms
DEF: 36-10, 21-18, 12-05
REF: document analysis 31-15 (BT), automatic indexing 31-06 (NT), classifying 31-12 (NT), other (NT) ref. section 35

information handling
F
D   Informationsbearbeitung
R   обработка информации
S   manejo de la información

s　manejo de la información
31-22 The storing and processing of *information* and its transmission from the source to the *user* (excluding creation and use of information)
DEF: 17-27/28
REF: documentation 31-19 (RT)

interlibrary loan
interlibrary lending
F　prêt entre bibliothèques
D　auswärtiger Leihverkehr
R　межбиблиотечный абонемент
s　préstamo interbibliotecario
31-23 A co-operative arrangement among *libraries* by which one library may borrow material from another library
DEF: 51-25
REF: circulation work 31-10 (RT)

librarianship
F　bibliothéconomie
D　Bibliothekswesen
R　библиотечное дело;
библиотечная деятельность
s　biblioteconomía
31-24 The application of *knowledge* of *books* and certain principles, theories and techniques to the establishment, preservation, organization and use of collections of books and other materials in *libraries* and to the extension of library service
DEF: 12-24, 21-08, 51-25
REF: special librarianship 31-28 (NT), documentation 31-19 (RT)

literature documentation
bibliographic documentation;
indirect documentation
F　bibliographie
D　Literaturdokumentation;
indirekte Dokumentation
R　документальное (библиографическое) информирование
s　biblioteconomía
31-25 'Documentation' providing the *user* with *references* to *documents*
DEF: 46-30, 22-17, 21-18
REF: documentation 31-19 (BT), data d. 31-14 (OT)

mechanized documentation
F　documentation automatique
D　maschinelle Dokumentation
R　автоматизированные информационные процессы
s　documentación automatizada
31-26 'Documentation' using *automatic* means at least for the purposes of *storage* and *retrieval*
DEF: 42-05, 312-28, 313-31
REF: automatic data processing 17-02 (BT), documentation 31-19 (BT), automatic abstracting 31-04 (RT), automatic classification 31-05 (RT), automatic indexing 31-06 (RT)

publishing
F　éditer; publier
D　Veröffentlichen; Publizieren
R　опубликование
s　publicación
31-27 Making a *record* of *knowledge* available to the public as a *publication*
DEF: 21-44, 12-24, 19-14
REF: publication 19-13 (RT)

special librarianship
F　bibliothéconomie spéciale
D　Spezialbibliothekswesen;
Fachbibliothekswesen
R　специализированная библиотечная деятельность
s　biblioteconomía especializada
31-28 'Librarianship' in a specific *subject field* or for specific purposes
DEF: 12-31
REF: librarianship 31-24 (BT)

32 Catalogues and cataloguing

accession list
F　liste d'acquisition
D　Zugangsliste
R　список новых поступлений (издаваемый периодически)
s　lista de adquisiciones
32-01 A periodical list of new acquisitions often issued monthly
REF: accessions register 32-02 (RT)

accessions register
F　registre d'acquisitions
D　Zugangsverzeichnis; Zugangsbuch
R　перечень новых поступлений
s　católogo de adquisiciones
32-02 A *record* of *volumes* added to a *library* in the order in which they are received
DEF: 21-43, 21-44, 51-25
REF: accession list 32-01 (RT)

alphabetical subject catalogue
F　catalogue-matières;
catalogue alphabétique de matières
D　alphabetischer Sachkatalog
R　алфавитно-предметный каталог
s　catálogo alfabético de materias
32-03 A *subject catalogue* in alphabetical order of the *index terms*
DEF: 36-10
REF: subject catalogue 32-27 (BT), classed c. 32-15 (OT)

annotated catalogue
F　catalogue annoté
D　annotierender Katalog

R аннотированный каталог
S catálogo anotado
32-04 A 'catalogue' containing *bibliographic descriptions* and additional *annotations* to the *documents*
DEF: 31-07, 314-05, 21-18
REF: catalogue 32-08 (BT)

author catalogue
F catalogue-auteurs;
catalogue alphabétique d'auteurs
D Autorenkatalog; Verfasserkatalog
R авторский каталог
S catálogo de autores
32-05 A 'catalogue' of *author entries*, alphabetically arranged, usually including *added entries* under *editors, translators*, etc., and entries under *titles* in the case of anonymous works
DEF: 33-03, 33-01, 52-11, 52-25, 22-23
REF: catalogue 32-08 (BT), shelflist 32-25 (OT), subject c. 32-27 (OT), title c. 32-29 (OT), name c. 32-20 (RT)

bookform catalog (U.S.A.)
ledger catalogue; page catalogue
F catalogue en forme de livre
D Bandkatalog
R печатный каталог
S catálogo impreso
32-06 A 'catalogue' in the form of a *book*.
DEF: 21-09
REF: catalogue 32-08 (BT), card c. 32-07 (OT), sheaf c. 32-24 (OT)

card catalogue
card index
F catalogue sur fiches
D Kartei;
Karteikatalog;
Zettelkatalog
R карточный каталог
S catálogo en fichas; catálogo en tarjetas
32-07 A 'catalogue' made up of cards, each usually bearing a single *entry*.
DEF: 33-08
REF: catalogue 32-08 (BT), bookform catalog 32-06 (OT), sheaf c. 32-24 (OT)

catalogue (Brit.)
catalog (U.S.A.)
F catalogue
D Katalog
R каталог
S catálogo
32-08 An ordered compilation of *bibliographic descriptions* and sufficient *information* to afford *access* to the *documents*
DEF: 31-07, 17-28, 313-01, 21-18
REF: file 33-11 (BT), annotated catalogue 32-04 (NT), author c. 32-05 (NT), bookform catalog 32-06 (NT), card c. 32-07 (NT), central c. 32-11/13 (NT),

dictionary c. 32-19 (NT), name c. 32-20 (NT), serial c. 32-23 (NT), sheaf c. 32-24 (NT), shelflist 32-25 (NT), split c. 32-26 (NT), subject c. 32-27 (NT), file 32-12 (RT)

cataloguing rules
cataloguing code
F règles catalographiques
D Katalogisierungsregeln
R каталогизационные правила
S reglas de catalogación
32-09 Rules for the construction of *entries* into a 'catalogue'
DEF: 33-08
REF: classification code 39-18 (RT)

catchword catalogue
F catalogue par mots typiques
D Stichwortkatalog; Titelstichwortkatalog
R каталог с расположением описаний по существенным словам заглавий
S catálogo por descriptores
32-10 A *catalogue* arranged by *catchwords* taken from the *title* of the *document*
DEF: 36-02, 22-23, 21-18
REF: subject catalogue 32-27 (BT), title c. 32-29 (RT)

central catalogue
main catalogue (1,3);
general catalogue (1,3);
master catalogue (1,3);
union catalogue (2); joint catalogue (2)
F catalogue général (1);
catalogue collectif
D Hauptkatalog (1,3); Gesamtkatalog (1,2); Zentralkatalog (1,2)
R центральный каталог (1, 2);
сводный каталог (2, 3);
генеральный каталог (3)
S catálogo centralizado
32-11 (1) The 'catalogue' of the central *library* of a library *system*
DEF: 51-25, 41-40
REF: catalogue 32-08 (BT), centralized cataloguing 32-14 (RT)
32-12 (2) The common 'catalogue' of the *collections* of several *libraries*
DEF: 312-05, 51-25
REF: catalogue 32-08 (BT), co-operative cataloguing 32-17 (RT)
32-13 (3) The complete 'catalogue' of all *collections* of one *library*
DEF: 312-05, 51-25
REF: catalogue 32-08 (BT)

centralized cataloguing
F catalogage centralisé
D zentrale Katalogisierung
R централизованная каталогизация
S catalogación centralizada
32-14 The *cataloguing* by one *library* or

cataloguing office within a *system* of libraries of all books acquired by all those libraries so that the results of such cataloguing are used by the individual libraries
DEF: 31-09, 51-25, 41-40
REF: cataloguing 31-09 (BT), central catalogue 32-11 (RT), co-operative c. 32-17 (RT)

classed catalogue
   class catalogue;
   classified subject catalogue;
   systematic catalogue; classified catalogue
F   catalogue systématique
D   systematischer Katalog;
   systematischer Sachkatalog
R   систематический каталог;
   реальный каталог
S   catálogo sistemático
   32-15 A 'catalogue' arranged by subject according to a *classification schedule*
   DEF: 39-19
   REF: subject catalogue 32-27 (BT), alphabetical subject c. 32-03 (OT)

collective cataloguing
F   catalogage groupé
D   Sammelkatalogisierung
R   групповая каталогизация
S   catalogación por grupo
   32-16 A method of *cataloguing* minor and fugitive material by assemblying a group of material and assigning it a *heading* and a collective *title*
   DEF: 31-09, 36-08, 22-23
   REF: cataloguing 31-09 (BT)

co-operative cataloguing
   shared cataloguing
F   catalogage partagé
D   gemeinsame Katalogisierung
R   кооперированная каталогизация;
   совместная каталогизация
S   catalogación cooperativa
   32-17 The sharing of common *cataloguing* operations by a number of *libraries* to avoid the duplication of effort
   DEF: 31-09, 51-25
   REF: cataloguing 31-09 (BT), central c. 32-12 (RT), centralized c. 32-14 (RT)

descriptive cataloguing
   description
F   catalogage
D   Titelaufnahme
R   описательная каталогизация
S   catalogación descriptiva
   32-18 That phase of *cataloguing* concerned with the *bibliographic description*.
   DEF: 31-09, 31-07
   REF: cataloguing 31-09 (BT), subject c. 32-28 (OT), bibliographic description 31-07 (RT)

dictionary catalogue
   cross catalogue;
   mixed alphabetical catalogue
F   catalogue-dictionnaire
D   Kreuzkatalog
R   перекрёстный каталог;
   словарный каталог
S   catálogo diccionario
   32-19 A 'catalogue' of *entries* under *authors, editors, translators*, etc., *titles*, subjects, form and *series* which together with the necessary *references* are arranged in general alphabetical sequence.
   DEF: 33-08 52-03, 52-11, 52-25, 22-23, 21-52, 22-17
   REF: catalogue 32-08 (BT), split c. 32-26 (OT)

name catalogue
F   catalogue par noms propres
D   Namenskatalog; Nominalkatalog
R   именной каталог;
   авторский каталог
S   catalogación por nombres propios
   32-20 An alphabetically arranged 'catalogue' of *entries* under the *names* of persons and places as author headings and as *subject headings*
   DEF: 33-08, 14-29, 36-28
   REF: catalogue 32-08 (BT), author c. 32-27 (RT)

pre-natal cataloguing
   cataloguing in source; self-cataloguing; cataloguing in publication
F   catalogage à la source
D   Vorauskatalogisierung
R   централизованная каталогизация
S   catalogación en la fuente
   32-21 The provision of *cataloguing data* within a *document* or *publication*
   DEF: 31-09, 17-12, 21-18, 19-14
   REF: cataloguing 31-09 (BT), in-source indexing 35-21 (RT)

selective cataloguing
F   catalogage sélectif
D   Auswahlkatalogisierung
R   выборочная каталогизация;
   дифференцированная каталогизация
S   catalogación selectiva
   32-22 The *cataloguing* of certain types of material in a *library* with either shorter or fuller cataloguing than that used for the bulk of the library *collection*
   DEF: 31-09, 51-25, 312-05
   REF: cataloguing 31-09 (BT)

serial catalogue
F   catalogue des publications en séries
D   Katalog von Reihenwerken;
   Zeitschriftenkatalog
R   каталог продолжающихся
   и периодических изданий

s catálogo de publicaciones seriadas
32-23 A 'catalogue' of *serials*
DEF: 21-52
REF: catalogue 32-08 (BT), title c. 32-29 (RT)

sheaf catalogue
F catalogue sur feuillets
D Blattkatalog
R листовой каталог;
блоккартный каталог
s catálogo en papeletas
32-24 A 'catalogue' having the *entries* on slips of paper inserted in some binder
DEF: 33-08
REF: catalogue 32-08 (BT), bookform catalog 32-06 (OT), card c. 32-07 (OT)

shelflist
topographical catalogue; shelf catalogue
F catalogue topographique
D Standortkatalog; Regalkatalog
R топографический каталог;
шкафная опись
s catálogo topográfico
32-25 A *record* of the *books* in the *library* arranged in the order in which they stand on the shelves
DEF: 21-44, 21-09, 21-23/24
REF: catalogue 32-08 (BT), author c. 32-05 (OT), name c. 32-20 (OT), subject c. 32-27 (OT), title c. 32-29 (OT), location index 35-28 (RT)

split catalogue
divided catalogue
F catalogue par nature d'entrées
D Einzelkatalog
R разделённый каталог
s catálogo dividido
32-26 A *library catalogue* in which the different varieties of *entry*, e.g. *subjects author, title*, are filed in separate alphabetical sequences
DEF: 51-25, 33-08, 33-25, 52-03, 22-23
REF: catalogue 32-08 (BT), dictionary c. 32-19 (OT)

subject catalogue
F catalogue-matières
D Sachkatalog
R предметный каталог;
реальный каталог
s catálogo por materias
32-27 A 'catalogue' consisting of *subject entries* only
DEF: 33-25
REF: catalogue 32-08 (BT), alphabetical s. c. 32-03 (NT), catchword c. 32-10 (NT), classed c. 32-15 (NT), author c. 32-05 (OT), shelflist 32-25 (OT), dictionary c. 32-19 (RT), name c. 32-20 (RT), title c. 32-29 (RT)

subject cataloguing
F catalogage-matières
D Sachkatalogisierung
R предметизация; описание под предметным заголовком
s catalogación por materias
32-28 That phase of *cataloguing* concerned with the construction of *subject entries*
DEF: 31-09, 33-25
REF: cataloguing 31-09 (BT), descriptive c. 32-18 (OT), indexing 31-21 (RT)

title catalogue
F catalogue-titres
D Titelkatalog; Sachtitelkatalog
R каталог заглавий
s catálogo de títulos
32-29 A catalogue consisting of *title entries* only
DEF: 33-28
REF: catalogue 32-08 (BT), author c. 32-05 (OT), shelflist 32-25 (OT), catchword c. 32-10 (RT), serial c. 32-23 (RT), subject c. 32-27 (RT)

33 Files and entries in files

added entry
secondary entry
F entrée secondaire
D Nebenaufnahme; Nebeneintrag(ung)
R добавочное описание;
вспомогательное описание
s asiento secundario
33-01 An 'entry', other than a 'subject entry' and additional to the 'main entry' under which a bibliographical entity is represented in a *catalogue*
DEF: 32-08
REF: entry 33-08 (BT), main e. 33-18 (OT), analytical e. 33-02 (RT)

analytical entry
analytic entry; analytical description
F entrée sous la vedette-matière
D analytische Titelaufnahme;
analytische Aufnahme
R аналитическое описание
s asiento analítico
33-02 An 'entry' for a part of a *document*, including a *reference* to that document
DEF: 21-18, 22-17
REF: entry 33-08 (BT), added e. 33-01 (RT)

author entry
F entrée sous la vedette-auteur
D Verfassereintrag (ung)
R авторское описание
s asiento por autor

33-03 'Entry' of a *document* in a 'file' under its *author's name*
DEF: 21-18, 52-03. 14-29
REF: entry 33-08 (BT), forename e. 33-13 (NT), form e. 33-14 (OT), subject e. 33-25 (OT), title e. 33-28 (OT), corporate e. 33-06 (RT)

authority file
F   liste de mots vedettes
D   verbindliche Liste; Schlagwortliste
R   ключ к заголовкам каталожных описаний
S   lista oficial de encabezamientos
33-04 A list of the *headings* selected for use in a *catalogue* and sources consulted to establish such headings
DEF: 36-08, 32-08
REF: name a. f. 33-21 (NT), subject a. f. 33-24 (NT), authority list 35-04 (RT)

catchword entry
F   entrée sous le mot typique
D   Stichworteintrag(ung)
R   описание под существенным словом
S   registro por palabra-clave; registro por descriptores
33-05 'Entry' of a *document* in a 'file' under a secondary part of its *title*
DEF: 21-18, 22-23
REF: subject entry 33-25 (BT), title e. 33-28 (RT)

corporate entry
   corporate heading
F   entrée sous la vedette de collectivité-auteur
D   Korporationeneintrag; korporativer Eintrag
R   описание под коллективным автором
S   asiento por autor corporativo
33-06 'Entry' of a *document* in a 'file' under the *name* of a corporate body
DEF: 21-18, 14-29
REF: entry 33-08 (BT), form e. 33-14 (OT), subject e. 33-25 (OT), title e. 33-28 (OT), author c. 33-03 (RT)

duplicate entry
   double entry
F   entrée sous des vedettes multiples
D   Doppeleintrag(ung); Doppelaufnahme
R   дублирующие описание
S   asiento doble por autor
33-07 'Entry' of a *document* in a 'file' under two aspects of it
DEF: 21-18
REF: entry 33-08 (BT), multiple e. 33-20 (RT), unit card 33-29 (RT)

entry
   catalogue entry; index entry
F   notice; entrée (dans le catalogue)
D   Eintrag(ung); Aufnahme

R   описание; (отдельная) запись
S   asiento
33-08 A set of *data* representing a *document* in a 'file' (e.g. in a *catalogue*, a *bibliography* or an *index*)
DEF: 17-12, 21-18, 32-08, 315-04, 35-22
REF: added entry 33-01 (NT), analytical e. 33-02 (NT), author e. 33-03 (NT), duplicate e. 33-07 (NT), corporate e. 33-06 (NT), form e. 33-14 (NT), indirect e. 33-15 (NT), item e. 33-17 (NT), main e. 33-18 (NT), multiple e. 33-20 (NT), series e. 33-33 (NT), subject e. 33-25 (NT), term e. 33-27 (NT), title e. 33-28 (NT)

entry word
   filing word; heading
F   vedette entrée
D   Ordnungswort; Registereingang
R   порядковое слово
S   palabra para el asiento
33-09 The *word* by which an 'entry' is arranged in a 'file'
DEF: 14-55
REF: word 14-55 (BT), heading 36-08 (RT)

extension card
   continuation card
F   fiche complémentaire
D   Fortsetzungskarte
R   карточка, служащая продолжением
S   tarjeta complementaria
33-10 A card that continues an 'entry' from the preceding card
REF: tally 33-26 (BT)

file
F   fichier
D   Datei; Kartei
R   массив; информационный массив
S   registro; archivo; fichero
33-11 An ordered *collection* of related *records*, treated as a unit
DEF: 312-05, 21-44
REF: collection 12-05 (BT), authority file 33-04 (NT), inverted f. 33-16 (NT), master f. 33-19 (NT), normal f. 33-22 (NT), catalogue 32-08 (NT), storage 312-28 (RT)

first-word entry
   given name entry; byname entry
F   entrée au premier mot du titre
D   Eintrag(ung) unter dem ersten Wort des Titels
R   описание под первым словом заглавия
S   asiento por palabra inicial
33-12 'Entry' of a *document* in a 'file' made under the first *word* other than an article of the *title* of the document
DEF: 21-18, 14-55, 22-23
REF: title entry 33-28 (BT)

forename entry
    given name entry; byname entry
F   entrée au prénom
D   Eintrag(ung) unter dem Vornamen
R   описание под личным именем
S   asiento por primer nombre
    33-13 'Entry' of a *document* in a 'file'
    under the personal name of an *author*
    (especially used for saints, sovereigns,
    ruling princes, popes, persons known
    under the first name only)
    DEF: 21-18, 52-03
    REF: author entry 33-03 (BT)

form entry
F   entrée sous une vedette de forme
D   Eintrag(ung) nach der Form;
    Formaleintrag(ung)
R   описание под заголовком формы
S   asiento por forma
    33-14 'Entry' of a *document* in a 'file'
    under a *heading* expressing formal
    characteristics, e.g. periodical, poetry,
    drama, etc.
    DEF: 21-18, 36-08
    REF: entry 33-08 (BT), author e. 33-03
    (OT), corporate e. 33-06 (OT), subject
    e. 33-25 (OT), title e. 33-28 (OT)

indirect entry
    inverted entry; rotated entry
F   entrée inversée
D   invertierter Eintrag;
    invertierte Eintragung
R   описание с инверсией; описание под
    инвертированной рубрикой
S   asiento invertido
    33-15 'Entry' of *documents* in a 'file'
    under the principal noun common to
    some *headings* consisting of more than
    one *word*
    DEF: 21-18, 36-08, 14-55
    REF: entry 33-08 (BT), natural word
    order 34-16 (OT), inverted heading
    36-11 (RT)

inverted file
F   fichier inversé
D   merkmalsbezogene Datei;
    invertierte Datei
R   инвертированная картотека
S   registro invertido
    33-16 A 'file' in which each card or
    analogous *storage* unit pertains to one
    term and identifies all *documents* to
    which that term has been assigned
    DEF: 312-28, 14-52, 21-18
    REF: file 33-11 (BT), normal f. 33-22
    (OT), term entry 33-27 (RT), term entry
    system 41-43 (RT)

item entry
    document entry

F   entrée univoque
D   Dokumenteintrag(ung)
R   описание документа;
    документационное описание
S   asiento unívoco
    33-17 An 'entry' containing *information*
    about one item
    DEF: 17-27
    REF: entry 33-08 (BT), term e. 33-27 (OT)
    normal file 33-22 (RT), i.e. system
    41-22 (RT)

main entry
    full description
F   entrée principale
D   Haupteintrag(ung); Hauptaufnahme
R   основное описание; полное описание
S   asiento principal
    33-18 'Entry' of a *document* to a 'file'
    giving all the *data* necessary to the
    complete identification of the item
    DEF: 21-18, 17-12
    REF: entry 33-08 (BT), added e. 33-01
    (OT), unit card 33-29 (RT)

master file
F   fichier principal
D   Stammdatei
R   основной массив
S   catálogo oficial
    33-19 A 'file' that is either relatively
    permanent or that is treated as an
    authority in a particular function
    REF: file 33-11 (BT)

multiple entry
F   vedette multiple
D   Mehrfacheintrag(ung)
R   многократное описание
S   asiento múltiple
    33-20 'Entry' of a *document* to a 'file'
    under several *headings*, each representing
    different aspects
    DEF: 21-18, 36-08
    REF: entry 33-08 (BT), duplicate e. 33-07
    (RT), unit card 33-29 (RT)

name authority file
F   liste d'entrées auteur autorisées
D   verbindliche Namensliste
R   ключ к заголовкам авторских
    каталожных описаний
S   registro autorizado de autores
    33-21 A 'file' listing the forms of *name*
    of both personal and corporate *authors*,
    editors, etc., authorized for use as
    headings in a *catalogue*
    DEF: 14-29, 52-03, 52-11, 36-08, 32-08
    REF: authority file 33-04 (BT), subject
    a. f. 33-24 (OT)

norma file
F   fichier direct
D   objektbezogene Datei
R   (массив информации, в котором каждая запись соответствует одному документу)
S   registro directo
33-22 A 'file' in which each item pertains to one *document* and identifies all descriptions disclosed in that document
DEF: 21-18
REF: file 33-11 (BT), inverted f. 33-16 (OT), item entry 33-17 (RT), item entry system 41-22 (RT)

series entry
F   entrée de suite
D   Serieneintrag(ung)
R   описание под названием серии
S   asiento de serie
33-23 'Entry' in a *catalogue* of the several works which belong to a *series* under the *name* of the series as a *heading*
DEF: 32-08, 21-54, 14-29, 36-08
REF: entry 33-08 (BT), title e. 33-28 (RT)

subject authority file
F   index de vedettes-matières autorisées
D   verbindliche Schlagwortliste
R   ключ к заголовкам предметных каталожных описаний
S   lista de encabezamientos de materias
33-24 A list of *subject headings* and subject references selected for use in subject *cataloguing*
DEF: 36-28, 31-09
REF: authority file 33-04 (BT), name a. f. 33-21 (OT), authority list 35-04 (RT)

subject entry
    subject-word entry
F   entrée par vedette-sujet
D   Sacheintrag(ung)
R   описание под предметным заголовком
S   asiento por materias
33-25 'Entry' of a *document* in a 'file' under a *heading* which indicates the subject of the document
DEF: 21-18, 36-08
REF: entry 33-08 (BT), catchword e. 33-05 (NT), author e. 33-04 (OT), corporate e. 33-06 (OT), form e. 33-14 (OT), title e. 33-28 (RT)

tally
F   recueil de données
D   physische Speichereinheit
R   носитель описания
S   compilación de datos
33-26 The physical unit which carries the 'entry'
REF: extension card 33-10 (NT)

term entry
F   entrée
D   Merkmaleingang
R   описание под рубрикой инвертированной картотеки
S   asiento de términos
33-27 'Entry' into an 'inverted file'
REF: entry 33-08 (BT), item e. 33-17 (OT), inverted file 33-16 (RT), t.e. system 41-43 (RT)

title entry
F   entrée au titre
D   Titeleintrag(ung)
R   описание под заглавием
S   asiento de títulos
33-28 'Entry' of a *document* in a 'file' made under a *word* of the document's *title*, usually the first word other than the article
DEF: 21-18, 14-55, 22-23
REF: entry 33-08 (BT), first-word e. 33-12 (NT), author e. 33-03 (OT), corporate e. 33-06 (OT), form e. 33-14 (OT), catchword e. 33-05 (RT), subject e. 33-25 (RT)

unit card
    unit entry
F   fiche de base; fiche principale
D   Einheitskarte; Stammkarte
R   единая карточка; единое описание
S   tarjeta principal
33-29 A basic *catalogue* card, in the form of a 'main entry' which, when duplicated, may be used as a unit for 'multiple entries'
DEF: 32-08
REF: duplicate entry 33-07 (RT), main entry 33-18 (RT), multiple entry 33-20 (RT)

34 Structuring of files

allocation
F   mise en ordre
D   Anordnung; Zuordnung
R   размещение; расположение; расстановка
S   ordenación
34-01 Placing one subject in context with, or near to, another subject
REF: collocation 34-08 (RT)

alphabetic-classed filing system
    alphabetic-classed catalogue
F   catalogue alphabético-systématique
D   Gruppenschlagwortverfahren; Gruppenschlagwortkatalog
R   алфавитно-систематическая расстановка; алфавитно-систематический каталог

s   catálogo alfabético-sistemático
34-02 A grouping of material into broad subject *classes* alphabetically arranged and subdivided by topics arranged alphabetically within each class
DEF: 39-15/16
REF: order 34-17 (BT), alphabetical order 34-03 (BT), classified f.s. 34-05 (RT)

alphabetical order
alphabetical arrangement
F   ordre alphabétique
D   alphabetische Ordnung
R   алфавитная расстановка; алфавитный порядок; алфавитное расположение
s   orden alfabético
34-03 Arranging items into a sequence according to an *alphabet*
DEF: 13-01/02

chronological filing system
chronological order
F   ordre chronologique
D   chronologische Ordnung
R   хронологическая расстановка; хронологический порядок; хронологическое расположение
s   archivo cronológico
34-04 Arranging items in a *file* according to date
DEF: 33-11
REF: order 34-17 (BT), alphabetical order 34-03 (OT), geographic filing method 34-14 (OT), classified filing system 34-05 (RT), chronological device 39-14 (RT)

classified filing system
classified arrangement; systematic arrangement; hypotaxis
F   ordre systématique
D   systematische Ordnung
R   систематическая расстановка; систематическое расположение
s   sistema de ordenación clasificado
34-05 Arranging items in a *file* according to a *classification system*
DEF: 33-11, 39-21
REF: order 34-17 (BT), alphabetical order 34-03 (OT), alphabetic-classed filing system 34-02 (RT), chronological f. s. 34-04 (RT), geographic filing method 34-14 (RT)

collating
F   fusionnement
D   Zusammenordnen; Vereinigen; Mischen
R   подборка (информации из нескольких массивов)
s   intercalación
34-06 Combining items from two or more ordered sets into one set having

a specified 'order' (not necessarily the same as any of the original sets)
REF: sorting 34-21 (RT), merging 43-12 (RT)

collating sequence
F   ordre de fusionnement
D   Sortierfolge; einheitliche Sortierfolge
R   принцип расположения
s   secuencia de intercalación
34-07 An ordering assigned to a set of items, such that any two sets in that assigned 'order' can be 'collated'

collocation
F   fusion
D   Gruppierung
R   смежная расстановка; смежное расположение; размещение тесно связанных предметов в непосредственной близости
s   colocación
34-08 Placing closely associated subjects in proximity
REF: allocation 34-01 (RT)

cross reference
reference
F   renvoi; renvoi réciproque; double renvoi
D   Verweis(ung); Kreuzverweis(ung)
R   (перекрёстная) ссылка
s   envío; referencia
34-09 A *symbol* in a *file* or *index* which directs from one *heading* or *entry* to another
DEF: 13-34, 33-11, 35-22, 36-08, 33-08
REF: general information reference 34-11 (NT), general r. 34-12 (NT), see also r. 34-19 (NT), see r. 34-20 (NT), subject r. 34-22 (NT), use r. 34-23 (NT), used for r. 34-24 (NT), broader term 37-02 (NT), narrower term 37-14 (NT), related term 37-16 (NT)

filing
file arrangement; file ordering
F   intercalation
D   Einordnung; Aufstellung; Ordnen
R   систематизирование; систематизация; расстановка
s   archivar
34-10 The action of arranging a number of *entries* into a sequence in accordance with a set of rules, and the subsequent insertion of further entries into their correct places within this sequence
DEF: 33-08
REF: order 34-17 (RT)

general information reference
F   renvoi générique
D   generische Verweisung; generischer Verweis

R   отсылка от вида к роду
S   envío genérico
34-11 A 'cross reference' in a *file* from a specific subject or *class* of *records* on which the file does not contain records to the general *heading* which includes the specific subject or class of records
DEF: 33-11, 39-15/16, 21-44, 36-08
REF: general r. 34-12 (BT), see r. 34-20 (BT), use r. 34-23 (RT), quasi-synonym 14-40 (RT)

general reference
general cross reference;
information entry
F   renvoi general
D   Generalanweis(ung)
R   общая (перекрёстная) ссылка; отсылка
S   encabezamiento general
34-12 A 'cross reference' in a 'file' to the *heading* under which one may expect to find entries for material on certain subjects or entries for particular kinds of *names*
DEF: 33-11, 36-08, 14-27
REF: cross reference 34-09 (BT), general information r. 34-11 (NT), see r. 34-20 (RT), see also r. 34-19 (RT)

generic posting
multilevel indexing
F   indexation hiérarchique
D   generische Aufnahme; Indexierung auf mehreren hierarchischen Niveaus
R   индексирование на нескольких иерархических уровнях
F   registro jerárquico de palabras clave
34-13 The 'posting' of items under *class headings* as well as under the appropriate *specific headings*
DEF: 36-03, 36-24
REF: posting 34-18 (BT), indexing 39-21 (BT)

geographic filing method
geographic filing system;
geographical order;
geographic arrangement
F   classement toponymique
D   geographische Ordnung
R   географическая расстановка; географическое расположение
S   clasificación geográfica o toponímica
34-14 Arranging items in a *file* according to geographical *characteristics*, e.g. place of publication
DEF: 33-11, 12-02
REF: order 34-17 (BT), alphabetical order 34-03 (OT), chronological filing method 34-04 (OT), classified filing system 34-05 (RT), geographical subdivision 39-43 (RT)

linking
F   relation
D   Koppelung
R   отражение отношений (при проставлении индексационных терминов к документу)
S   enlazamiento
34-15 Indicating that two *index terms* assigned to the same *document* are connected in some way
DEF: 36-10, 21-18
REF: link 36-13 (RT)

natural word order
F   ordre des mots du langage naturel
D   natürliche Wortfolge
R   естественный порядок слов
S   orden natural de palabras
34-16 Arranging the *words* contained in *phrases* or *terms* consisting of more than one word in the sequence which is used in spoken *language*
DEF: 14-55, 14-34, 14-52, 15-13
REF: indirect entry 33-15 (OT), inverted heading 36-11 (OT)

order
arrangement
F   ordre; arrangement
D   Ordnung; Anordnung
R   порядок; последовательность; расстановка; расположение
S   ordenación
34-17 Arranging items according to a specified set or rules
REF: alphabetic-classed filing system 34-02 (RT), alphabetical order 34-03 (NT), chronological filing system 34-04 (NT), classified filing system 34-05 (NT), geographic filing method 34-14 (NT), o. in array 39-57 (NT), filing 34-10 (RT)

posting
F   enregistrement
D   Aufnahme
R   проставление (номеров документов под рубриками в инвертированной картотеке)
S   registro de palabras clave
34-18 To enter the *document* numbers under each relevant *term entry* in an *inverted file*
DEF: 21-18, 32-22, 33-16
REF: generic posting 34-13 (NT)

see also reference
F   renvoi 'voir aussi'; renvoi d'orientation
D   Siehe-auch-Verweis(ung)
R   ссылка "смотри также"; отсылка
S   envío de 'véase también'
34-19 'Cross reference in *catalogues* and *indexes* to indicate that under another *heading* similar material may be found
DEF: 32-08, 35-22, 36-08

REF: cross reference 34-09 (BT), general r. 34-12 (RT), broader term 37-02 (RT), narrower term 37-14 (RT), related term 37-16 (RT)

see reference
F   renvoi 'voir'
D   Siehe-Verweis(ung)
R   ссылка "смотри"; отсылка
S   envío de 'véase'
    34-20 'Cross reference' in *catalogues* and *indexes* to indicate that the kind of material sought under a heading may be found under another heading
    DEF: 32-08, 35-22
    REF: cross reference 34-09 (BT), general information r. 34-11 (RT), general r. 34-12 (RT), use r. 34-23 (RT)

sorting
F   tri
D   Sortierung; Sortieren
R   сортировка
S   clasificar
    34-21 Arranging physical units into a sequence
    REF: collating 34-06 (RT)

subject reference
    subject cross reference
F   renvoi-matière
D   Sachverweis(ung)
R   предметная ссылка
S   envío de un tema a otro
    34-22 A 'cross reference' from one *subject heading* to another
    DEF: 36-28
    REF: cross reference 34-09 (BT)

use reference
F   renvoi 'utiliser'
D   Benutze-Verweis(ung)
R   ссылка "используй"
S   envío de 'úsese'
    34-23 A 'cross reference' in an *indexing language* indicating that another *index term* has to be used
    DEF: 15-10, 36-10
    REF: cross reference 34-09 (BT), used for r. 34-24 (OT), general information r. 34-11 (RT), general r. 34-12 (RT), see r. 34-20 (RT)

used for reference
F   renvoi 'utilisé pour'
D   Benutzt-für-Verweis(ung)
R   ссылка "использовано вместо"
S   envío de 'usado por'
    34-24 A 'cross reference' in an *indexing language* indicating that the *index term* from which the reference leads to another is allowed for *indexing*, while the other is deprecated
    DEF: 15-10, 36-10, 31-21

REF: cross reference 34-09 (BT), use r. 34-23 (OT)

35 Indexing and indexes

alphabetical index
    alphabetical register
F   index alphabétique
D   alphabetisches Register; alphabetischer Index; alphabetisches Verzeichnis
R   алфавитный указатель
S   índice alfabético
    35-01 'Index' in which the *index terms* are arranged in *alphabetical order*
    DEF: 36-10, 34-03
    REF: index 35-22 (BT), co-ordinate i. 35-14 (NT), KWAC i. 35-25 (NT), KWIC i. 35-26 (NT), KWOC i. 35-27 (NT), permuted i. 35-32 (NT), rotated i. 35-35 (NT), classified i. 35-11 (OT)

associative indexing
F   indexation associative
D   assoziative Indexierung
R   ассоциативное индексирование
S   indizado por asociación
    35-02 *Indexing*, by means of a *computer* which records associations between *terms* without there necessarily being a specified functional relationship between them
    DEF: 31-21, 42-10, 14-52
    REF: automatic indexing 31-06 (BT)

asyndetic index
F   index à entrée unique
D   nicht-verweisendes Register; Register ohne Verweisungen
R   указатель без связующих ссылок
S   índice asindético
    35-03 An 'index' without *cross references*
    DEF: 34-09
    REF: index 35-22 (BT), syndetic i. 35-36 (OT)

authority list
    controlled term list
F   liste (normalisée) de termes
D   verbindliche Deskriptorenliste; kontrollierte Schlagwortliste
R   нормализованный перечень индексационных терминов
S   lista autorizada de términos
    35-04 List of *terms* that is used as an authority in *indexing*
    DEF: 14-52, 31-21
    REF: term list 16-14 (NT), word list 16-17 (RT), indexing language 15-10 (RT), authority file 33-04 (RT), thesaurus 37-22 (RT)

bibliographic coupling
F   référence bibliographique couplée
D   bibliographische Koppelung
R   индексирование на основе общих
     библиографических ссылок (1);
     библиографическая совместимость (2)
S   referencia bibliográfica acoplada
     35-05 (1) A method of *indexing* by the
     number of cited *references* which two
     documents have in common
     DEF: 31-21, 22-17, 21-18
     REF: citation indexing 35-10 (RT)
     35-06 (2) The link formed between two
     sources of *documents* by their common
     citation of one or more documents
     DEF: 21-18

catchword indexing
F   indexation par mots typiques
D   Stichwortindexierung
R   индексирование по существенным
     словам (заглавий)
S   indizado por palabras clave
     35-07 A method of *indexing* in which
     significant *words* in a title are used as
     index terms
     DEF: 31-21, 14-55, 36-10
     REF: indexing 31-21 (BT), keyword i.
     35-24 (RT), KWAC index 35-25 (RT),
     KWIC index 35-26 (RT), KWOC index
     35-27 (RT)

chain indexing
     chain procedure
F   indexation en arbre
D   Kettenindexierung
R   цепной метод составления указателей
S   indizado en cadena
     35-08 A method of producing an 'alpha-
     betical index' of the *terms* or *phrases*
     corresponding to the parts of a *compound*
     classified *entry* of a *document* where
     distributed relatives are displayed in
     relation to superior terms
     DEF: 14-52, 14-35, 14-09, 33-08, 21-18
     REF: relative index 35-34 (RT), rotated
     index 35-35 (RT), faceted classification
     311-11 (RT)

citation index
F   index des citations
D   Zitierungsindex; Zitierungsregister
R   указатель библиографических ссылок
S   índice de citas
     35-09 An 'index' of published *documents*
     in which each of the earlier documents
     cited in the *bibliography* appended to the
     later document being indexed
     DEF: 21-18, 315-04
     REF: index 35-22 (BT), bibliographic
     coupling 35-05 (RT), citation i. 35-10 (RT)

citation indexing
F   indexation par citation
D   Rückwärtsdokumentation;
     Zitierungsnachweis
R   индексирование на основе
     библиографических ссылок
S   indizado por citas
     35-10 The method of preparing a 'cita-
     tion index' by 'bibliographic coupling'
     REF: indexing 31-21 (BT), bibliographic
     coupling 35-05 (RT), citation index 35-09
     (RT)

classified index
F   index systématique
D   systematisches Register
R   систематический указатель
S   índice clasificado
     35-11 'Index' in which the *index terms*
     are arranged according to a *classification
     system*
     DEF: 36-10, 39-21
     REF: index 35-22 (BT), alphabetic i. 35-01
     (NT)

concordance
     internal index (1)
F   concordance
D   Konkordanz
R   конкорданция
S   concordancia
     35-12 (1) An 'index' of the meaningful
     words, terms or *phrases* in a *book* or the
     work of an *author*
     DEF: 14-55, 14-52, 14-34, 21-09
     REF: index 35-22 (BT), in-source-indexing
     35-20 (RT)
     35-13 (2) An 'index' to a *documentary
     language* in *terms* of an arrangement of
     another language
     DEF: 15-08, 14-52
     REF: index 35-22 (BT), chain indexing
     35-08 (RT), relative index 35-34 (RT)

co-ordinate index
     concept co-ordinate index
F   index coordonné
D   koordinierter Index;
     Register gleichrangiger Begriffe
R   координатный указатель
S   índice coordinado
     35-14 An 'index' in which more than one
     entry in the index *file* identifies or de-
     scribes the subject content of each
     indexed unit
     DEF: 33-08, 33-11
     REF: alphabetical index 35-01 (BT), classi-
     fied i. 35-11 (OT), correlative i. 35-16
     (OT), syndetic i. 35-36 (OT), co-ordinate
     indexing 35-15 (RT)

co-ordinate indexing
     multiaspect indexing;
     inverted co-ordinate indexing

F   indexation coordonnée
D   koordiniertes Indexieren;
    koordinierte Indexierung
R   координатное индексирование;
    многоаспектное индексирование
S   indizado coordinado
    35-15 A method of 'indexing' by which
    the subject content of the indexed item is
    described by *index terms* of equal rank
    which may be co-ordinated in *retrieval*
    DEF: 31-21, 36-10, 313-31
    REF: indexing 31-21 (BT), uniterm i. 35-37
    (NT), manipulative i. 35-29 (OT), re-
    lational i. 35-33 (OT), co-ordinate index
    35-15 (RT), keyword i. 35-24 (RT),
    semantic factoring 36-23 (RT)

correlative index
F   index corrélatif
D   korrelativer Index;
    korrelatives Register
R   координатный указатель;
    коррелятивный указатель
S   índice correlativo
    35-16 An 'index' having, indicating or
    involving relations among the *index terms*
    DEF: 36-10
    REF: index 35-22 (BT), co-ordinate i.
    35-14 (OT), asyndetic i. 35-03 (OT),
    classified i. 35-11 (RT), relational index-
    ing 35-33 (RT), syndetic i. 35-36 (RT)

cumulative index
F   index cumulatif; index récapitulatif
D   kumuliertes Register;
    kumulierendes Register
R   кумулятивный указатель
S   índice acumulativo
    35-17 An 'index' to a *periodical* that
    combines new *entries* with those of one or
    more earlier indexes to the same periodi-
    cal
    DEF: 21-38, 33-08
    REF: index 35-22 (BT), periodical i.
    35-31 (RT)

depth of indexing
    specificity
F   degré d'indexation
D   Indexierungsgenauigkeit;
    Indexierungstiefe
R   глубина индексирования
S   grado de indizado
    35-18 The degree to which an assigned
    index term is co-extensive with the *concept*
    treated in the *document*
    DEF: 36-10, 12-05, 21-18
    REF: exhaustivity of indexing 35-19 (RT)

exhaustivity of indexing
F   indexation exhaustive
D   Indexierungsumfang; Indexierungstiefe
R   полнота индексирования
S   indizado exhaustivo
    35-19 Number of *index terms* assigned to
    an indexed item
    DEF: 36-10
    REF: depth of indexing 35-18 (RT)

in-source indexing
    pre-natal indexing (2)
F   indexation à la source
D   Eigenindexierung (1);
    Vorausindexierung (2)
R   индексирование в источнике;
    индексирование до опубликования
    документа
S   indizado en la fuente
    35-20 (1) Preparing an 'index' to one
    document that is appended to the *text* of
    the document
    DEF: 21-18, 22-21
    REF: indexing 31-21 (BT), concordance
    35-12 (RT)
    35-21 (2) The provision of *index terms*
    within a *document* or *publication*
    DEF: 36-10, 21-18, 19-14
    REF: pre-natal cataloguing 32-21 (RT)

index
F   index
D   Register
R   указатель
S   índice
    35-22 An ordered reference list of the
    contents of a *file* or *document* together
    with *references* for identification or loca-
    tion of those contents
    DEF: 17-10, 33-11, 21-18, 22-17
    REF: alphabetical index 35-01 (NT), asyn-
    detic i. 35-03 (NT), citation i. 35-09 (NT),
    classified i. 35-11 (NT), concordance 35-
    12/13 (NT), correlative i. 35-16 (NT),
    cumulative i. 35-17 (NT), location i. 35-28
    (NT), manipulative i. 35-29 (NT),
    periodical i. 35-30/31 (NT), relative i.
    35-34 (NT), syndetic i. 35-36 (NT)

inter-indexer consistency
F   cohérence d'indexation
D   Indexierungskonsistenz
R   идентичность индексирования;
    стабильность индексирования
S   coherencia de indizado
    35-23 The capability of a prescribed set
    of rules for *indexing* to lead different
    indexers to identical *index terms* in
    indexing the same items
    DEF: 31-21, 52-12, 36-10

keyword indexing
F   indexation par mots clés
D   Stichwortindexierung;
    Stichwortverfahren;
    Schlüsselwortverfahren
R   индексирование по ключевым словам

s indizado por palabras clave
35-24 *Indexing* by selecting a group of *keywords* out of the *document*
DEF: 31-21, 36-12, 21-18
REF: indexing 31-22 (BT), catchword i. 35-07 (RT), co-ordinate i. 35-15 (RT), KWAC index 35-25 (RT), KWIC index 35-26 (RT), KWOC index 35-27 (RT)

keyword-and-context index
KWAC index
F index 'KWAC'
D KWAC-Register; KWAC-Index
R указатель ключевых слов вне контекста (заглавия документов приводятся полностью)
s índice 'KWAC'
35-25 A 'keyword-out-of-context index' with the *title* quoted each time in full
DEF: 22-23
REF: alphabetical index 35-01 (BT), catchword indexing 35-07 (RT), keyword indexing 35-24 (RT), KWIC i.35-26 (RT), KWOC i. 35-26 (RT), permuted i. 35-32 (RT)

keyword-in-context index
KWIC index; permuted title index
F index 'KWIC'
D KWIC-Register; KWIC-Index
R указатель ключевых слов в контсксте; пермутационный указатель ключевых слов заглавий
s índice 'KWIC'
35-26 An 'alphabetical index' containing *titles*, *phrases* or *sentences* of *documents* with each title phrase or sentence repeated so that it appears with each significant *word* in *alphabetical order* in a single central column with as much of the remainder of the title sentence or phrase before and after the word as space permits
DEF: 22-23, 14-34, 14-44, 21-18, 14-56, 34-03
REF: alphabetical index 35-01 (BT), catchword indexing 35-07 (RT), keyword indexing 35-24 (RT), KWAC i. 35-26 (RT), permuted i. 35-32 (RT)

keyword-out-of-context-index
KWOC index
F index 'KWOC'
D KWOC-Register; KWOC-Index
R указатель ключевых слов вне контекста (заглавия документов приводятся в объёме одной печатной строки указателя)
s índice 'KWOC'
35-27 An 'index' containing *titles* of *documents* listed with all significant *words* in *alphabetical order* each followed by its respective title within a given line length

DEF: 22-23, 21-18, 14-56, 34-03
REF: alphabetical index 35-01 (BT), catchword indexing 35-07 (RT), keyword indexing 35-24 (RT), KWAC i. 35-25 (RT), KWOC i. 35-26 (RT), permuted i. 35-32 (RT)

location index
location register
F index de localisation
D Standortregister; Fundortregister
R топографический указатель; схема расстановки
s índice de localización
35-28 An 'index' of items indicating their physical location
REF: index 35-22 (BT), shelflist 32-25 (RT)

manipulative index
F index manipulatif
D
R (укзатель, пользование которым требует выполнения нетрадиционных операций, напр., координатный)
s índice manipulativo
35-29 An 'index' in which manipulations other than turning pages, reading *entries*, following *cross references*, and locating *documents* are necessary
DEF: 33-08, 34-09, 21-18
REF: index 35-22 (BT), co-ordinate i. 35-14 (RT)

periodical index
index of periodicals (1)
F index de périodique (1)
D Zeitschriftenregister (1); periodisches Register (2)
R указатель периодических изданий (1); указатель к периодическому изданию (1); периодический указатель (2)
s índice de publicaciones periódicas; índice de revistas
35-30 (1) An 'index' to a *volume*, several volumes or a set of one or more *periodicals*
DEF: 21-63, 21-37
REF: index 35-22 (RT), in-source indexing 35-20 (RT)
35-31 (2) A 'index' issued periodically, usually a 'cumulative' index
REF: index 36-22 (BT), cumulative i. 35-17 (RT)

permuted index
permutational index
F index permuté
D Permutationregister; Permutationsindex; permutiertes Register
R пермутационный указатель
s índice permutado
35-32 An 'alphabetical index' repeating

every *index term* or other kind of textual material so that it appears with each significant element as an *entry*
DEF: 36-10, 33-08
REF: alphabetical index 35-01 (BT), KWAC i. 35-25 (RT), KWIC i. 35-26 (RT), KWOC i. 35-27 (RT), rotated i. 35-35 (RT)

relational indexing
F   indexation par relations
D   Beziehungsindexierung
R   индексирование с отражанием отношений (между отдельными аспектами сложных предметов)
S   indizado por relaciones
     35-33 *Indexing* in which complex subjects are represented structurally by the interposition of relations formally stated between *terms*
DEF: 31-22, 14-52
REF: indexing 31-22 (BT), co-ordinate i. 35-15 (OT), syndetic index 35-36 (RT), semantic code 18-24 (RT)

relative index
F   index de relations
D   mehrdimensionales Klassifikationsregister
R   многоаспектный алфавитно--предметный указатель (к таблицам классификации)
S   índice de relaciones
     35-34 An 'index' to a *classification system* in which all relationships and aspects of the subject are brought together under each index *entry*
DEF: 39-21, 33-08
REF: index 35-22 (BT), chain indexing 35-08 (RT), concordance 35-13 (RT)

rotated index
     rotational index
F   index par rotation
D   Rotationsindex; Rotationsregister
R   перестановочный указатель
S   índice por rotación
     35-35 An 'alphabetical index' containing *titles, phrases* or *sentences* or their coded representations in which a selected element appears first, followed by any subsequent elements in their original order and then by any *terms* preceding the selected term in their original order each selected element constituting a single *entry*
DEF: 22-23, 14-34, 14-44, 14-52, 33-08
REF: alphabetical index 35-01 (BT), permuted i. 35-32 (RT)

syndetic index
     connective index
F   index connectif

D   syndetisches Register
R   указатель с отражением связей между рубриками (не только путем последовательности их расположения, но и при помощи вспомогательных приёмов)
S   índice sindético
     35-36 An 'index' displaying relations between *headings* by auxiliary devices, e.g. *cross references*, in addition to the order in which the index itself is arranged
DEF: 36-08, 34-09
REF: index 35-22 (BT), asyndetic i. 35-03 (OT), relational indexing 35-33 (RT)

uniterm indexing
F   indexation par mots clés univoques
D   Uniterm-System; Uniterm-Verfahren
R   индексирование унитермами
S   indizado por unitérminos
     35-37 'Co-ordinate indexing' by using single *words* as *index terms* (*uniterms*)
DEF: 14-55, 36-10, 36-29
REF: co-ordinate index 35-15 (BT)

36 Elements of documentary languages

(excluded classifications, ref. to section 39)

bound terms
F   termes reliés
D   gebundene Modifikatoren; unselbständige Schlagwörter
R   уточняющие термины (к предметным рубрикам)
S   términos asociados
     36-01 *Terms* that are used to modify the meaning of 'subject headings' but may not be used as 'index terms' solely
DEF: 14-52, 14-27
REF: modifier 36-15 (BT), role indicator 36-21 (RT)

catchword
F   mot typique
D   Stichwort; Titelstichwort
R   существенное слово
S   palabra clave
     36-02 A significant *word* out of the *title* of a *document* used for an *entry* into a *file* or *index*
DEF: 14-55, 22-23, 21-18, 33-08, 33-11, 35-22
DEF: descriptor 36-05 (BT), index term 36-10 (BT), descriptor 36-06 (OT), keyword 36-12 (RT), subject heading 36-28 (RT), uniterm 36-29 (RT)

class heading
generic heading
F   vedette générique
D   generisches Schlagwort;
Gruppenschlagwort
R   название отдела (в классификации)
S   encabezamiento genérico
36-03 A 'heading' designating a *class which* is subdivided
DEF: 39-15/16
REF: heading 36-08 (BT), specific h. 36-24 (OT), subdivided h. 36-25 (RT)

composite heading
compound heading
F   vedette composée
D   zusammengesetztes Schlagwort;
zusammengesetztes Ordnungswort
R   рубрика-словосочетание;
сложный заголовок описания
S   encabezamiento compuesto
36-04 A single 'heading' representing one *concept* by more than one *word*
DEF: 12-05, 14-55
REF: heading 36-08 (BT), docuterm 36-07 (RT)

descriptor
F   descripteur
D   Deskriptor
R   дескриптор
S   descriptor
36-05 (1) Each single *term* or *phrase* of a *documentary language* which may be used as an *index term*
DEF: 14-52, 14-34, 15-03, 36-10
REF: catchword 36-02 (NT), keyword 36-12 (NT), subject heading 36-28 (NT), uniterm 36-29 (NT), notation 310-23 (NT), descriptor 36-06, 37-05 (NT), index term 36-10 (RT)
36-06 (2) A well-defined, unequivocal *technical term* used in a *documentary language*
DEF: 14-51, 15-08
REF: descriptor 36-05 (BT), index term 36-10 (BT), subject heading 36-28 (NT), descriptor 37-05 (NT), notation 310-23 (OT), catchword 36-02 (OT), keyword 36-12 (OT), uniterm 36-29 (OT)

docuterm
structerm
F
D   Deskriptor mit Rollenindikator
R   (индексационный термин,
состоящий из дескриптора
и указателя роли)
S
36-07 'Index term' formed of a 'descriptor' and a 'role indicator'
REF: index term 36-10 (BT), composite

heading 36-04 (RT), qualified heading 36-17 (RT)

heading
F   vedette
D   Ordnungswort; Registerwort; Schlagwort
R   заголовок описания; рубрика
S   encabezamiento
36-08 A *name, word* or *phrase* placed at the head of an *entry* to indicate some special aspect of the item referred to
DEF: 14-29, 14-55, 14-34, 33-08
REF: classe heading 36-03 (NT), ideographic h. 36-09 (NT), inverted h. 36-11 (NT), main h. 36-14 (NT), qualified h. 36-17 (NT), specific h. 36-24 (NT), subdivided h. 36-25 (NT), subheading 36-26/27 (NT), subject h. 36-28 (NT), entry word 33-09 (RT), descriptor 36-05 (RT), index term 36-10 (RT)

ideographic heading
F   vedette idéographique
D   künstliches Ordnungswort
R   рубрика, состоящая
из символических обозначений
S   encabezamiento ideográfico
36-09 A 'heading' which consists of *symbols* other than *words*
DEF: 13-34, 14-55
REF: heading 36-08 (BT), notation 310-23 (RT)

index term
indexing term
F   terme d'indexation
D   Index-Terminus
R   индексационный термин
S   término de indizado
36-10 Each set of *words* or other *symbols* allocated to an item in *indexing* used to form one *entry*
DEF: 14-55, 13-33, 31-21, 33-08
REF: catchword 36-02 (NT), descriptor 36-06 (NT), keyword 36-12 (NT), docuterm 36-07 (NT), notation 310-23 (NT), subject heading 36-28 (NT), uniterm 36-29 (NT), descriptor 36-05 (RT), heading 36-08 (RT)

inverted heading
F   vedette inversée
D   invertiertes Schlagwort;
invertiertes Ordnungswort;
permutiertes Schlagwort;
permutiertes Ordnungswort
R   инвертированная рубрика ;
инвентированный заголовок
S   encabezamiento invertido
36-11 A 'heading' in which the *natural word order* is reversed to place the significant noun at the beginning of the heading
DEF: 34-16

REF: heading 36-08 (BT), natural word order 34-16 (OT), indirect entry 33-15 (RT)

keyword
keyterm
F mot clé
D Stichwort; Schlüsselwort
R ключевое слово
S palabra clave
36-12 A *word* or *term* selected out of a *document* to represent a given item of *information* for use in *indexing*
DEF: 14-55, 14-52, 21-18, 17-27/29, 31-21
REF: index term 36-10 (BT), descriptor 36-05 (BT), descriptor 36-06 (OT), notation 310-23 (OT), catchword 36-02 (RT), subject heading 36-28 (RT), uniterm 36-29 (RT)

link
F indicateur de liaison; lien
D Koppelungsindikator
R указатель связи
S enlace
36-13 A *symbol* attached to two or more 'index terms' in order to indicate that these index terms have some unspecified interrelation, and in order to prevent the *association* of these index terms with other index terms accidentally
DEF: 13-34, 38-06
REF: linking 34-15 (RT), relator 36-20 (RT), role indicator 36-21 (RT)

main heading
F vedette principale ;
vedette matière générale
D Hauptordnungswort; Hauptschlagwort
R основная рубрика;
рубрика основного описания
S encabezamiento principal
36-14 The 'heading' adopted for a *main entry*
DEF: 33-18
REF: heading 36-08 (BT)

modifier
F modificateur
D Modifikator
R определитель; пояснительная помета
S modificador
36-15 A *term* or a *symbol* used to modify the *meaning* of a 'descriptor' (1) which is usually not used as an 'index term' solely
DEF: 14-52, 13-34, 14-27
REF: qualifier 36-18 (NT), quantifier 36-19 (NT), role indicator 36-21 (NT), subheading 36-26 (NT), bound term 36-01 (RT)

preferred term
F terme préférentiel
D Vorzugsbenennung
R предпочтительный индексационный термин; рекомендуемый индексационный термин
S término preferido
36-16 (2) *Term* which should be used in *indexing* instead of another (deprecated) term
DEF: 14-52, 31-21
REF: non-descriptor 37-15 (OT), preferred term 14-37 (RT), descriptor 37-05 (RT)

qualified heading
F vedette identifiée
D spezifiziertes Schlagwort;
spezifiziertes Ordnungswort
R рубрика с пояснительной пометой
S encabezamiento calificado
36-17 A 'heading' followed by a 'qualifier' which is usually enclosed in parentheses; mostly used to distinguish the different *meanings* of *homonyms* and *polysemes*
DEF: 14-27, 14-22, 14-36
REF: heading 36-08 (BT), docuterm 36-07 (RT)

qualifier
identifier
F qualificatif
D Qualifikator; Spezifikator; Identifikator
R пояснительная помета
(качественного характера)
S calificador
36-18 A *symbol* used to qualify the *meaning* of a 'descriptor', e.g. to distinguish the different meanings of *homonyms*
DEF: 13-34, 14-27, 14-22
REF: modifier 36-15 (BT), quantifier 36-19 (OT), role indicator 36-21 (RT), subheading 36-27 (RT)

quantifier
F indicateur de quantification
D Quantifikator
R пояснительная помета
(количественного характера)
S cuantificador
36-19 A *symbol* or numeral used to modify or to indicate the *meaning* of a 'descriptor' in a quantitative way
DEF: 13-34, 14-27
REF: modifier 36-15 (BT), weight 36-30 (NT), qualifier 36-18 (OT)

relator
relational symbol; operator
F indicateur de relation

D Relator
R отсылочная помета;
указательная помета
S indicador de relación
36-20 A *symbol* used to establish a definite relation between two 'descriptors, or 'index terms' in *indexing*
DEF: 13-34, 31-21
REF: connector 39-25 (NT), linking 34-15 (RT), link 36-13 (RT), role indicator 36-21 (RT)

role indicator
F indicateur de rôle
D Rollenindikator; Funktionsindikator
R указатель роли
S indicador de función
36-21 A *symbol* used to modify the *meaning* of a 'descriptor' in indexing, when the descriptor is capable of assuming different functions in different subject-matter descriptions so that the function ascribed to it in a given context may be identified
DEF: 13-34, 14-27, 31-21
REF: modifier 36-15 (BT), bound term 36-01 (RT), qualifier 36-18 (RT)

semantic factors
F facteurs sémantiques
D semantische Faktoren
R семантические факторы
S factores semánticos
36-22 Generic *concepts* used to indicate important aspects of *meaning* of *terms* of a more specific nature and by the combination of which the more *specific concept* can be defined
DEF: 12-05, 14-27, 14-52, 12-29
REF: semantic factoring 36-23 (RT)

semantic factoring
F indexation sémantique par facteurs
D semantische Begriffszerlegung; semantische Zerlegung
R (представление понятий при индексировании путем комбинации сематических факторов)
S indizado semántico por factores
36-23 The representation of *specific concepts* in *indexing* by a combination of 'semantic factors'
DEF: 12-29, 31-21
REF: co-ordinate indexing 35-15 (RT)

specific heading
F vedette spécifique; vedette-matière spécifique
D spezifisches Schlagwort; spezifisches Ordnungswort
R узкая предметная рубрика
S encabezamiento específico
36-24 A 'heading' whose *meaning* des-

cribes the subject content covered by it
DEF: 14-27, 17-10
REF: heading 36-08 (BT), class h. 36-03 (OT)

subdivided heading
F vedette subdivisée
D unterteiltes Schlagwort; unterteiltes Ordnungswort
R подразделённая рубрика
S encabezamientos subdivididos
36-25 A 'class heading' which is split up into more 'specific headings' by the addition of 'modifiers' indicating the *characteristic* of subdivision
DEF: 12-02
REF: heading 36-08 (BT), subheading 36-27 (OT), class h. 36-25 (RT)

subheading
F sous-vedette
D Unterschlagwort
R подрубрика; подзаголовок
S subencabezamiento
36-26 (1) A subsidiary or modifying part of a 'heading', added to subdivide a given heading
REF: modifier 36-15 (BT), qualifier 36-18 (RT)
36-27 (2) A 'heading' subordinated to a 'subdivided heading'
REF: heading 36-08 (BT), subdivided h. 36-25 (RT)

subject heading
subject word
F vedette-matière; mot-matière; mot-sujet
D Schlagwort; Schlagworteingang
R предметная рубрика; предметный заголовок
S encabezamiento de materia
36-28 A *word*, *term* or a *phrase* chosen to express a *concept* or a concept combination in *indexing* and to constitute an *entry*
DEF: 14-55, 14-52, 14-34, 12-05, 31-21, 33-08
REF: descriptor 36-05 (BT), heading 36-08 (BT), index term 36-10 (BT), notation 310-23 (OT), catchword 36-02 (RT), descriptor 36-06, 37-06 (RT), keyword 36-12 (RT)

uniterm
F terme univoque
D Uniterm
R унитерм
S unitérmino
36-29 The most simple single *word* usable to denote a simple *concept* in *uniterm indexing*
DEF: 14-55, 12-05, 35-37

REF: descriptor 36-05 (BT), index term
36-10 (BT), descriptor 36-06 (OT),
notation 310-23 (OT), catchword 36-02
(RT), keyword 36-12 (RT)

weight
F   pondération
D   Gewichtung
R   весовой коэффициент
S   ponderador
      36-30 A 'quantifier' expressing the signif-
      icance a 'descriptor' has in relation to
      the whole indexed item
      REF: quantifier 36-19 (BT)

37 Thesaurus-type descriptor languages

alphabetical thesaurus
F   thesaurus alphabétique
D   alphabetischer Thesaurus
R   алфавитный тезаурус;
      дескрипторный словарь
S   tesauro alfabético
      37-01 A 'thesaurus' the 'main part'
      of which is arranged alphabetically
      REF: thesaurus 37-22 (BT), systematic
      th. 37-20 (OT)

broader term
F   terme générique
D   Oberbegriff
R   родовой дескриптор; вышестоящий
      дескриптор; подчиняющий дескриптор
S   término genérico
      37-02 A *cross reference* in the 'main
      part' of a 'thesaurus' indicating that
      the 'descriptor' (3) to which the reference
      is directed is superordinated to the
      descriptor from which the reference is
      made
      DEF: 34-09
      REF: cross reference 34-09 (BT), narrower
      term 37-14 (OT), related t. 37-16 (RT)
      general reference 34-12 (RT), see also
      reference 34-19 (RT)

classificatory structure (of thesaurus)
F   structure classificatoire d'un thesaurus
D   klassifikatorische Struktur
      (des Thesaurus)
R   классификационная схема
      (структурная основа тезауруса)
S   estructura clasificatoria de un tesauro
      37-03 The *classification system* which is
      incorporated in the 'broader term' and
      'narrower term' references of a thesaurus
      DEF: 39-21

REF: classification system 39-21 (BT),
descriptor network 37-07 (RT)

complex structured thesaurus
F   thesaurus à structure complexe
D   komplex strukturierter Thesaurus
R   тезаурус, отражающий сложные типы
      отношений между понятиями
S   tesauro de estructura compleja
      37-04 A 'thesaurus' that makes use of
      concept relationships other than the
      equivalence relation
      DEF: 38-12, 38-15
      REF: thesaurus 37-22 (BT), simple
      structured th. 37-18 (OT)

descriptor
F   descripteur
D   Deskriptor
R   дескриптор
S   descriptor
      37-05 (3) A well-defined, unequivocal
      term in a 'thesaurus' cross referenced
      to other terms and permitted for *indexing*
      DEF: 14-52, 31-21
      REF: index term 36-10 (BT), descriptor
      36-05/06 (BT), non-descriptor 37-15
      (OT), preferred term 36-16 (RT), subject
      heading 36-28 (RT)

descriptor association list
F   liste d'association des descripteurs
D   Deskriptorenassoziationsliste;
      Assoziationsklasse eines Deskriptors
R   указатель дескрипторных групп
S   lista de asociación de descriptores
      37-06 A list of *descriptors* associated
      with a particular descriptor or a group
      of particular descriptors in a given
      documentation system
      DEF: 36-05, 41-13
      REF: term list 16-14 (RT), graphic
      display 37-08 (RT)

descriptor network
F   réseau des descripteurs
D   Deskriptorennetzwerk
R   схема отношений между
      дескрипторами
S   red de descriptores
      37-07 The whole of relationships 'de-
      scriptors' (3) are indicated to have by
      cross references in the 'main part' of
      the 'thesaurus'
      DEF: 34-09
      REF: classificatory structure 37-03 (RT),
      graphic display 37-08 (RT)

graphic display
F   représentation graphique
D   Beziehungsgraph
R   графическое представление
      (отношений между дескрипторами)

S   representación gráfica
37-08 A graphical representation of 'descriptor networks'
REF: main part 37-09 (OT), descriptor network 37-07 (RT), thesaurus index 37-26 (RT), diagram 44-08 (RT)

main part (of thesaurus)
F   partie principale d'un thesaurus
D   Thesaurushauptteil
R   основная часть (тезауруса)
S   parte principal (de un tesauro)
37-09 Representation of all 'descriptors' (3) of a 'thesaurus', alphabetical or systematical, whereby all relevant relations to descriptors and 'non-descriptors' and all additional *informations* (like 'scope notes', *definitions*, etc.) are included at each descriptor *entry*
DEF: 17-28, 12-11, 33-08
REF: graphic display 37-08 (OT), thesaurus index 37-26 (OT)

macrothesaurus
F   macrothesaurus
D   Dachthesaurus; Makrothesaurus
R   макротезоурус
S   macrotesauro
37-10 A 'thesaurus' the 'thesaurus content' of which covers a broad *subject field* on a rather general level of specificity
DEF: 12-31
REF: thesaurus 37-22 (BT), microthesaurus 37-11 (OT)

microthesaurus
F   microthesaurus
D   Mikrothesaurus; Hilfsthesaurus
R   микротезаурус
S   microtesauro
37-11 A group of 'descriptors' (3) dedicated to a special field or a small *facet* of a *basic class* derived from the easy identification of the *characteristics* of the study to which it is applicable
DEF: 39-33, 39-05, 12-02
REF: thesaurus 37-22 (BT), macrothesaurus 37-10 (OT)

mission-oriented thesaurus
F   thesaurus sectoriel
D   aufgabenbezogener Thesaurus
R   тезаурус специального назначения (ориентированный на выполнение конкретной разработки)
S   tesauro especial
37-12 A 'thesaurus' the 'thesaurus content' of which covers the *concepts* necessary for a specific project within one *subject field* or across the boundaries of several subject fields
DEF: 12-05, 12-31
REF: thesaurus 37-22 (BT), subject-oriented th. 37-19 (OT)

multilingual thesaurus
F   thesaurus multilingue
D   mehrsprachiger Thesaurus
R   многоязычный тезаурус
S   tesauro multilingüe; tesauro políglota
37-13 A 'thesaurus' containing equivalent 'descriptors' (3) of more than two *natural languages* and the relationships between them according to the usage within each language
DEF: 15-18
REF: thesaurus 37-22 (BT)

narrower term
F   terme spécifique
D   Unterbegriff
R   видовой дескриптор; нижестоящий дескриптор; подчинённый дескриптор
S   término específico
37-14 A *cross reference* in the 'main part' of a 'thesaurus' indicating that the 'descriptor' (3) to which the reference is directed is subordinated to the descriptor from which the reference is made
DEF: 34-09
REF: cross reference 34-09 (BT), broader term 37-02 (OT), related t. 37-16 (RT), general reference 34-12 (RT), see also reference 34-19 (RT)

non-descriptor
F   non-descripteur
D   Nicht-Deskriptor
R   недескриптор
S   no-descriptor
37-15 A *deprecated term* in a 'thesaurus' from which a *use reference* is made to the *preferred term*, the 'descriptor' (3)
DEF: 14-15, 34-23, 36-16
REF: preferred term 36-16 (OT), descriptor 37-05 (OT), deprecated term 37-15 (RT)

related term
F   terme associé
D   assoziierter Begriff
R   ассоциативный дескриптор; смежный дескриптор
S   término asociado
37-16 A *cross reference* in the 'main part' of a 'thesaurus' indicating that two 'descriptors' (3)' are somewhat related in *meaning*
DEF: 34-09, 14-27
REF: cross reference 34-09 (BT), broader term 37-02 (RT), narrower t. 37-14 (RT), general reference 34-12 (RT), see also reference 34-19 (RT)

scope note
F   notice de contenu
D   Anwendungsnotiz
R   ограничительная помета

S   especificación de alcance
    37-17 A short indication of the scope and intended use of a 'descriptor (3)'

simple structured thesaurus
F   thesaurus à structure simple
D   einfach strukturierter Thesaurus
R   тезаурус, отражающий простые типы отношений между понятиями и обеспечивающий полноту терминологического контроля
S   tesauro de estructura simple
    37-18 A *term list* having complete 'terminological control'
    DEF: 16-14
    REF: authority list 35-04 (BT), thesaurus 37-22 (BT), complex structured th. 37-04 (OT)

subject-oriented thesaurus
F   thesaurus sectoriel
D   fachbezogener Thesaurus
R   отраслевой тезаурус
S   tesauro especializado
    37-19 A 'thesaurus' the 'thesaurus content' of which covers the concepts of a particular *subject field*
    DEF: 12-31
    REF: thesaurus 37-22 (BT), mission-oriented th. 37-12 (OT)

systematic thesaurus
F   thesaurus systématique
D   systematischer Thesaurus
R   систематический тезаурус
S   tesauro sistemático
    37-20 A 'thesaurus' the 'main part' of which is arranged systematically
    REF: thesaurus 37-22 (BT), alphabetical th. 37-01 (OT)

terminological control
F   contrôle de la terminologie
D   terminologische Kontrolle
R   терминологический контроль
S   control terminológico
    37-21 *Control* that *synonyms* and *quasi-synonyms* are cross referenced equivalently and *homonyms* and *polysemes* are distinguished by *qualifiers*
    DEF: 44-06, 14-49, 14-40, 14-22, 14-36, 36-18

thesaurus
F   thesaurus
D   Thesaurus
R   тезаурус; информационно-поисковый тезаурус
S   tesauro
    37-22 A controlled and dynamic *documentary language* containing semantically and generically related *terms*, which comprehensively covers a specific domain of *knowledge*

DEF: 15-08, 14-52, 12-24
REF: documentary language 15-08 (BT), alphabetical thesaurus 37-01 (NT), complex structured th. 37-04 (NT), macrothesaurus 37-10 (NT), microthesaurus 37-11 (NT), mission-oriented th. 37-12 (NT), multilingual th. 37-13 (NT), simple structured th. 37-18 (NT), subject-oriented th. 37-19 (NT), systematic th. 37-20 (NT), classification 311-05 (OT), authority list 35-04 (RT)

thesaurus content
F   contenu d'un thesaurus
D   Thesaurusinhalt
R   содержание тезауруса
S   contenido de un tesauro
    37-23 The subject area, i.e. the whole set of *concept systems*, a 'thesaurus' is intended to cover
    DEF: 12-34

thesaurus format
F   format d'un thesaurus
D   Thesaurusformat
R   формат тезауруса; формат записей тезауруса
S   formato de un tesauro
    37-24 (1) The format according to which the *data* necessary for 'thesaurus' development are recorded
    DEF: 17-12
    37-25 (2) The format according to which the *entries* within the 'main part' of the thesaurus are designed
    DEF: 33-08

thesaurus index
F   index d'un thesaurus
D   Thesaurusregister
R   дескрипторный словарь; алфавитный указатель дескрипторов (тезауруса)
S   índice de un tesauro
    37-26 An 'index' to the 'main part' of the 'thesaurus'; usually arranged in *alphabetical order* when the main part is arranged systematically and vice versa
    DEF: 35-22, 34-03
    REF: main part 37-09 (OT), graphic display 37-08 (RT)

38 Concept, term and class relations

abstraction
    generalization
F   généralisation
D   Abstraktion; Verallgemeinerung
R   абстрагирование; обобщение

S   generalización
38-01 Building up very general *concepts* or classesby generalizing the *characteristics* of *specific concepts* or classes
DEF: 12-05, 38-16/17, 12-02, 12-29

affective relation
F   relation d'influence
D   Beeinflussungsbeziehung; Beeinflussungsrelation
R   отношение воздействия
S   relación de influencia
38-02 An 'analytical relation' indicating that something makes use of, is determined by or is influenced by something
REF: analytical relations 38-03 (BT), instrumental relation 38-21 (RT), productive r. 38-26 (RT), appurtenance r. 38-05 (RT)

analytical relations
F   relation analytique
D   analytische Beziehungen; analytische Relationen
R   аналитические отношения
S   relaciones analíticas
38-03 'Relations' which exist between *terms* by virtue of their scope of *meaning*
DEF: 14-52, 14-27
REF: affective relation 38-02 (NT), attributive r. 38-09 (NT), categorical r. 38-10 (NT), comprehensive r. 38-12 (NT), inclusive r. 38-20 (NT), instrumental r. 38-21 (NT), intrinsic r. 38-22 (NT), negative r. 38-24 (NT), productive r. 38-26 (NT), simulative r. 38-28 (NT), synthetic relations 38-35 (OT)

antonymic relation
    antonymy
F   antonymie
D   Antonymie; Gegensatzbeziehung
R   антонимия
S   antonimia
38-04 A 'concept relation' where one *concept* is the opposite of the other
DEF: 12-05
REF: concept relation 38-13 (BT), equivalence r. 38-16 (OT)

appurtenance relation
F   relation d'appartenance
D   Zugehörigkeitsbeziehung
R   отношение принадлежности
S   relación de atingencia
38-05 A 'concept relation' expressing the combination of fixed association with non-distinctness as exemplified in the relational situation between a thing, activity or abstraction and its physical or invariant properties, parts or species.
REF: concept relation 38-13 (BT), affec-

tive r. 38-02 (RT), instrumental r. 38-21 (RT), productive r. 38-26 (RT)

association
F   association
D   Assoziation
R   ассоциация
S   asociación
38-06 The cognitive process of relating *concepts* to another
DEF: 12-05
REF: association relation 38-07 (RT), concept relation 38-12 (RT)

associative relation
    non-hierarchical relation (1)
F   relation associative
D   Assoziationsrelation (2); assoziative Relation 38-08 ; assoziative Beziehung
R   ассоциативное отношение; неиерархическое отношение
S   relación asociativa
38-07 (1) 'Relation' between *concepts* or *classes* which is non-hierarchical
DEF: 12-05, 39-15/16
REF: relation 38-27 (BT), hierarchical r. 38-19 (OT)
38-08 (2) 'Concept relation' based on the psychological process of 'association'
REF: concept relation 38-13 (BT), hierarchical r. 38-19 (RT), association 38-06 (RT), similarity r. 38-28 (RT)

attributive relation
F   relation attributive
D   attributive Beziehung ; attributive Relation
R   атрибутивное отношение
S   relación atributiva
38-09 An 'analytical relation' indicating that something is characterized by something
REF: analytical relation 38-03 (BT), negative r. 38-24 (OT)

categorical relation
F   relation catégorique
D   kategoriale Beziehung; kategoriale Relation
R   категориальное отношение
S   relación categórica
38-10 The analytical form of the 'generic relation'
REF: analytical relation 38-03 (BT), generic r. 38-17 (RT)

class relation
F   relation de classes
D   Relation zwischen Klassen ; Klassenbeziehung
R   отношение классов
S   relación de clases

38-11 A relation between at least two
classes
DEF: 39-15/16
REF: relation 38-27 (BT), co-ordinate r.
38-14 (NT), hierarchical r. 38-19 (NT),
syntagmatic relations 38-34 (NT), concept r. 38-13 (RT)

comprehensive relation
F   relation de compréhension
D   Beziehung der Umfassung; Umfassungs-
     relation
R   отношение включения
S   relación comprensiva
38-12 An 'analytical relation' indicating
that a *term* represents a composite of
several members of a *class* which is repre-
sented by another term
DEF: 14-52, 39-15/16
REF: analytical relation 38-03 (BT),
whole-part r. 38-36 (RT)

concept relation
F   relation entre notions
D   Begriffsbeziehung
R   отношение между понятиями
S   relación de conceptos
38-13 A 'relation' between at least two
concepts
DEF: 12-05
REF: relation 38-27 (BT), antonymic r.
38-04 (NT), associative r. 38-08 (NT),
co-ordinate r. 38-14 (NT), hierarchical
r. 38-19 (NT), kinetic r. 38-23 (NT),
paradigmatic relations 38-25 (NT), similarity r. 38-28 (NT), spatial r. 38-30 (NT),
syntagmatic relations 38-34 (NT), synthetic relations 38-35 (NT), class r. 38-11
(RT)

co-ordinate relation
     co-ordination; concept co-ordination
F   relation coordonnée
D   Gleichordnung;
     Gleichordnungsbeziehung
R   отношение соподчинения
S   relación coordinada
38-14 Relation between *concepts or
classes* which are 'subordinate' to the
same concept or class
DEF: 12-05, 39-15/16
REF: class relation 38-11 (BT), concept r.
38-13 (BT), hierarchical r. 38-19 (OT),
array 39-03 (RT)

definitive relation
F   relation définitive
D   Definitionsbeziehung;
     definierende Beziehung
R   дефинитивное отношение
S   relación definitoria
38-15 The 'relation' of a 'term' to the
set of *words* which makes up its *defini-
tion*
DEF: 14-52, 14-55, 12-11

REF: relation 38-27 (BT)

equivalence relation
F   relation d'équivalence
D   Äquivalenzbeziehung;
     Äquivalenzrelation
R   отношение равнозначности;
     отношение эквивалентности
S   relación de equivalencia
38-16 A relation between *terms* indicat-
ing that they may be used equivalent,
i.e. treated as *synonyms*.
DEF: 14-52, 14-49
REF: relation 38-27 (BT), quasi-synonym
14-40 (RT), synonym 14-49 (RT)

generic relation
     abstraction relation; categorical relation;
     logical relation
F   relation générique
D   Abstraktionsbeziehung;
     Abstraktionsrelation;
     generische Relation;
     generische Beziehung
R   отношение «род-вид»
S   relación genérica
38-17 'Relation' between *concepts or
classes* in which one is the 'genus' and
the others are the 'species'
DEF: 12-05, 39-15/16
REF: hierarchical relation 38-19 (BT),
whole-part r. 38-36 (OT), categorical r.
38-10 (RT), intrinsic r. 38-22 (RT)

genus
F   genre
D   Genus; Oberbegriff
R   род
S   género
38-18 A *concept* 'a' or a *class* 'A' is a
genus in 'relation' to another concept 'b'
or class 'B' if b/B is defined by the same
attributes as a/A and one or more additional attributes
DEF: 12-05, 39-15/16, 12-01
REF: species 38-31 (OT), generic relation
38-17 (RT)

hierarchical relation
F   relation hiérarchique
D   Hierarchie-Relation;
     hierarchische Relation;
     hierarchische Beziehung
R   иерархическое отношение;
     отношение подчинения
S   relación jerárquica
38-19 'Relation' between *concepts or
classes* in which one is superordinate
to the others
DEF: 12-05, 39-15/16
REF: class relation 38-11 (BT), concept
r. 38-13 (BT), generic r. 38-17 (NT),
whole-part-r. 38-36 (NT), associative
r. 38-07 (OT), co-ordinate r. 38-14 (OT),

genus 38-18 (RT), species 38-31 (RT), subordination 38-32 (RT), superordination 38-33 (RT), basis of division 39-07 (RT), hierarchy 39-45 (RT), associative r. 38-08 (RT)

inclusive relation
F   relation d'inclusion
D   Einschlußbeziehung; Einschlußrelation
R   отношение «часть-целое»; отношение подчинения; отношение включения
S   relación inclusiva
38-20 An 'analytical relation' indicating that a *term* represents something that is part of a whole represented by another term
DEF: 14-52
REF: analytical relations 38-03 (BT), intrinsic relation 38-22 (OT), whole-part r. 38-36 (RT)

instrumental relation
F   relation instrumentale
D   instrumentelle Beziehung; instrumentelle Relation
R   инструментальное отношение
S   relación instrumental
38-21 An 'analytical relation' indicating that something is produced by, acts on, or is acted on by something
REF: analytical relations 38-03 (BT), affective relation 38-02 (RT), appurtenance r. 38-05 (RT), productive r. 38-26 (RT)

intrinsic relation
F   relation intrinsèque
D   Beziehung des Enthaltenseins
R   отношение «целое-часть»; отношение вхождения
S   relación intrínseca
38-22 An 'analytical relation' indicating that a *term* represents a whole of which that which is represented by the other term forms a part of
DEF: 14-52
REF: analytical relations 38-03 (BT), inclusive r. 38-20 (OT), whole-part r. 38-36 (RT)

kinetic relation
F   relation cinétique
D   Bewegungszusammenhang
R   кинетическое отношение
S   relación cinética
38-23 A 'concept relation' indicating that two *concepts* are related by some kind of motion
DEF: 12-05
REF: concept relation 38-13 (BT)

negative relation
F   relation négative

D   Ausschlußbeziehung; Ausschlußrelation
R   негативное отношение; отношение внеположенности
S   relación negativa
38-24 An 'analytical relation' indicating that one *term* represents something that is absent in another
DEF: 14-52
REF: analytical relations 38-03 (BT), attributive relation 38-09 (OT)

paradigmatic relations
F   relations paradigmatiques
D   paradigmatische Relationen; paradigmatische Beziehungen
R   парадигматические отношения
S   relaciones paradigmáticas
38-25 Relations between *concepts* which are shown by the structure of the *documentary language*, i.e. which are explicit before *indexing*
DEF: 12-05, 15-08, 31-21
REF: concept relation 38-13 (BT), synthetic relations 38-35 (OT)

productive relation
F   relation productive
D   Beziehung der Erzeugung; Relation der Erzeugung; Herstellungsrelation
R   продуктивное отношение
S   relación productiva
38-26 An 'analytical relation' indicating that something produces or is used for or to something
REF: analytical relations 38-03 (BT), affective relation 38-02 (RT), appurtenance r. 38-05 (RT), instrumental r. 38-21 (RT)

relation
F   relation
D   Relation; Beziehung
R   отношение
S   relación
38-27 The intellectual connexion between two or more *elements*
DEF: 12-12
REF: section 38 for NT

similarity relation
F   relation de similitude
D   Ähnlichkeitsrelation
R   отношение сходства
S   relación de similitud
38-28 A 'concept relation' based on some kind of physical similarity
REF: concept relation 38-13 (BT), associative r. 38-07 (RT)

simulative relation
F   relation d'apparence
D   simulative Beziehung; simulative Relation

R отношение (внешнего) подобия
S relación simulativa
38-29 An 'analytical relation' indicating that one *term* resembles but is not the other term
DEF: 14-52
REF: analytical relations 38-03 (BT)

spatial relation
F relation spatiale
D räumliche Beziehung; räumliche Relation
R пространственное отношение
S relación espacial
38-30 A 'concept relation' indicating the position of things to each other
REF: concept relation 38-13 (BT)

species
F espèces
D Spezies; Unterbegriff
R вид
S especie
38-31 A *concept* 'b' or *class* 'B' is species of another concept 'a' or class 'A' if a/A is 'genus' to b/B
DEF: 12-05, 39-15/16
REF: genus 38-18 (OT), generic relation 38-17 (RT)

subordination
F subordination
D Unterordnung
R подчинение; субординация
S subordinación
38-32 A *concept* or *class* having hierarchically superordinated concepts or classes
DEF: 12-05, 39-15/16
REF: hierarchical relation 38-19 (RT), chain 39-13 (RT)

superordination
F relation de supériorité
D Überordnung
R суперординация
S superordinación
38-33 A *concept* or *class* having hierarchically subordinated concepts or classes
DEF: 12-05, 39-15/16
REF: hierarchical relation 38-19 (RT), chain 39-13 (RT)

syntagmatic relations
F relation syntagmatique
D syntagmatische Relationen
R синтагматические отношения
S relaciones sintagmáticas
38-34 'Relations' between *concepts, classes* or *terms* which are established during *indexing* and having not before explicitly pointed out by the structure of the *documentary language*

DEF: 12-05, 39-15/16, 14-52, 31-21, 15-08
REF: class relation 38-11 (BT), concept relation 38-13 (BT), paradigmatic relations 38-25 (OT), phase relation 39-59 (RT)

synthetic relations
F relations synthétiques
D synthetische Relationen
R синтетические отношения
S relaciones sintéticas
38-35 'Concept relations' which pertain to empirical observation
REF: concept relation 38-13 (BT), analytical relations 38-03 (OT)

whole-part relation
partitive relation
F relation partitive
D Bestandsbeziehung; Bestandsrelation; partitive Beziehung; partitive Relation
R отношение «целое-часть»
S relación partitiva
38-36 'Relation' between *concepts* or *classes* in which one represents a whole and the others are the *elements*
DEF: 12-05, 39-15/16, 12-12
REF: hierarchical relation 38-19 (BT), generic r. 38-17 (OT), comprehensive r. 38-12 (RT), inclusive r. 38-28 (RT), intrinsic r. 38-22 (RT)

39 Elements and principles of classification

analet
F
D (zusammengesetzte Notation)
R аналет
S
39-01 A linear arrangement of 'isolates' linked by *relators*, which represents a specific subject
DEF: 36-20
REF: notation 310-23 (BT)

analytical subdivisions
F subdivision analytique
D besondere Anhängezahlen
R аналитические определители
S subdivisiones analíticas
39-02 'Auxiliary tables' for subdivision applying only in one 'main class' or a group of 'classes'
REF: auxiliary tables 39-04 (BT), common subdivisions 39-24 (OT)

array
F   rang
D   (Begriffs-) Reihe;
     klassifikatorische Reihe
R   ряд (взаимоисключающих
     подразделений класса, которые
     образованы его делением на основе
     какого-либо признака)
S   serie
     39-03 The series of 'classes' derived from
     a superordinated class by one step of
     subdivision
     REF: closed array 39-22 (NT), octave
     39-56 (NT), telescoped a. 39-61 (NT),
     chain a. 39-13 (OT)

auxiliary tables
     categorical tables; systematic schedules
F   table auxiliaire
D   Hilfstafeln; Anhängezahlen
R   вспомогательные таблицы;
     таблицы определителей
S   cuadros auxiliares;
     tablas de subdivisiones comunes
     39-04 'Classification schedules' which
     are used to subdivide 'classes' of the
     'main tables' according to 'facets'
     applying to all 'main classes' or a group
     of classes
     REF: classification schedule 39-19 (BT),
     analytical subdivisions 39-02 (NT), com-
     mon subdivisions 39-24 (NT), main
     table 39-55 (OT)

basic class
F   classe de base
D   Grundklasse
R   основной класс; основной раздел
     (классификации)
S   categoría básica
     39-05 A 'main class' or a 'canonical
     class'
     REF: class 39-15/16 (BT), basic focus
     39-06 (NT), canonical c. 39-09 (NT),
     main c. 39-54 (NT), infima species
     39-46 (OT)

basic focus
F   foyer de base
D   Hauptfacettenunterteilung
R   главный фокус (законченное
     подразделение в классификации,
     выделенное на основе определенного
     фасета)
S   foco básico
     39-06 The 'canonical classes' derived
     by the first step of subdivision of a
     'facet'
     REF: canonical class 39-09 (BT), focus
     39-38 (BT), isolate 39-52 (OT)

basis of division
     basis of subdivision; difference

F   base de division
D   Untergliederungsgesichtspunkt;
     Unterteilungsgesichtspunkt
R   основание деления
S   base de la división
     39-07 The *characteristics* added to a
     superordinated 'class' to build an
     'array'
     DEF: 12-02
     REF: hierarchical relation 38-19 (RT)

bias
F   biais
D   Ausrichtung
R   (соотношение между фазами
     (в классификации), при котором
     основная фаза рассматривается
     с точки зрения вторичной)
S
     39-08 A 'phase relation' between two
     terms indicating that a subject has been
     treated as background for *users* who
     are specialists in another field
     DEF: 14-52, 46-30
     REF: phase relations 39-59 (BT)

canonical class
F   classe formelle
D   traditionelle Hauptunterteilung;
     kanonische Klasse
R   традиционное подразделение
     основного класса
S   clase canónica
     39-09 A class derived by the first step
     of subdivision of a 'main class', where
     no principle of subdivision is dis-
     coverable
     REF: basic class 39-05 (BT), main c. 39-54
     (BT), basic forms 39-06 (NT), infima
     species 39-46 (OT)

canonical order
     mathematical order
F   ordre canonique
D   formale Ordnung
R   традиционная последовательность;
     традиционное расположение
S   orden canónico
     39-10 The 'order in an array' not
     following subject *characteristics*, but the
     formal characteristics of *notation*
     DEF: 12-02, 310-23
     REF: order in array 39-57 (BT), chrono-
     logical device 39-14 (OT), evolutionary
     o. 39-32 (OT), form subdivision 39-39
     (OT), geographical subdivision 39-43
     (OT), language subdivision 39-52 (OT)

category
F   catégorie
D   Kategorie
R   категория
S   categoría
     39-11 (1) A 'class' of very high generality

REF: class 39-15/16 (BT), facet 39-33/34 (RT), main class 39-54 (RT)
39-12 (2) A general 'facet' applying to a lot of *subject fields*
DEF: 12-31
REF: facet 39-33 (NT), fundamental category 39-41 (NT)

chain
F   chaîne
D   (Begriffs-) Kette; (Begriffs-) Leiter; klassifikatorische Leiter; klassifikatorische Kette
R   иерархия соподчинённых классов (подразделений), образованных последовательным делением
S   cadena
39-13 A 'hierarchy of classes' of decreasing *extension* and increasing *intension* derived by successive subdivision
DEF: 12-14, 12-20
REF: hierarchy 39-45 (BT), generic chain 39-42 (NT), array 39-03 (RT), subordination 38-32 (RT), superordination 38-33 (RT)

chronological device
chronological subdivision
F   subdivision chronologique
D   zeitliche Unterteilung
R   хронологическое подразделение
S   subdivisión cronológica
39-14 The subdivision of a 'class' by *characteristics* of date or time
DEF: 12-02
REF: basis of division 39-07 (BT), common subdivision 39-24 (BT), order in array 39-57 (BT), canonical order 39-10 (OT), evolutionary order 39-32 (OT), form subdivision 39-39 (OT), geographical subdivision 39-43 (OT), language subdivision 39-52 (OT), chronological filing system 34-04 (RT)

class
F   classe
D   Klasse
R   класс
S   clase
39-15 (1) A set of *elements* having at least one *characteristic* in common
DEF: 12-12, 12-02
REF: basic class 39-05 (NT), category 39-11 (NT), infima species 39-46 (NT), focus 39-38 (NT), facet 39-33 (RT), isolate 39-51 (RT)
39-16 (2) A set of *characteristics* defining a set of *elements*
DEF: 12-02, 12-12
REF: see 39-15

class description
F   description d'une classe
D   Klassenbeschreibung

R   описание класса; определение класса
S   descripción de una clase
39-17 The verbal description or *definition* of the *elements* or *characteristics* constituting the 'class'
DEF: 12-11, 12-12, 12-02
REF: notation 310-22/23 (OT)

classification code
F   code de classification
D   Klassifizierungsregeln
R   свод правил классифицирования; классификационный код
S   código de clasificación
39-18 A set of rules for applying a *classification* in *indexing*
DEF: 311-05, 31-21
REF: classifying 31-12 (RT), cataloguing rules 32-09 (RT)

classification schedule
classification table
F   cadre de classification
D   Klassifikationstafel; Klassifikationsplan
R   классификационная таблица; таблица классификации
S   esquema de clasificación
39-19 The readable representation of a 'classification system' presenting the 'classes' in their *hierarchical relations* by *notations* and 'class descriptions'
DEF: 38-19, 310-22/23
REF: auxiliary tables 39-04 (NT), main table 39-55 (NT), classification scheme 39-20 (RT), classification system 39-21 (RT), generic coding 18-21 (RT)

classification scheme
F   plan de classification
D   Klassifikationsschema
R   классификационная схема; схема классификации
S   plan de clasificación
39-20 The conceptional scheme lying behind a 'classification schedule'
DEF: 38-19, 38-25, 15-08
REF: classification schedule 39-19 (RT), classification system 39-21 (RT)

classification system
F   système de classification
D   Klassifikationssystem
R   классификация; классификационная система
S   sistema de clasificación
39-21 The set of *hierarchical relations* indicated as *paradigmatic relations* within a *documentary language*
DEF: 38-19, 38-25, 15-08
REF: classificatory structure 37-03 (NT), classification schedule 39-19 (RT), classification scheme 39-20 (RT), hierarchy 39-45 (RT)

closed array
F   série fermée
D   geschlossene Reihe
R   закрытый ряд; полный ряд
     (в классификации)
S   serie cerrada
39-22 An 'array' which cannot be extended, either because of the notational base or completeness of subdivision
DEF: array 39-03 (BT), hospitality of notation 310-14 (RT)

common facet
F   facette commune
D   Allgemeinfacette
R   общий фасет
S   faceta común
39-23 A 'facet' which is common to all subjects of a specific *subject field*
DEF: 12-31
REF: facet 39-34 (BT), differential f. 39-29 (OT)

common subdivisions
     common auxiliaries
F   subdivisions communes
D   allgemeine Anhängezahlen
R   общие определители
S   subdivisiones auxiliares
39-24 'Auxiliary tables' applicable to all the 'main tables' of a *classification*
DEF: 311-05
REF: auxiliary tables 39-04 (BT), chronological device 39-14 (NT), form subdivisions 39-40 (NT), geographical subdivision 39-44 (NT), language s. 39-53 (NT)

connector
     intra-facet connector
F   connecteur
D   Konnektor; Intrafacettenkonnektor
R   указатель межфасетной связи
S   conector
39-25 A *special character* for forming *compounds* by 'intrafacet relations'.
DEF: 13-32, 14-09
REF: relator 36-20 (BT), separator 39-60 (BT)

co-ordinate classes
F   classes coordonnées
D   gleichgeordnete Klassen
R   координированные классы
S   clases coordinadas
39-26 The 'classes' within one 'array'

cross classification
     alternative location
F   classification croisée
D   Mehrfacheinordnung (einer Klasse)
R   перекрёстная классификация;
     параллельная классификация
S   clasificación cruzada

39-27 The possibility of having one 'class' on two or more places in the *classification*, arising in *hierarchical classifications* by the problems of polyhierarchy
DEF: 311-05, 311-12
REF: monohierarchical classification 311-15 (RT)

dependent facet
F   facette dépendante
D   abhängige Facette
R   зависимый фасет; подчинённый фасет
S   faceta dependiente
39-28 A 'facet' which cannot manifest itself unless the 'focus' in the preceding facet also manifests itself
REF: facet 39-34 (BT)

differential facet
     secondary facet
F   facette différentielle
D   Unterscheidungsfacette
R   отличительный фасет
S   faceta diferencial
39-29 A 'facet' which applies only to a restricted group of *concepts* of a more general facet
DEF: 12-05
REF: facet 39-34 (BT), common f. 39-23 (OT)

dimensionality
F   dimensionnalité
D   Dimensionalität
R   размерность
S   dimensionalidad
39-30 (1) The quality of a 'class' being subdivided by different trains of *characteristics* or 'facets'
DEF: 12-02
REF: monodimensional classification 311-14 (RT), polydimensional classification 311-17 (RT)
39-31 (2) The length of the longest downward chain from a 'class'

evolutionary order
     evolutionary sequence
F   ordre de complexité croissante
D   Ordnung vom Einfachen zum Komplexen
R   эволюционная последовательность
S   orden de complejidad creciente
39-32 'Order in an array' going from simple to complex
REF: order in array 39-57 (BT), canonical o. 39-10 (OT), chronological device 39-14 (OT), form subdivision 39-39 (OT), geographical subdivision 39-43 (OT), language subdivision 39-52 (OT)

facet
F   facette
D   Facette

R   фасет
s   faceta
39-33 (1) An aspect under which a group of *concepts* may be looked at to have something general in common
DEF: 12-05
REF: class 39-15/16 (RT), category 39-11 (RT)
39-34 (2) In a *faceted classification* any one group of 'classes' having certain common *characteristics*, constituting a 'category (1)'
DEF: 311-11, 12-02
REF: category 39-12 (BT), common facet 39-23 (NT), dependent f. 39-28 (NT), differential f. 39-29 (NT), category 39-11 (RT)

facet analysis
F   analyse par facettes
D   Facettenanalyse
R   фасетный анализ
s   análisis por facetas
39-35 The analysis of the *concepts* of a *subject field* to detect the 'facets' suitable in this subject field
DEF: 12-05, 12-31
REF: classifying 31-11 (RT)

facet order
facet formula; combination order; citation order
F   ordre de facettes
D   Facettenfolge; Facettenformel
R   фасетная формула
s   orden de facetas
39-36 The order in which the 'facets' are represented in the *notation*
DEF: 310-22/23
REF: expressive notation 310-10 (RT), labelled notation 310-18 (RT)

facet indicator
F   indicateur de facette
D   Facettenindikator
R   указатель начала фасета (в индексе)
s   indicador de faceta
39-37 A *character* indicating in *notation* the starting of a 'facet'
DEF: 13-10, 310-22/23
REF: separators 39-60 (BT)

focus
F   foyer
D   Fokus; Facettenunterteilung
R   фокус (подразделение фасета)
s   foco (de faceta)
39-38 A 'class' or 'isolate' in the context of a 'facet'
REF: class 39-15/16 (BT), isolate 39-51 (RT)

form subdivisions
auxiliary subdivisions of form (2)
F   subdivision formelle (1); subdivisions de formes (2)
D   formale Unterteilung (1); Anhängezahlen der Form (2)
R   формальное подразделение (1); определители формы (2)
s   subdivisiones de forma
39-39 (1) The subdivision of a 'class' by *characteristics* of form
DEF: 12-02
REF: order in array 39-57 (BT), basis of division 39-07 (BT), canonical order 39-10 (BT), chronological device 39-14 (OT), evolutionary order 39-32 (OT), geographical subdivision 39-43 (OT), language subdivision 39-52 (OT)
39-40 (2) 'Auxiliary tables' for subdivision by *characteristics* of form
DEF: 12-05
REF: common subdivisions 39-24 (BT), chronological device 39-14 (OT), geographical subdivision 39-44 (OT), language subdivision 39-53 (OT)

fundamental category
F   catégorie fondamentale
D   Fundamentalkategorie
R   основная категория
s   categoría fundamental
39-41 A 'category (2)' applicable to all fields of *knowledge*
DEF: 12-24
REF: category 39-12 (BT)

generic chain
scalar series
F   chaîne générique
D   generische Kette; Abstraktionskette
R   иерархия соподчинённых классов (связанных родовыми отношениями)
s   cadena genérica
39-42 A 'chain' constituted by *generic relations* only, i.e. excluding *whole-part-relations*
DEF: 38-17, 38-36
REF: chain 39-13 (BT)

geographical subdivision
geographical device; local subdivision; subdivisions of place (2)
F   subdivision géographique (1); subdivision de lieu (2)
D   geographische Unterteilung (1); Anhängezahl des Ortes (2)
R   географическое подразделение (1); географические определители (2); определители места (2)
s   subdivisión geográfica
39-43 (1) The subdivision of a 'class' by *characteristics* of geographical location
DEF: 12-02

REF: basis of division 39-07 (BT), order in array 39-57 (BT), canonical order 39-10 (OT), chronological device 39-14 (OT), evolutionary order 39-32 (OT), form subdivisions 39-39 (OT), language s. 39-52 (OT), geographic filing method 34-14 (RT)
39-44 (2) 'Auxiliary tables' for subdivision by *characteristics* of geographical location
DEF: 12-02
REF: common subdivision 39-24 (BT), chronological device 39-14 (OT), form subdivisions 39-40 (OT), language s. 39-53 (OT)

hierarchy
F hiérarchie
D Hierarchie; hierarchische Struktur
R иерархия
S jerarquía
39-45 The *network* between *concepts* constituted by *hierarchical relations*
DEF: 41-28, 12-05, 38-19
REF: chain 39-13 (NT), classification system 39-21 (RT), hierarchical relation 38-19 (RT), hierarchical classification 311-12 (RT), monohierarchical classification 311-15 (RT), polyhierarchical classification 311-18 (RT)

infima species
smallest subdivision; ultimate class
F espèce minimale
D kleinste Unterteilung
R низшее подразделение (классификации)
S subdivisión infima
39-46 The last 'class' in a 'chain', i.e. the class which has not been subdivided further
REF: class 39-15/16 (BT), basic class 39-05 (OT), canonical class 39-09 (OT), main class 39-54 (OT)

integrative level
F niveau d'intégration
D Komplexitätsniveau
R (вышестоящий уровень в иерархии классов понятий; расположенных по возрастающей сложности)
S nivel de integración
39-47 In a series of 'classes' arranged in an order of complexity, any level at which the *concepts* exhibit a combination of the properties of concepts of lesser complexity together with additional *characteristics*
DEF: 12-05, 12-02

intercalation
F intercalation
D Interkalation
R введение новой классификационной рубрики

S intercalación
39-48 The introduction of *notations* from other 'classification schedules' into notations taken from a specific classification schedule
DEF: 310-23

intercalator
intercalation mark
F intercalaire
D Interkalator
R условный знак при дополнительно введённой классификационной рубрике
S intercalador
39-49 A *character* indicating 'intercalation'
DEF: 13-10
REF: separators 39-60 (BT)

intra-facet relations
F relations intra-facette
D Intrafacettenrelationen
R отношения внутри фасета
S relaciones intra-faceta
39-50 *Relations* between 'isolates' within one 'facet'
DEF: 38-27
REF: phase relation 39-59 (RT)

isolate
F isolat
D Isolat; Einzelklasse; singuläre Klasse
R изолат
S clase elemental
39-51 A single *concept* of any degree of complexity which can be considered in isolation for purposes of *definition*, or for placing in a *classification*
DEF: 12-05, 12-11, 311-05
REF: class 39-15/16 (RT), focus 39-38 (RT)

language subdivision
F subdivision par langues
D sprachliche Unterteilung (1); Anhängezahlen der Sprache (2)
R подразделение по языку (1); определители языка (2)
S subdivisión por lenguaje
39-52 (1) The subdivision of a 'class' according to *characteristics* of *language*
DEF: 12-02, 15-13
REF: basis of division 39-07 (BT), order in array 39-57 (BT), canonical order 39-10 (OT), chronological device 39-14 (OT), evolutionary order 39-32 (OT), form subdivisions 39-39 (OT), geographical subdivisions 39-34 (OT)
39-53 (2) 'Auxiliary schedules' for subdivision of 'classes' by 'languages' in which the *document* is written
DEF: 15-13, 21-18

REF: common subdivisions 39-24 (BT), chronological device 39-14 (OT), form s. 39-40 (OT), geographical subdivisions 39-44 (OT)

main class
F classe principale
D Hauptklasse
R основной класс; основной раздел (классификации)
S clase principal
39-54 A major division of a *classification*, often a traditional discipline
DEF: 311-05
REF: basic class 39-05 (BT), canonical c. 39-09 (NT), infima species 39-46 (OT)

main table
main schedule
F table principale
D Haupttafel
R основная таблица
S cuadro principal; esquema principal
39-55 The 'classification schedule' exposing the subjects to be classified by the *classification*
DEF: 311-05
REF: classification schedule 39-19 (BT), auxiliary table 39-04 (OT)

octave
F octave
D Oktave
R октава (область или комплекс в классификационном ряду, отделённый от других при восьмеричной системе индексации)
S octava
39-56 A zone or region of an 'array' marked off from others
REF: array 39-03 (BT), octave device 310-26 (RT), octave notation 310-27 (RT)

order in array
F ordre séquentiel
D Anordnung der Reihe
R принцип расположения классов в ряду
S orden en serie
39-57 The principle of arrangement of 'classes' in an 'array'
REF: canonical order 39-10 (NT), chronological device 39-14 (NT), evolutionary order 39-32 (NT), form subdivision 39-39 (NT), geographical subdivision 39-43 (NT), language subdivision 39-52 (NT), basis of division 39-07 (RT)

phase
F phase
D Phase
R фаза (в классификации)
S fase

39-58 Any one of two or more 'classes' brought into relation to one another in *classifying*
DEF: 31-12
REF: phase relations 39-59 (RT)

phase relations
F relations de phase
D Phasenbeziehungen; Phasenrelationen
R фазовые отношения
S relaciones de fase
39-59 Relations between 'classes' other than that implied between the 'categories' or 'facets'
REF: phase 39-58 (RT), syntagmatic relations 38-34 (RT)

separators
F séparateurs
D Separatoren
R разделительные знаки (в индексах)
S separadores
39-60 *Characters* marking different parts of a *notation*
DEF: 13-10, 310-23
REF: connector 39-25 (NT), facet indicator 39-37 (NT), intercalator 39-49 (NT), octave device 310-26 (RT)

telescoped array
cross classification
F classification hétérogène
D mehrdimensionale (Begriffs-) Reihe
R (ряд в классификации, образованный путём параллельного деления вышестоящего класса по нескольким принципам)
S serie heterogéna
39-61 An 'array' in a 'classification schedule' which includes 'classes' stemming from more than one subdivision of the superordinated class on the same level, i.e. by using more than one train of *characteristics* or 'facet (1)'
DEF: 12-02
REF: array 39-04 (BT), polydimensional classification 311-17 (RT)

310 Notation and numbers

accession number
F numéro d'entrée; numéro d'ordre
D Zugangsnummer
R инвентарный номер
S número de registro; número de acceso
310-01 The number assigned to an acquired *document* indicating the order of its entry into the *collection*
DEF: 21-18, 312-05
REF: accession 31-02 (RT)

alphabetic notation
F   notation alphabétique
D   alphabetische Notation; Alpha-Notation
R   буквенная нотация
S   notación alfabética
310-02 A 'notation' consisting of *letters* and *special characters*
DEF: 13-23, 13-32
REF: pure notation 310-31 (BT), alpha-numeric n. 310-03 (OT), numeric n. 310-25 (OT)

alphanumeric notation
F   notation alphanumérique
D   alphanumerische Notation
R   буквенно-цифровая нотация
S   notación alfanumérica
310-03 A 'notation' consisting of *letters, digits* and *special characters*
DEF: 13-23, 13-18, 13-32
REF: mixed notation 310-20 (BT), alpha-betic n. 310-02 (OT), numeric n. 310-25 (OT)

binary notation
F   notation binaire
D   binäre Notation
R   двоичная нотация
S   notación binaria
310-04 A 'numeric notation' consisting of *binary digits* and *special characters*
DEF: 13-06, 13-32
REF: numeric notation 310-25 (BT), decimal n. 310-08 (OT), octave n. 310-27 (OT), polydecimal n. 310-28 (OT)

call number
     location mark; shelf-mark; shelf-number
F   cote
D   Standortnummer; Signatur
R   расстановочный индекс; шифр
S   signatura de ubicación; signatura topográfica
310-05 A number used to indicate the location of a *book* on the shelves
DEF: 21-09
REF: document number 310-09 (RT)

class number
F   indice
D   Klassennummer
R   индекс отдела; индекс раздела (в классификации)
S   número de clase
310-06 A number used for the identifi-cation of *classes*
DEF: 39-15/16
REF: notation 310-23 (RT)

current number
     running number
F   numéro courant
D   laufende Nummer

R   порядковый номер
S   número progresivo
310-07 A number identifying items in the order of occurrence
REF: serial number 310-23 (NT), linear notation 310-19 (RT)

decimal notation
F   notation décimale
D   Dezimalnotation
R   десятичная нотация
S   notación decimal
310-08 A 'numeric notation' where the 'notational base' is 10
REF: numeric notation 310-25 (BT), binary n. 310-04 (OT), polydecimal n. 310-28 (OT), decimal classification 311-07 (RT)

document number
F   numéro de document
D   Dokumentnummer
R   номер документа
S   número de documento
310-09 The number given to a *document* to be used as a means for *reference* and *retrieval*
DEF: 21-18, 22-17, 313-31
REF: call number 310-05 (RT)

expressive notation
     structured notation; structural notation
F   notation expressive
D   strukturierte Notation; semantische Notation
R   нотация с отражением отношений между понятиями
S   notación expresiva
310-10 A 'notation' emphasizing *symbol* structure which corresponds to the *concept relations*
DEF: 13-34, 38-13
REF: notation 310-22/23 (BT), hier-archical n. 310-13 (NT), linear n. 310-19 (OT), facet order 39-36 (RT)

flexibility of notation
F   flexibilité de notation
D   Flexibilität der Notation
R   гибкость нотации
S   flexibilidad de notación
310-11 The quality of a 'notation' which permits the insertion of new *classes* and mobility of its semantic elements
DEF: 39-15/16
REF: hospitality of notation 310-14 (RT)

group notation
F   notation de groupe
D   Gruppennotation
R   групповая нотация
S   notación de grupo
310-12 A variation in an otherwise

'hierarchical notation' in which a single conceptual *array* is represented by several notational arrays
DEF: 39-03
REF: notation 310-22/23 (BT), hierarchical n. 310-13 (RT)

hierarchical notation
F   notation hiérarchique
D   hierarchische Notation
R   иерархическая нотация
S   notación jerárquica
310-13 A 'notation' in which each *character* symbolizes one step of subdivision
DEF: 13-10
REF: expressive notation 310-10 (BT), linear n. 310-19 (OT), group n. 310-12 (RT), basis of division 39-07 (RT)

hospitality of notation
F   réserve de notation
D   Erweiterungsfähigkeit der Notation
R   гибкость нотации;
     растяжимость нотации
S   flexibilidad de notación
310-14 The quality of a 'notation' to permit interpolation or extrapolation of *arrays*
DEF: 39-03
REF: flexibility of notation 310-14 (RT), octave device 310-26 (RT), closed array 34-22 (RT)

inclusive notation
F   notation inclusive
D   Erstreckungsangabe
R   система записи ряда
     последовательных номеров чере тире
S   notación inclusiva
310-15 Representation of consecutive numbers or notation (2) by a symbol consisting of the first number, a dash, and the last number
DEF: 13-34

international standard book number (ISBN)
F   numéro international normalisé des livres
D   internationale Standard-Buchnummer (ISBN)
R   система международных стандартных номеров для книг
S   número internacional normalizado para libros
310-16 An internationally standardized number assigned to *books* by the *publishing houses* used for *reference*
DEF: 21-09, 51-32, 22-17
REF: international standard serial number 310-17 (RT)

international standard serial number (ISSN)
F   numéro international normalisé des publications en série

D   internationale Standard-Seriennummer (ISSN)
R   система международных стандартных номеров для продолжающихся изданий
S   número internacional normalizado para publicaciones seriadas o revistas
310-17 An internationally standardized number assigned to *serials* used for *reference*
DEF: 21-52, 22-17
REF: international standard book number 310-16 (RT)

labelled notation
F
D   markierte Notation
R   нотация с выделением символов для основных классов
S   notación marcada
310-18 A 'notation' in which there are distinctive 'main class symbols'
DEF: 13-34
REF: notation 310-22/23 (BT), facet order 39-16 (RT)

linear notation
     ordinal notation
F   notation linéaire
D   lineare Notation
R   линейная нотация
S   notación lineal
310-19 A 'notation' which does not try to reflect the hierarchical structure of the *classification system*
DEF: 39-21
REF: notation 310-22/23 (BT), expressive n. 310-10 (OT)

mixed notation
F   notation mixte
D   gemischte Notation; Mischnotation
R   смешанная нотация
S   notación mixta
310-20 A 'notation' using more than one type of *characters* (except *special characters*), e.g. an 'alphanumeric notation'
DEF: 13-10, 13-32
REF: notation 310-22/23 (BT), alphanumeric n. 310-03 (NT), pure n. 310-31 (OT)

mnemonic notation
F   notation mnémonique;
     notation mnémotechnique
D   mnemotechnische Notation;
     mnemonische Notation
R   мнемоническая нотация
S   notación mnemotécnica;
     notación mnemónica
310-21 A 'notation' where identical or analogous *classes* arising in different

contexts are allocated to the same *symbol*
DEF: 39-15/16, 13-34
REF: notation 310-22/23 (BT)

notation
     notational system (1);
     notational symbol (2)
F   notation
D   Notation; Notationssystem (1)
R   нотация
S   notación
     310-22 (1) An *artificial language* to express the relations between the *classes* of a *classification*
     DEF: 15-02, 39-15/16, 311-05
     REF: artificial language 15-02 (BT), expressive notation 310-10 (NT), group n. 310-12 (NT), labelled n. 310-18 (NT), linear n. 310-19 (NT), mixed n. 310-20 (NT), mnemonic n. 310-21 (NT), positional n. 310-29 (NT), polydecimal n. 310-28 (NT), pure n. 310-31 (NT), classification 311-05 (RT), generic coding 18-21 (RT)
     310-23 (2) A 'class number' obtained from a *classification schedule*
     DEF: 39-19
     REF: index term 36-10 (BT), analet 39-01 (NT), for further (NT) see 310-22, descriptor 36-05/06 (OT), keyword 36-12 (OT), subject heading 36-28 (OT), index term 36-10 (BT), uniterm 36-29 (OT), ideographic heading 36-09 (RT)

notational base
     radix of notation; base of notation
F   base de notation
D   Notationsbasis
R   основа нотации
S   base de notación
     310-24 The *character set* used in a 'notation' (1)
     DEF: 13-12

numeric notation
     digital notation
F   notation numérique
D   numerische Notation; Ziffernnotation
R   цифровая нотация
S   notación numérica
     310-25 A 'notation' using only *digits* and *special characters*
     DEF: 13-18, 13-32
     REF: pure notation 310-31 (BT), binary n. 310-04 (NT), decimal n. 310-08 (NT), alphabetic n. 310-02 (OT), alphanumeric n. 310-03 (OT)

octave device
F   principe de l'octave
D   Oktavenprinzip
R   принцип восьмеричной нотации
S   principio de octavas

310-26 The use of the *digit* 9 as an 'empty' digit (or octavizing digit) in order to accommodate an unlimited number of *classes* in an *array*
DEF: 13-18, 39-15/16, 39-03
REF: octave 39-56 (RT), octave notation 310-27 (RT)

octave notation
F   notation par octave
D   Oktavennotation
R   восьмеричная нотация
S   notación por octavas
     310-27 A notation permitting 'hospitability of notation' by the 'octave device'
     REF: decimal notation 310-08 (BT), binary n. 310-04 (OT), polydecimal n. 310-28 (RT), octave 34-56 (RT), octave device 310-26 (RT)

polydecimal notation
F   notation polydécimale
D   polydezimale Notation; Polydezimalnotation
R   полидесятичная нотация
S   notación polidecimal
     310-28 A 'notation' which allows more than ten subdivisions of a *class* by its *character set* and/or structure
     DEF: 39-15/16, 13-12
     REF: notation 310-22/23 (BT), decimal n. 310-08 (BT), octave n. 310-27 (RT)

positional notation
     positional representation
F   notation positionnelle
D   Positionsnotation
R   позиционная нотация
S   notación posicional
     310-29 A 'notation' in which the *concept* is represented by means of an ordered set of *characters* such that the value contributed by each character depends on its position as well as upon its value
     DEF: 12-05, 13-10
     REF: notation 310-22/23 (BT)

pronounceable notation
F   notation prononçable
D   sprechbare Notation
R   произносимая нотация
S   notación pronunciable
     310-30 A 'notation' which is designed to produce notational *symbols* whose pronunciation is internationally recognized
     DEF: 13-34
     REF: alphabetic notation 310-02 (BT), ramisyllabic n. 310-32 (NT), syllabic n. 310-34 (NT)

pure notation
uniform notation
F notation pure
D reine Notation
R однородная нотация
S notación pura
310-31 A 'notation' using only one type of *characters* (excluded *special characters*)
DEF: 13-10, 13-32
REF: notation 310-22/23 (BT), alphabetic n. 310-02 (NT), numeric n. 310-25 (NT), mixed 310-20 (OT)

ramisyllabic notation
F notation ramisyllabique
D zusammengesetzte Silbennotation
R (нотация, включающая последовательность произносимых слогов)
S notación ramisilábica
310-32 A 'notation' wherein the *symbols* are formed of a succession of pronounceable *syllables*
DEF: 13-34, 14-47/48
REF: pronounceable notation 310-30 (BT), syllabic n. 310-34 (RT)

serial number
F numéro de série
D Seriennummer
R номер выпуска (продолжающегося издания)
S número de serie
310-33 A number denoting the place of a single publication in a *serial*
DEF: 21-52
REF: current number 310-07 (RT)

syllabic notation
F notation syllabique
D Silbennotation
R слоговая нотация
S notación silábica
310-34 A 'notation' which is in the form of pronounceable *syllables*
DEF: 14-47/48
REF: pronounceable notation 310-30 (BT), ramisyllabic n. 310-32 (RT)

311 Types of classification

analytic classification
F classification analytique
D analytische Klassifikation
R аналитическая классификация
S clasificación analítica
311-01 A 'classification' dividing the *subject field* from the general to the specific by *hierarchical relations*
DEF: 12-31, 38-19

REF: classification 311-05 (BT), hierarchical c. 311-12 (NT), synthetic c. 311-21 (OT), analytico-synthetic c. 311-02 (RT), enumerative c. 311-09 (RT)

analytico-synthetic classification
F classification analytico-synthétique
D analytisch-synthetische Klassifikation
R аналитико-синтетическая классификация
S clasificación analítico-sintética
311-02 A 'classification' combining the principles of 'analytic' and 'synthetic classification', i.e. dividing the *subject field* into some *main classes* and splitting the main classes into *facets*
DEF: 12-31, 39-54, 39-33/34
REF: classification 311-05 (BT), analytic c. 311-01 (RT), synthetic c. 311-21 (RT)

artificial classification
F classification artificielle
D künstliche Klassifikation
R искусственная классификация
S clasificación artificial
311-03 A 'classification' where artificial *characteristics* like outward likeness, analogy, etc., are used for subdivision
DEF: 12-02
REF: classification 311-05 (BT), natural c. 311-16 (OT)

broad classification
F classification à grandes divisions
D Grobklassifikation
R классификация по широким комплексам
S clasificación amplia
311-04 A 'classification' which arranges the subjects only in broad general divisions with a minimum of subdivision
REF: classification 311-05 (BT), close c. 311-06 (OT)

classification
documentary classification
F classification
D Klassifikation; dokumentarische Klassifikation
R классификация
S clasificación
311-05 A *documentary language* which groups *concepts* into *classes*, uses mostly *hierarchical relations* for arrangement of classes, and reflects the structure of arrangement by *notation*
DEF: 15-08, 12-05, 39-15/16, 38-19, 310-22
REF: documentary language 15-08 (BT), for (NT) see section 311, thesaurus 37-22 (OT)

close classification
minute classification; exact classification
F   classification détaillée
D   detaillierte Klassifikation
R   детализированная классификация;
    дробная классификация
S   clasificación detallada
311-06 A 'classification' which arranges
the subjects in detailed subdivisions
REF: classification 311-05 (BT), broad
c. 311-04 (OT)

decimal classification
F   classification décimale
D   Dezimalklassifikation
R   десятичная классификация
S   clasificación decimal
311-07 A 'classification' using a *decimal
notation*, i.e. including up to ten *classes*
in an *array*
DEF: 310-08, 39-15/16, 39-03
REF: classification 311-05 (BT), dicho-
tomized c. 311-08 (OT)

dichotomized classification
bifurcate classification
F   classification par dichotomie
D   dichotomische Klassifikation
R   дихотомическая классификация
S   clasificación por dicotomía
311-08 An 'analytic classification' sub-
dividing each class only into two mutual
exclusive *classes*
DEF: 39-15/16
REF: analytic classification 311-01 (BT),
decimal c. 311-07 (OT)

enumerative classification
linear classification
F   classification linéaire
D   enumerative Klassifikation
R   линейная классификация
S   clasificación lineal
311-09 A 'classification' enumerating all
the subjects to be classified by it in
its *main tables*
DEF: 39-55
REF: classification 311-05 (BT), faceted
c. 311-11 (OT), synthetic c. 311-21 (OT),
analytic c. 311-01 (RT), hierarchical
c. 311-12 (RT)

expansive classification
F   classification extensive
D   expansive Klassifikation
R   растяжимая классификация
S   clasificación expansiva
311-10 A 'classification' having several
complete *classification schedules*, each
after the first being more minutely
subdivided than the previous are
DEF: 39-19
REF: classification 311-05 (BT)

faceted classification
multi-aspect classification
F   classification à facettes
D   facettierte Klassifikation;
    Facettenklassifikation
R   многоаспектная классификация;
    фасетная классификация
S   clasificación por facetas
311-11 A 'synthetic classification' arranging *concepts* in a series of *facets*
and synthesizing the *notation* of a
subject by combination of facets
DEF: 12-05, 39-34, 310-22
REF: synthetic classification 311-21 (BT),
polydimensional c. 311-17 (BT), poly-
hierarchical c. 311-18 (BT), hierarchical
c. 311-12 (OT), semantic code 18-24 (RT)

hierarchical classification
F   classification hiérarchique
D   hierarchische Klassifikation
R   иерархическая классификация
S   clasificación jerárquica
311-12 An 'analytic classification' using
only *hierarchical relations* for subdivision, thus leading to a mostly
'monohierarchical' and 'monodimensional classification', introducing *facets*
only by *auxiliary tables*
DEF: 38-19, 39-33/34, 39-04
REF: analytic classification 311-01 (BT),
faceted c. 311-11 (OT), enumerative
c. 311-09 (RT), monodimensional c.
311-14 (RT), monohierarchical c. 311-15
(RT), hierarchy 39-45 (RT)

library classification
bibliographical classification;
bibliothecal classification;
book classification
F   classification bibliologique
D   Bibliotheksklassifikation;
    bibliothekarische Klassifikation;
    bibliographische Klassifikation;
    bibliothekarisch-bibliographische
    Klassifikation
R   библиотечная классификация;
    библиотечно-библиографическая
    классификация; классификация книг
S   clasificación bibliográfica
311-13 A 'classification' designed for
the purposes of *libraries* to label each
volume with only one *notation*
DEF: 52-24, 21-62, 310-23
REF: classification 311-05 (BT), universal
c. 311-22 (RT), subject c. 311-20 (RT)

monodimensional classification
uni-dimensional classification
F   classification unidimensionnelle
D   monodimensionale Klassifikation;
    eindimensionale Klassifikation
R   одноаспектная классификация
S   clasificación unidimensional

311-14 A 'classification' permitting sub-division of *classes* only by one train of *characteristics* or *facet*
DEF: 39-15/16, 12-02, 39-33/34
REF: classification 311-05 (BT), poly-dimensional c. 311-17 (OT), hierarchical c. 311-12 (RT), dimensionality 39-30 (RT)

monohierarchical classification
F classification monohiérarchique
D monohierarchische Klassifikation
R моноиерархическая классификация
S clasificación unijerárquica
311-15 A 'classification' where each *class* has only one directly superordinated class
DEF: 39-15/16
REF: classification 311-05 (BT), poly-hierarchical c. 311-18 (OT), hierarchical c. 311-12 (RT), hierarchy 39-45 (RT)

natural classification
F classification naturelle
D natürliche Klassifikation
R естественная классификация
S clasificación natural
311-16 A 'classification' in which *intrinsic characteristics* are used for sub-division
DEF: 12-22
REF: classification 311-05 (BT), artificial c. 311-03 (OT)

polydimensional classification
  multi-aspect classification;
  multi-dimensional classification
F classification multidimensionnelle
D polydimensionale Klassifikation
R многоаспектная классификация;
  многомерная классификация
S clasificación multidimensional
311-17 A 'classification' permitting sub-division of *classes* by more than one train of *characteristics* or *facets*
DEF: 39-15/16, 12-02, 39-33/34
REF: classification 311-05 (BT), faceted c. 311-11 (NT), monodimensional c. 311-14 (OT), dimensionality 39-30 (RT)

polyhierarchical classification
F classification multihiérarchique
D polyhierarchische Klassifikation
R полииерархическая классификация
S clasificación multijerárquica
311-18 A 'classification' in which each *class* may have more than one directly superordinated class
DEF: 39-15/16
REF: classification 311-05 (BT), faceted c. 311-11 (NT), monohierarchical c. 311-15 (OT), hierarchy 39-45 (RT)

special classification
F classification spécifique
D Spezialklassifikation; Fachklassifikation
R отраслевая классификация;
  специальная классификация
S clasificación especifica
311-19 A 'classification' of a specific *subject field* or designed for specific purposes
DEF: 12-31
REF: subject classification 311-20 (BT), universal c. 311-22 (OT)

subject classification
F classification-matières
D Sachklassifikation
R предметная классификация
S clasificación por materías
311-20 A 'classification' designed to classify the subject *contents* of *documents*
DEF: 17-10, 21-18
REF: classification 311-05 (BT), special c. 311-19 (NT), universal c. 311-22 (NT), library c. 311-13 (RT)

synthetic classification
  composite classification
F classification synthétique
D synthetische Klassifikation
R синтетическая классификация;
  составная классификация
S clasificación sintética
311-21 A 'classification' which synthe-sizes the subject by combination of its *characteristics*
DEF: 12-02
REF: classification 311-05 (BT), faceted c. 311-11 (NT), analytic c. 311-01 (OT), analytico-synthetic c. 311-02 (RT)

universal classification
F classification universelle
D Universalklassifikation
R универсальная классификация
S clasificación universal
311-22 A 'classification' designed to cover the whole universe of *knowledge*
DEF: 12-24
REF: subject classification 311-20 (BT), special c. 311-19 (OT), library c. 311-13 (RT)

312 Storage of data

address
F adresse
D Adresse
R адрес
S dirección
312-01 A *symbol* that designates the 'storage location' of a device or of an item of *data*

DEF: 13-34, 17-12
REF: direct address 312-10 (NT), indirect
a. 312-17 (NT), symbolic a. 312-34
(NT), addressing system 312-02 (RT)

addressing system
F   système d'adressage
D   Adressierungssystem; Adressiersystem
R   система адресации
S   sistema de dirección
      312-02 The procedure used to label
      'storage locations' in a *computer*
      DEF: 42-10
      REF: address 312-01 (RT)

associative storage
      content-addressed storage
F   mémoire associative;
      mémorisation associative
D   assoziativer Speicher;
      assoziative Speicherung
R   ассоциативное запоминающее
      устройство
S   memoria asociativa
      312-03 'Storage' or a 'storage device'
      in which 'storage locations' are identified
      by their *contents*, not by *names* or
      positions
      DEF: 17-10, 14-29
      REF: storage 312-28 (BT), storage device
      312-32 (BT)

chaining
F   chaînage
D   Verkettung; Folgeadressenspeicherung;
      Adreßverkettung
R   (система накопления информации
      для последующего цепного поиска)
S   encadenamiento
      312-04 A *system* of 'storage' in which
      each unit belongs to a group of units
      and has a linking 'field' for tracing the
      chain
      DEF: 41-40
      REF: storage 312-28 (BT), chaining
      search 313-04 (RT)

collection
F   collection
D   Sammlung
R   коллекция; массив; собрание; фонд
S   colección
      312-05 (2) An organized body of stored
      items
      REF: data base 312-07 (NT), deposit
      collection 312-08 (NT), archives 51-01
      (NT), data bank 51-07 (NT), library
      21-25 (NT)

core storage
      core memory; magnetic core storage
F   mémoire à tores de ferrite
D   Kernspeicher; Magnetkernspeicher

R   запоминающее устройство
      на магнитных сердечниках
S   memoria de ferritas
      312-06 A 'magnetic storage' in which
      the magnetic medium consists of mag-
      netic cores
      REF: magnetic storage 312-22 (BT),
      magnetic card 312-19 (RT), magnetic
      disc 312-20 (RT), magnetic drum 312-21
      (RT), magnetic tape 312-23 (RT)

data base
F   base de données
D   Datenbasis
R   массив данных; массив информации
S   banco de datos
      312-07 A 'collection' of *data*, part or
      the whole of another collection of data
      and consisting of at least one *file*, that
      is sufficient for a given purpose or
      for a given *data processing system*
      DEF: 17-12, 33-11, 41-09
      REF: collection 312-05 (BT), data bank
      51-07 (RT)

deposit collection
F   collection de dépôt
D   Depotsammlung
R   архивное собрание;
      собрание обязательных экземпляров
S   colección de depósito
      312-08 A 'collection' of materials, from
      a single *publisher* or owner placed in a
      library for public *access* and preservation
      DEF: 52-20, 51-25, 313-01
      REF: collection 313-05 (BT), deposit
      library 51-11 (RT)

direct access storage
      random access storage
F   mémoire à accès direct;
      mémoire à accès sélectif
D   Direktzugriffsspeicher;
      Speicher mit wahlfreiem Zugriff
R   запоминающее устройство
      с произвольной выборкой
S   memoria de acceso directo
      312-09 A 'storage device' in which the
      access time is effectively independent of
      the 'storage location' of the *data*
      DEF: 313-01, 17-12
      REF: storage device 312-32 (BT)

direct address
      one-level address
F   adresse directe
D   direkte Adressierung; direkte Adresse
R   прямой адрес;
      непосредственный адрес
S   dirección directa
      312-10 An 'address' that designates the
      'storage location' of an item of *data*
      to be treated as an operand
      DEF: 17-12

REF: address 312-01 (BT), indirect a. 312-17 (OT)

dynamic storage
F   mémoire dynamique
D   dynamischer Speicher
R   запоминающее устройство динамического типа
S   memoria dinámica
312-11 A 'storage device' storing 'data' in a manner that permits the data to move or vary with time such that the specified data are not always available for recovery
DEF: 17-12
REF: storage device 312-32 (BT), fixed st. 312-16 (OT)

external storage
peripheral storage
F   mémoire externe; mémorisation externe
D   externer Speicher; peripherer Speicher; externe Speicherung; periphere Speicherung
R   внешнее запоминающее устройство
S   memoria externa
312-12 'Storage' in a 'storage device', or the device itself, which is not an integral part of a *computer*, but in a form prescribed for use by the computer
DEF: 42-10
REF: storage 312-28 (BT), storage device 312-32 (BT), internal st. 312-18 (OT)

field
F   zone
D   Datenfeld; Speicherfeld; Feld
R   зона (запоминающего устройства)
S   campo
312-13 A specified area of a 'storage device' used for a particular category of *data*
DEF: 17-12
REF: punched-card field 43-21 (NT), field length 312-14 (RT)

field length
F   longueur de zone
D   Feldlänge
R   величина зоны
S   longitud de campo
312-14 The physical extent of a 'field'
REF: field 312-13 (RT), fixed field 312-15 (NT)

fixed field
F   zone fixe
D   feste Positionierung
R   фиксированное поле; постоянное поле
S   campo fijo

312-15 Location on a *punched card* or other search medium, that is reserved for *information* of a particular type, form or length
DEF: 43-20, 17-28
REF: field 312-13 (BT)

fixed storage
read-only storage; non-erasable storage; permanent storage; read-only memory
F   mémoire permanente
D   Festspeicher
R   долговременное запоминающее устройство; запоминающее устройство с нестираемой записью; постоянное запоминающее устройство
S   memoria fija; memoria permanente
312-16 A 'storage device' whose contents are inherently non-erasable, non-erasable by a particular *user* or non-erasable when operating under particular conditions
DEF: 46-30
REF: storage device 312-32 (BT), dynamic st. 312-11 (OT)

indirect address
multilevel address
F   adresse indirecte
D   indirekte Adressierung; indirekte Adresse
R   непрямой адрес; косвенный адрес
S   dirección indirecta
312-17 An 'address' that specifies a 'storage location' that contains either a 'direct address' or another indirect address
REF: address 312-01 (BT), direct 312-10 (OT)

internal storage
F   mémoire interne
D   interner Speicher; maschineninterner Speicher; Zentralspeicher
R   внутреннее запоминающее устройство
S   memoria interna
312-18 An addressable 'storage device' directly controlled by the *central processing unit* of a *digital computer*
DEF: 42-07, 42-16
REF: storage device 312-32 (BT), register 42-39 (NT), external storage 312-12 (OT)

magnetic card
F   carte magnétique
D   Magnetkarte; Magnetstreifen
R   магнитная карта
S   tarjeta magnética
312-19 A card with a magnetic surface in which *data* can be stored by selective magnetization of portions of the flat surface

DEF: 17-12
REF: magnetic storage 312-22 (BT), core storage 312-06 (RT), magnetic disc 312-20 (RT), magnetic drum 312-21 (RT), magnetic tape 312-23 (RT)

magnetic disc
F   disque magnétique
D   Magnetplatte
R   магнитный диск
S   disco magnético
312-20 A flat circular plate with a magnetic surface on which *data* can be stored by selective magnetization of portions of the flat surface
DEF: 17-12
REF: magnetic storage 312-22 (BT), core storage 312-06 (RT), magnetic card 312-19 (RT), magnetic drum 312-21 (RT), magnetic tape 312-23 (RT)

magnetic drum
F   tambour magnétique
D   Magnettrommel
R   магнитный барабан
S   tambor magnético
312-21 A light circular cylinder with a magnetic surface on which *data* can be stored by selective magnetization of portions of the curved surface
DEF: 17-12
REF: magnetic storage 312-22 (BT), core storage 312-06 (RT), magnetic card 312-19 (RT), magnetic disc 312-20 (RT), magnetic tape 312-23 (RT)

magnetic storage
     magnetic memory
F   mémoire magnétique
D   Magnetspeicher
R   магнитное запоминающее устройство
S   memoria magnética
312-22 A 'storage device' that uses the magnetic properties of materials to store *data*
DEF: 17-12
REF: storage device 312-32 (BT), core storage 312-06 (NT), magnetic card 312-19 (NT), magnetic disc 312-20 (NT), magnetic drum 312-21 (NT), magnetic tape 312-23 (NT)

magnetic tape
F   bande magnétique; ruban magnétique
D   Magnetband
R   магнитная лента
S   cinta magnética
312-23 A tape with magnetic surface on which *data* can be stored by selective polarization of portions on the surface
DEF: 17-12
REF: magnetic storage 312-22 (BT), core storage 312-06 (RT), magnetic card 312-

19 (RT), magnetic disc 312-20 (RT), magnetic drum 312-21 (RT)

matrix storage
F   mémoire à sélection matricielle
D   Matrixspeicher; Matrizenspeicher
R   матричное запоминающее устройство
S   memoria de matriz
312-24 A 'storage device' whose elements are so arranged that *access* to a 'storage location' requires two or more co-ordinates
DEF: 314-01
REF: storage device 312-32 (BT)

microfilm storage
F   mémoire sur microfilm
D   Mikrofilmspeicher
R   запоминающее устройство на микрофильме
S   almacenamiento en micropelícula
312-25 A 'storage device' using *microfilm*
DEF: 110-33
REF: storage device 312-32 (BT)

off-line storage
F   mémoire autonome
D   off-line-Speicher; off-line-Speicherung; rechnerabhängiger Speicher
R   автономное запоминающее устройство
S   memoria indirecta; memoria autónoma
312-26 A 'storage device' not under *control* of the *central processing unit* of a *computer*
DEF: 44-06, 42-07, 42-10
REF: storage device 312-32 (BT), on-line storage 312-27 (OT)

on-line storage
F   mémoire en ligne
D   on-line-Speicher; on-line-Speicherung; rechnerunabhängiger Speicher
R   запоминающее устройство для работы в реальном масштабе времени
S   memoria directa
312-27 A 'storage device' which is readily accessible to the *central processing unit* of a *computer*
DEF: 42-07, 42-10
REF: storage device 312-32 (BT), off-line storage 312-26 (OT)

storage
     storing
F   mise en mémoire; mémorisation
D   Speicherung
R   накопление; хранение
S   almacenamiento; memorización
312-28 The process involving placement and retention of *data* or *documents* for subsequent use

DEF: 17-12, 21-18
REF: associative storage 312-03 (NT), chaining 312-04 (NT), external st. 312-12 (NT), storage allocation 312-29 (NT)

storage allocation
F   attribution de mémoire
D   Speicherzuordnung
R   распределение памяти
S   asignación de memoria
312-29 The assignment of blocks of items to specified blocks of a 'storage device'
REF: storage 312-28 (BT)

storage capacity
F   capacité de mémoire
D   Speicherkapazität
R   ёмкость запоминающего устройства
S   capacidad de memoria
312-30 The amount of items that can be contained in a 'storage device'

storage cell
F   cellule de mémoire; élément de mémoire
D   Speicherelement; Speicherzelle
R   ячейка запоминающего устройства
S   elemento de memoria
312-31 An elementary unit of a 'storage device'
REF: storage device 312-32 (BT)

storage device
   store (Brit.); memory; storage
F   mémoire
D   Speicher; Speichereinrichtung
R   запоминающее устройство; память; накопитель
S   memoria
312-32 A device into which *data* can be entered, in which they can be retained, and from which they can be retrieved
DEF: 17-12
REF: storage and retrieval d. 313-44 (BT), associative storage 312-03 (NT), direct access storage 312-09 (NT), dynamic storage 312-11 (NT), external storage 312-12 (NT), fixed storage 312-16 (NT), internal storage 312-18 (NT), magnetic storage 312-22 (NT), matrix storage 312-24 (NT), microfilm storage 312-25 (NT), off-line storage 312-26 (NT), on-line storage 312-27 (NT), storage cell 312-31 (NT), storage location 312-33 (NT), punched card 43-20 (NT), punched tape 43-22 (NT), verge perforated card 43-27 (NT)

storage location
F   emplacement de mémoire
D   Speicherplatz; Speicherzelle
R   ячейка запоминающего устройства; адрес ячейки запоминающего устройства

S   localización de memoria
312-33 A part of a 'storage device' that can be explicitly and uniquely specified by means of an 'address'
REF: storage device 312-33 (RT), punch position 43-18 (RT)

symbolic address
F   adresse symbolique
D   symbolische Adressierung; symbolische Adresse
R   символический адрес; условный адрес
S   dirección simbólica
312-34 An 'address' explained in a form convenient to a *programmer*
DEF: 52-18
REF: address 312-01 (BT)

313 Retrieval

access
F   accès
D   Zugriff
R   выборка; обращение; доступ
S   acceso
313-01 Methods by which the 'search question' may be brought into coincidence with the stored items
REF: immediate access 313-13 (NT), list processing 313-16 (NT), multilevel a. 313-22 (NT), multiple a. 313-23 (NT), parallel a. 313-26 (NT), random a. 313-28 (NT), remote a. 313-30 (NT), sequential a. 313-42 (NT)

binary search
   dichotomized search
F   recherche binaire
D   binäre Suche; dichotomische Suche
R   двоичный поиск; дихотомический поиск
S   búsqueda binaria
313-02 A 'search procedure' (2) in which the number of items of the stored set is divided into two equal parts at each step of the 'search'
REF: search procedure 313-35 (BT), chaining search 313-04 (RT), dialogous s. 313-06 (RT), fractional scanning 313-11 (RT)

browsability
F   recherche libre
D   freie Durchsuchmöglichkeit
R   возможность свободного просмотра
S   búsqueda casual
313-03 The ability of a *retrieval system* to lend itself to unsystematic or random searches
DEF: 41-34

chaining search
F   recherche en chaîne
D   Kettensuche; Suche mit Folgeadressen
R   цепной поиск
S   búsqueda en cadena
313-04 A 'search procedure (2)' in which each item contains an *identifier* for locating the next item to be considered
DEF: 13-22
REF: search procedure 313-35 (BT), binary search 313-02 (RT), dialogous s. 313-06 (RT), fractional scanning 313-11 (RT), chaining 312-04 (RT)

data retrieval
     fact retrieval
F   recherche automatique de données
D   Datenretrieval
R   фактографический информационный поиск; поиск данных
S   recuperación de datos
313-05 The action of or methods and procedures for recovering specific *data* about *facts* from a *collection* of stored data
DEF: 17-12, 12-17, 312-05
REF: information retrieval 313-14 (BT), document r. 313-07 (RT), reference r. 313-29 (RT)

dialogous search
F   recherche conversationnelle
D   Dialogsuche
R   информационный поиск с обратной связью; информационный поиск в режиме диалога
S   búsqueda conversacional
313-06 A 'search procedure (2)' in which the searcher interacts with the *retrieval system* by altering his 'search questions' according to search outcomes
DEF: 41-34
REF: search procedure 313-35 (BT), binary search 313-02 (RT), chaining s. 313-04 (RT), fractional scanning 313-11 (RT)

document retrieval
F   recherche automatique des documents
D   Dokumentretrieval
R   документальный информационный поиск; поиск документов
S   recuperación de documentos
313-07 The action of or methods and procedures for recovering specific *documents* from a *collection* of documents
DEF: 21-18, 312-05
REF: information retrieval 313-14 (BT), data r. 313-05 (RT), reference r. 313-29 (RT)

encoded question
F   question codée
D   verschlüsselte Sachfrage

R   кодированный запрос
S   pregunta codificada
313-08 A 'search question' set up and *encoded* in the form appropriate for operating, programming or conditioning a 'search device'
DEF: 18-18
REF: search question 313-36 (BT)

false drop
F   réponse non pertinente
D   Fehlselektion
R   поисковый шум (ошибочная выдача)
S   datos errados
313-09 In 'reference retrieval' a retrieved *reference* that does not pertain to the subject sought
DEF: 22-17
REF: noise 313-24 (BT), hit 313-12 (OT), false retrievals 313-10 (RT)

false retrieval
F   recherche non pertinente
D   ungenügende Suchergebnisse
R   поисковый шум (неточная выдача)
S   recuperación irrelevante
313-10 In 'reference retrieval' retrieved *references* which are not pertinent to but are vaguely related to the subject sought
DEF: 22-17
REF: noise 313-24 (BT), hit 313-12 (OT), false drop 313-09 (RT)

fractional scanning
F   balayage fractionnaire
D   schrittweises Durchsuchen
R   поэтапный просмотр (массива)
S   barrido fraccional
313-11 Scanning a *file* in a series of stages
DEF: 33-11
REF: search procedure 313-35 (BT), binary search 313-02 (RT), chaining search 313-04 (RT), dialogous search 313-06 (RT)

hit
F   réponse pertinente
D   Treffer; Hit
R   точная выдача
S   acierto
313-12 A relevant item found by the 'search'
REF: false drop 313-09 (OT), false retrieval 313-10 (OT), miss 313-21 (OT)

immediate access
F   accès immédiat
D   Sofortzugriff; unmittelbarer Zugriff
R   непосредственный доступ; быстрый доступ
S   acceso inmediato
313-13 'Access' to items in a *storage device* directly without serial delay and usually in a relative short period of time
DEF: 312-32

REF: access 313-01 (BT), list processing 313-16 (OT), sequential a. 313-42 (NT)

information retrieval
F   recherche automatique de l'information
D   Informationswiedergewinnung; Informationsrückgewinnung; Informationsretrieval
R   информационный поиск; поиск информации
S   recuperación de información
313-14 The action of or methods and procedures for recovering specific *information* from a collection of stored *data*
DEF: 17-27/29, 312-05, 17-12
REF: retrieval 313-31 (BT), data r. 313-05 (NT), document r. 313-07 (NT), reference r. 313-29 (NT)

inquiry
  request
F   demande de l'information
D   Anfrage
R   информационный запрос
S   consulta
313-15 A request for *information*
DEF: 17-27
REF: search question 313-36 (RT)

list processing
F   traitement par listes
D   listengeleitete Suche; Listenverarbeitung
R   поиск в массиве со списочной структурой
S   tratamiento de listas en cadena
313-16 A method of *file* organization whereby the searcher is first directed through a *dictionary* to the latest *record* associated with a *term*, this record also contains the chain address of the next record having the same *descriptor*, and so on
DEF: 33-11, 16-03, 21-44, 14-52, 36-05
REF: access 313-01 (BT), immediate a. 313-13 (OT)

locator
F   localisateur
D   Lokalisator
R   определитель адреса
S   localizador
313-17 A device for determining the position of an item in a *file* or *storage device*
DEF: 33-11, 312-32
REF: searching device 313-39 (BT)

literature search
F   recherche bibliographique
D   Literatursuche; Literaturrecherche
R   библиографический информационный поиск; поисклитературы
S   investigación bibliográfica
313-18 A systematic and exhaustive

'search' for published material on a specific subject
REF: search 313-33 (BT)

manual selection
F   sélection manuelle
D   manuelle Selektion; Handauswahl
R   ручная выборка; ручной отбор
S   selección manual
313-19 'Selection' of items out of a *storage device* manually
DEF: 312-32
REF: selection 313-41 (BT), needle sorting 43-15 (NT), mechanical s. 313-20 (OT)

mechanical selection
  automatic selection
F   sélection mécanique; sélection automatique
D   mechanische Selektion; automatische Selektion
R   машинный отбор; автоматический отбор
S   selección mecánica
313-20 'Selection' of items out of a *storage device* by mechanical or *automatic* means
DEF: 312-31, 42-05
REF: selection 313-41 (BT), manual s. 313-19 (OT)

miss
F   élément non retrouvé
D   verfehlte Sucheinheit
R   пропуск; невыдача
S   dato fallido
313-21 A relevant item of the *collection* not to be found by the 'search procedure'
DEF: 312-05
REF: hit 313-12 (OT)

multilevel access
F   accès à plusieurs niveaux
D   Zugriff auf mehreren Ebenen
R   выборка на различных уровнях иерархии; доступ на различных уровнях иерархии
S   acceso a niveles múltiples
312-22 'Access' to items in a *storage device* possible on different levels of *hierarchy*
DEF: 312-32, 39-45
REF: access 313-01 (BT)

multiple access
F   accès multiple
D   Mehrfachzugriff
R   многократная выборка; множественная выборка
S   acceso múltiple
313-23 'Access' to items in a *storage device* by two or more independent searchers or 'search devices'
DEF: 312-32
REF: access 313-01 (BT), parallel a. 313-25 (RT)

noise
F   bruit
D   Ballast
R   поисковый шум;
     нерелевантная информация
S   ruido
     313-24 (3) In 'reference retrieval' the
     amount of unrelevant *references* contained
     in the drop-out of a 'retrieval run'
     DEF: 22-17
     REF: false drop 313-09 (NT), false
     retrieval 313-10 (NT)

parallel access
F   accès parallèle
D   Parallelzugriff
R   параллельная выборка;
     параллельный доступ
S   acceso paralelo
     313-25 'Access' to items in a *storage
     device* by a single searcher or 'search
     device' capable of two or more simul-
     taneous matchings
     DEF: 312-32
     REF: access 313-01 (BT), multiple a.
     313-23 (RT)

postcoordination
F   postcoordination
D   Postkoordination
R   посткоординация
S   postcoordinación
     313-26 The co-ordination of *concepts* to
     complex subjects during 'retrieval', e.g.
     by performing conjunctive or disjunctive
     'searches'
     DEF: 12-05
     REF: precoordination 313-27

precoordination
F   précoordination
D   Präkoordination
R   предкоординация
S   precoordinación
     313-27 The combination of *concepts* to
     complex subjects during *indexing*, e.g. by
     using a *classification*
     DEF: 12-05, 31-21, 311-05
     REF: postcoordination 313-26 (OT)

random access
     arbitrary access
F   accès aléatoire
D   wahlfreier Zugriff; Direktzugriff
R   произвольная выборка;
     произвольный доступ
S   acceso aleatorio
     313-28 'Access' to items in a *storage
     device* under conditions in which the next
     location from which *data* are to be ob-
     tained is in no way dependent on the
     location of the previously obtained data
     DEF: 312-32, 17-12
     REF: access 313-01 (BT), sequential a.
     313-42 (OT)

reference retrieval
F   recherche automatique de références
D   Dokumentnachweisretrieval;
     Nachweisretrieval
R   библиографический информационный
     поиск; поиск документов
S   recuperación de referencias
     313-29 The action of or methods and
     procedures for recovering *references*
     from a *collection* of references in order to
     permit recovering of specific *information*
     DEF: 22-17, 312-05, 17-27/29
     REF: information retrieval 313-14 (BT),
     data r. 313-05 (RT), document r. 313-07
     (RT)

remote access
F   accès à distance
D   Fernzugriff
R   дистанционная выборка;
     дистанционный доступ
S   acceso remoto
     313-30 'Access' to items in a *storage
     device* by one or more stations that are
     distant from the store itself
     DEF: 312-31
     REF: access 313-01 (BT)

retrieval
F   recherche automatique
D   Retrieval
R   поиск (с выдачей)
S   recuperación
     313-31 The action of recovering some-
     thing
     REF: information retrieval 313-14 (NT),
     specific r. 313-43 (NT), selection 313-41
     (NT), retrieval run 313-32 (RT), search
     313-33 (RT), search procedure 313-35
     (RT)

retrieval run
     search run
F   phase de recherche
D   Suchgang; Suchdurchgang; Suchlauf
R   поисковый цикл; прогон
     (поисковой программы)
S   corrida de recuperación
     313-32 The matching of an 'encoded
     question' with the *collection*
     DEF: 312-05
     REF: retrieval 313-31 (RT), search proce-
     dure 313-35 (RT)

search
F   recherche
D   Suche
R   поиск
S   búsqueda
     313-33 To examine a set of items for one
     or more having a desired property
     REF: literature search 313-18 (NT),
     retrieval 313-31 (RT), search procedure
     313-35 (RT)

search procedure
search process
F   procédé de recherche (1);
      opération de recherche (2)
D   Suchverfahren (1); Suchvorgang (2)
R   методика поиска (1);
      процесс поиска (2)
S   procedimiento de búsqueda
      313-34 (1) The plan of 'search' used in a
      particular *retrieval system* for certain
      types or categories of searchers
      DEF: 41-34
      REF: search strategy 313-37 (RT)
      313-35 (2) The whole process of 'search'
      including one or more 'retrieval runs'
      REF: binary search 313-02 (NT), chaining
      search 313-04 (NT), dialogous search
      313-06 (NT), fractional scanning 313-11
      (NT), retrieval 313-31 (RT), retrieval run
      313-32 (RT), search 313-33 (RT)

search question
F   question
D   Suchfrage
R   информационный запрос
S   consulta para la búsqueda
      313-36 The question the searcher has
      before it becomes to be *encoded*
      DEF: 18-18
      REF: encoded question 313-08 (BT), inqui-
      ry 313-05 (RT)

search strategy
F   stratégie de recherche
D   Suchstrategie
      стратегия поиска
S   estrategía de búsqueda
      313-37 An analysis and formulation of
      the optimum methods by which a partic-
      ular 'search question' may be answered
      by a *retrieval system*
      DEF: 41-34
      REF: search procedure 313-34 (RT)

search time
F   temps de recherche
D   Suchzeit
R   время поиска
S   tiempo de búsqueda
      313-38 The amount of time needed to
      perform the 'search procedure *(2)*'

searching device
F   dispositif de recherche
D   Sucheinrichtung
R   поисковое устройство
S   dispositivo de búsqueda
      313-39 The physical or operational device
      used to perform a 'search procedure (2)'
      REF: storage and retrieval device 313-44
      (BT), locator 133-17 (NT), selecting d.
      313-40 (NT)

selecting device
F   dispositif de sélection
D   Selektionseinrichtung
R   селектор
S   selector
      313-40 The physical or operational device
      used to select items out of the *storage
      device*
      DEF: 312-32
      REF: searching device 313-39 (BT)

selection
F   sélection
D   Selektion
R   выбор; отбор
S   selección
      313-41 A physical process subsequent to
      the successful matching of a 'search
      question' against the *collection*, in which
      the item successfully matched is indicated
      DEF: 312-05
      REF: retrieval 313-31 (BT), manual selec-
      tion 313-19 (NT), mechanical s. 313-20
      (NT), specific retrieval 313-43 (RT)

sequential access
F   accès séquentiel
D   sequentieller Zugriff
R   последовательная выборка;
      последовательный доступ
S   acceso secuencial
      313-42 'Access to items of a *storage device*
      by considering every item in turn
      DEF: 312-32
      REF: access 313-01 (BT), immediate a.
      313-13 (OT), random a. 313-28 (OT)

specific retrieval
F   recherche automatique spécifique
D   gezielte Auswahl
R   поиск определённого
      информационного источника
S   recuperación específica
      313-43 'Retrieval' of a specific item
      known to exist and describable, at least
      to some extent, by the searcher
      REF: retrieval 313-31 (BT), selection
      313-41 (RT)

storage and retrieval device
F   dispositif de mise en mémoire et de
      recherche automatique
D   Speicher- und Retrievaleinrichtung
R   устройство для накопления
      и поиска информации
S   dispositivo para el almacenamiento y la
      recuperación
      313-44 The *storage device* and the con-
      nected 'searching' and 'selection devices'
      DEF: 312-32
      REF: storage device 312-32 (NT), search-
      ing d. 313-19 (NT)

314 Abstracting and information services

abstract
F   analyse; résumé; abstract
D   Kurzreferat
R   реферат
S   resumen; extracto
314-01 The usually non-critical indication of the subject *contents* of a *document*, aiming to permit the *user* a decision about the *relevance* of the document
DEF: 17-10, 21-18, 46-30, 45-32
REF: author's abstract 314-06 (NT), auto-abstract 314-07 (NT), descriptive a. 314-13 (NT), encoded a. 314-14 (NT), slanted a. 314-26 (NT), structured a. 314-28 (NT), telegraphic a. 314-30 (NT), annotation 314-05 (OT), critical review 314-11 (OT), extract 314-17 (OT), excerpt 314-16 (RT), summary 314-29 (RT)

abstract bulletin
F   bulletin analytique;
    bulletin des résumés analytiques;
    bulletin d'abstract
D   Referatedienst
R   реферативный бюллетень
S   boletín de resúmenes;
    boletín de extractos
314-02 A printed or mimeographed *bulletin* containing 'abstracts' of currently published *periodical* articles, *pamphlets* etc., and distributed monthly, weekly or daily to the *users* of an *information* or *documentation system*
DEF: 21-12, 21-38, 21-33, 46-30, 41-19/20, 41-13
REF: abstracting service 314-04 (BT), abstract journal 314-03 (RT)

abstract journal
    abstracting journal
F   bulletin d'analyses; revue d'analyses
D   Referatezeitschrift
R   реферативный журнал
S   revista de resúmenes;
    revista de extractos
314-03 A *journal* containing 'abstracts' of currently published *documents*
DEF: 21-24, 21-18
REF: abstracting service 314-04 (BT), abstract bulletin 314-02 (RT)

abstracting service
F   service d'analyses
D   Referatedienst
R   реферативная служба;
    реферативное издание
S   servicio de resúmenes;
    servicio de extractos

314-04 The preparation and dissemination of 'abstracts' of currently published *documents*; e.g. in the form of 'abstract bulletins', 'abstract journals', etc.
DEF: 21-18
REF: abstract bulletin 314-02 (NT), abstract journal 314-03 (NT), comprehensive abstracting service 314-09 (NT), selective a. s. 314-24 (NT), information s. 314-20 (RT), bibliography 315-04 (RT)

annotation
    note; bibliographic note; contents note
F   annotation; note
D   Annotation
R   аннотация
S   anotación bibliográfica
314-05 The short, descriptive indication of the subject *contents* of a *document*, giving *information* that is not contained in the *title* of the document
DEF: 17-10, 21-18, 17-27/29, 22-23
REF: abstract 314-01 (OT), telegraphic abstract 314-30 (RT)

author's abstract
    synopsis
F   résumé d'auteur
D   Autorenreferat
R   авторский реферат; автореферат
S   resumen de autor
314-06 An 'abstract' which has been produced by the *author* of the *document* himself
DEF: 52-03, 21-18
REF: abstract 314-01 (BT), auto-a. 314-07 (OT), summary 314-29 (RT)

auto-abstract
    auto-extract; automatic abstract;
    machine abstract
F   analyse automatique
D   maschinell erstelltes Kurzreferat;
    maschinell erstellter Auszug
R   машинный реферат
S   resumen automatizado;
    extracto automatizado
314-07 An 'abstract' which has been produced by *automatic* means
DEF: 42-05
REF: abstract 314-01 (BT), author's abstract 314-06 (OT), extract 314-17 (RT)

alerting service
F   service de signalement rapide
D   Schnellinformation
R   служба сигнального (библиографического) информирования; служба текущего оповещения
S   servicio de alerta
314-08 A service designed to make

potential readers aware of new *documents* relevant to their work
DEF: 21-18
REF: information service 314-20 (BT), contents list bulletin 314-10 (RT), current awareness s. 314-12 (RT), express information 314-15 (RT)

comprehensive abstracting service
F   service d'analyse complet
D   vollständiger Referatedienst
R   реферативная служба
     с исчерпывающим охватом;
     реферативное издание
     с исчерпывающим охватом
S   servicio exhaustivo de resúmenes
     o extractos
314-09 An 'abstracting service' aiming to abstract every *document* in its specific *subject field*
DEF: 21-18, 12-31
REF: abstracting service 314-04 (BT) selective a. s. 314-24 (OT)

contents list bulletin
     current contents bulletin
F   bulletin de sommaires;
     revue des sommaires
D   laufende Zeitschrifteninhaltsübersicht
R   бюллетень оглавлений (текущих номеров периодических изданий)
S   boletín de tablas de materias
314-10 A periodical *bulletin* consisting of *copies* of the *contents lists* of selected *periodicals* assembled into some form of *cover*
DEF: 21-12, 110-05, 22-06, 21-38, 22-08
REF: information service 314-20 (BT), alerting service 314-08 (RT)

critical review
F   compte rendu
D   Rezension; Besprechung
R   аналитический обзор;
     критический обзор
S   revisión crítica
314-11 Literature surveying, evaluation and synthesizing newly published *documents*
DEF: 21-18
REF: abstract 314-01 (OT), progress report 314-22 (RT), slanted abstract 314-26 (RT)

current awareness service
F   service de signalement courant
D   Schnellinformationen
R   служба текущего оповещения
     (по тематическому принципу)
S   servicio de actualización permanente
314-12 A service which provides *users* with the latest *information*, or published literature, on their particular subject interest

DEF: 46-30, 17-27/30
REF: information service 314-20 (BT), alerting s. 314-12 (RT), express information 314-15 (RT)

descriptive abstract
F   analyse descriptive
D   deskriptives Kurzreferat;
     deskriptives Referat
R   описательный реферат
S   resumen descriptivo;
     extracto descriptivo
314-13 An 'abstract' describing the subject *contents* of a *document*, but not evaluating it
DEF: 17-10, 21-18
REF: abstract 314-01 (BT), indicative a. 314-18 (NT), indicative-informative a. 314-19, informative a. 314-21 (NT), slanted a. 314-26 (OT)

encoded abstract
F   analyse codée
D   kodiertes Kurzreferat
R   кодированный реферат
S   resumen codificado;
     extracto codificado
314-14 An 'abstract' not written in *natural language* but *encoded* to some kind of formal representation enabling *electronic data processing* machines to scan it easily
DEF: 15-18, 18-18, 17-21
REF: abstract 314-01 (BT)

express information
F   informations express
D   Schnellinformationen;
     Expreß-Informationen
R   экспресс-информация
S   información expedita
314-15 An 'information service' disseminating 'excerpts' or translations from significant *documents*
DEF: 21-18
REF: information service 314-20 (BT), alerting service 314-12 (RT), current awareness service 314-12 (RT)

excerpt
F   citation
D   Exzerpt; Zitat
R   выдержка; извлечение
S   excerpta; excerta
314-16 A passage reproduced verbatim from a *document*
DEF: 21-18
REF: abstract 314-01 (OT), extract 314-17 (RT)

extract
F   extrait
D   Auszug
R   выдержка; подборка отрывков

s   extracto
314-17 A set of passages out of a *document* indicating the subject *contents* of the document
DEF: 21-18, 17-10
REF: auto-abstract 314-07 (NT), abstract 314-01 (RT), excerpt 314-16 (RT)

Indicative abstract
F   analyse indicative
D   indikatives Referat
R   аннотация; указательный реферат
S   resumen indicativo
314-18 A brief 'abstract' to indicate to the reader the scope and *content* of a *document*
DEF: 17-10, 21-18
REF: descriptive abstract 314-13 (BT), informative a. 314-21 (OT), indicative-informative a. 314-19 (RT), telegraphical a. 314-30 (RT)

indicative-informative abstract
F   analyse indicative-informative
D   indikativ-informatives Referat
R   указательно-информативный реферат
S   resumen indicativo-informativo
314-19 An 'abstract' summarizing some significant elements of the subject *contents* of a *document* in the way of an 'informative abstract' and indicating the other elements only shortly
DEF: 17-10, 21-18
REF: descriptive abstract 314-13 (BT), indicative a. 314-18 (RT), informative a. 314-21 (RT)

information service
F   service d'information
D   Informationsdienst
R   информационная служба; информационное издание; информационное обслуживание
S   servicio de información
314-20 A service aiming at the actual *information* of its *users*
DEF: 17-31, 46-30
REF: alerting service 314-08 (NT), contents list bulletin 314-10 (NT), current awareness s. 314-12 (NT), express information 314-15 (NT), selective dissemination of information 314-25 (NT), abstracting s. 314-04 (RT), bibliography 315-04 (RT)

informative abstract
information abstract
F   analyse informative
D   informatives Referat
R   информативный реферат
S   resumen informativo
314-21 An 'abstract' summarizing the principal arguments and giving the

significant *data* contained in the *document*
DEF: 17-12, 21-18
REF: descriptive abstract 314-13 (BT), indicative a. 314-18 (OT), indicative-informative a. 314-19 (RT)

progress report
F   état des travaux en cours
D   Fortschrittsbericht
R   тематический обзор литературы (типа "Итоги...", "Успехи в...")
S   estado de trabajos en curso
314-22 A *report* of the state of the art and the future developments of a specific *subject field* or problems by evaluating the literature of a certain period
DEF: 21-46, 12-31
REF: report 21-46 (BT), state of the art r. 314-27 (RT)

reader's advisory service
F   service d'orientation des lecteurs
D   Literaturhinweisdienst; Leserberatung
R   консультативная служба для читателей; справочно--библиографическое обслуживание
S   servicio de orientación a los lectores
314-23 A service aiming to give the reader of the literature of a particular *subject field* advice for orientation
DEF: 12-31

selective abstracting service
F   service sélectif d'analyses
D   auswählender Referatedienst
R   служба выборочного реферирования; реферативное издание с выборочным охватом
S   servicio selectivo de resúmenes o extractos
314-24 An 'abstracting service' selecting only those *documents* which it considers are likely to be of use to a specific *class* of *users*
DEF: 21-18, 39-15/16, 46-30
REF: abstracting service 314-04 (BT), comprehensive a. s. 314-09 (OT)

selective dissemination of information
SDI; SDI service
F   diffusion sélective de l'information; service de diffusion sélective de l'information
D   gezielte Informationsverbreitung; SDI; SDI-Dienst
R   избирательное распространение информации; направленное распределение информации
S   diseminación selectiva de información; difusión selectiva de información
314-25 A service which continually disseminates *documents, references,* 'ab-

stracts' or *data* selected according to the *interest profiles* of the *users*
DEF: 21-18, 22-17, 17-12, 46-19, 46-30
REF: information service 314-20 (BT), active dissemination 19-01 (RT)

slanted abstract
F   analyse orientée
D   wertendes Referat; auswählendes Referat
R   специализированный реферат
S   resumen orientado
314-26 An 'abstract' giving emphasis to a particular aspect of a *document* to cater for the specialized interest of a particular group of readers
DEF: 21-18
REF: abstract 314-01 (BT), descriptive a. 314-13 (OT), critical review 314-11 (RT)

state-of-the-art report
analytical survey
F   synthèse; état de la question
D   Literaturbericht; Übersichtsbericht; Überblicksbericht
R   аналитический тематический обзор литературы
S   estado de la cuestión; síntesis de la cuestión
314-27 A *report* of the state of the art of a specific *subject field* or problem by evaluating the literature of a certain period
DEF: 21-46, 12-31
REF: report 21-46 (BT), progress r. 314-22 (RT)

structural abstract
positioned abstract
F   analyse structurée
D   Positionsreferat; Strukturreferat
R   анкетный реферат
S   resumen estructural
314-28 An 'abstract' which structures the description of the subject *contents* of the *document* by a prefixed scheme of positions or *categories*
DEF: 17-10, 21-18, 39-11
REF: abstract 314-01 (BT)

summary
F   résumé
D   Zusammenfassung
R   выводы; резюме
S   conclusiones
314-29 The summarizing of the most important arguments and conclusions of a *document*, which has not necessarily to be intelligible without the original document, usually produced by the author and placed at the end of the document
DEF: 21-18

REF: abstract 314-29 (RT), author's abstract 314-06 (RT)

telegraphic abstract
telegraphic style abstract; skeleton abstract
F   analyse 'ou style télégraphique'
D   Schlagwortreferat; Telegrammstilreferat
R   реферат телеграфного стиля
S   resumen telegráfico
314-30 An 'abstract' consisting of a set of *keywords* indicating the subject *content* of the *document*
DEF: 36-12, 17-10, 21-18
REF: abstract 314-01 (BT), indicative a. 314-18 (RT)

315 Bibliographical services

alphabetical bibliography
F   bibliographie alphabétique
D   alphabetische Bibliographie
R   алфавитная библиография
S   bibliografía alfabética
315-01 A 'bibliography' which is arranged alphabetically by the *names* of the *authors*
DEF: 14-29, 52-03
REF: bibliography 315-04 (BT), systematic b. 315-21 (OT)

annotated bibliography
F   bibliographie annotée
D   annotierende Bibliographie
R   аннотированная библиография
S   bibliografía anotada
315-02 A 'bibliography' including not only formal descriptions but additionally *annotations*
DEF: 314-05
REF: bibliography 314-05 (BT)

author bibliography
F   biobliographie
D   Autorenbibliographie; Biobibliographie; Personalbibliographie
R   персональная библиография; биобиблиография
S   bibliografía de autor
315-03 A 'bibliography' of the works of a single *author*
DEF: 52-03
REF: bibliography 315-04 (BT), subject b. 315-20 (OT)

bibliography
F   bibliographie
D   Bibliographie
R   библиография
S   bibliografía

315-04 A printed list of *documents* containing formal descriptions of the documents
DEF: 21-18
REF: abstracting service 314-04 (RT), information service 314-20 (RT), for (NT) see section 315

collectanea
F   collectanea
D   Kollektaneen
R   (систематическая библиография, включающая тексты важнейших документов или выдержки из них)
S   colectánea
315-05 A 'systematic bibliography' which includes significant *documents*, parts of documents or *excerpts* within the bibliography itself, duplicating them where required by the structure of analysis
DEF: 21-18, 314-16
REF: systematic bibliography 315-21 (BT)

comprehensive bibliography
F   bibliographie exhaustive
D   vollständige Bibliographie
R   исчерпывающая библиография; полная библиография
S   bibliografía exhaustiva
315-06 A 'bibliography' trying to include all relevant *documents* of its subject
DEF: 21-18
REF: bibliography 315-05 (BT), selective b. 315-18 (OT)

current bibliography
F   bibliographie courante
D   laufende Bibliographie
R   текущая библиография
S   bibliografía actual
315-07 A 'bibliography' including descriptions of current *documents* being published or distributed concurrently
DEF: 21-18
REF: bibliography 315-04 (BT), periodical b. 315-14 (NT)

general bibliography
F   bibliographie encyclopédique
D   Allgemeinbibliographie
R   общая библиография
S   bibliografía general
315-08 A 'bibliography' the scope of which is not limited to particular *subject fields*
DEF: 12-31
REF: bibliography 315-04 (BT), local b. 315-11 (NT), municipal b. 315.12 (NT), national b. 315-13 (NT), regional b. 315-16 (NT), special b. 315-19 (OT), subject b. 315-20 (OT), technical b. 315-22 (OT), universal b. 315-23 (RT)

hidden bibliography
F   bibliographie cachée

D   versteckte Bibliographie
R   неявная библиография
S   bibliografía oculta
315-09 A list of *documents* which is not designated to be a 'bibliography', but may act as one
DEF: 21-18
REF: bibliography 315-04 (RT)

international bibliography
F   bibliographie internationale
D   internationale Bibliographie
R   международная библиография
S   bibliografía internacional
315-10 A 'bibliography' containing *documents* without regard where they are published
DEF: 21-18
REF: bibliography 315-04 (BT), local b. 315-11 (OT), municipal b. 315-12 (OT), national b. 315-13 (OT), regional b 315-16 (OT), universal b. 315-23 (RT)

local bibliography
F   bibliographie locale
D   lokale Bibliographie; Ortsbibliographie
R   местная библиография; библиография местных публикаций
S   bibliografía local
315-11 A 'bibliography' listing *documents* published in a certain geographic area
DEF: 21-18
REF: general bibliography 315-08 (BT), national b. 315-13 (OT), municipal b. 315-12 (RT), regional b. 315-16 (RT)

municipal bibliography
F   bibliographie municipale
D   Munizipalbibliographie Stadtbibliographie
R   библиография публикаций выпущенных в определённом городе
S   bibliografía municipal
315-12 A 'bibliography' listing *documents* published in a particular town
DEF: 21-18
REF: general bibliography 315-08 (BT), national b. 315-13 (OT), regional b. 315-16 (OT), local b. 315-11 (RT)

national bibliography
F   bibliographie nationale
D   Nationalbibliographie
R   государственная библиография; национальная библиография
S   bibliografía nacional
315-13 A 'bibliography' of 'books' produced in one country whatever their *language* and/or in the language of one country
DEF: 21-09, 15-13

REF: general bibliography 315-08 (BT), local b. 315-11 (OT), municipal b. 315-12 (OT), regional b. 315-16 (OT)

periodical bibliography
F   bibliographie périodique
D   periodische Bibliographie
R   периодическое библиографическое издание
S   bibliografía periódica
     315-14 A 'current bibliography' being published periodically
     REF: current bibliography 315-07 (BT)

prospective bibliography
F   liste de documents à paraître
D   prospektive Bibliographie
R   проспективная библиография
S   bibliografía prospectiva
     315-15 A 'bibliography' of *documents* to be published
     DEF: 21-18
     REF: bibliography 315-04 (BT), retrospective b. 315-17 (OT)

regional bibliography
F   bibliographie régionale
D   Regionalbibliographie
R   краевая библиография; региональная библиография
S   bibliografía regional
     315-16 A 'bibliography' of the *documents* being published in a particular geographical region
     DEF: 21-18
     REF: general bibliography 315-08 (BT), municipal, b. 315-12 (OT), national b. 315-13 (OT), local b. 315-11 (RT)

retrospective bibliography
F   bibliographie rétrospective
D   retrospektive Bibliographie; Sammelbibliographie
R   ретроспективная библиография
S   bibliografía retrospectiva
     315-17 A bibliography containing published *documents* of a *subject field* or particular problem back into history as much as possible or desired
     DEF: 21-18, 12-31
     REF: bibliography 315-04 (BT), prospective b. 315-15 (OT)

selective bibliography
     selected bibliography
F   bibliographie sélective
D   selektive Bibliographie; Auswahlbibliographie
R   выборочная библиография
S   bibliografía selectiva
     315-18 A 'bibliography' of *documents* selected for some specific purpose
     DEF: 21-18

REF: bibliography 315-04 (BT), comprehensive b. 315-06 (OT)

special bibliography
F   bibliographie spécialisée
D   Spezialbibliographie
R   специальная библиография; отраслевая библиография
S   bibliografía especial
     315-19 A 'bibliography' of *documents* of a specific *subject field* or problem
     DEF: 21-18, 12-31
     REF: bibliography 315-04 (BT), general b. 315-08 (OT), subject b. 315-20 (RT), technical b. 315-22 (RT)

subject bibliography
     thematic bibliography; topical bibliography
F   bibliographie par sujets
D   Sachbibliographie
R   предметная библиография; тематическая библиография
S   bibliografía temática
     315-20 A 'bibliography' of *documents* about a given subject, whether the subject be a person, place or thing
     DEF: 21-18
     REF: bibliography 315-04 (BT), general b. 315-08 (OT), special b. 315-19 (RT), technical b. 315-22 (RT)

systematic bibliography
F   bibliographie systématique
D   systematische Bibliographie
R   систематическая библиография
S   bibliografía sistemática
     315-21 A 'bibliography' which is arranged according to a *classification scheme*
     DEF: 39-20
     REF: bibliography 315-04 (BT), alphabetical b. 315-01 (OT)

technical bibliography
F   bibliographie spécialisée
D   Fachbibliographie
R   специальная библиография; отраслевая библиография
S   bibliografía técnica
     315-22 A 'bibliography' of *documents* on a particular scientific or technological discipline
     DEF: 21-18
     REF: bibliography 315-04 (BT), general b. 315-08 (OT), special b. 315-19 (RT), subject b. 315-20 (RT)

universal bibliography
F   bibliographie universelle
D   Universalbibliographie
R   универсальная библиография; всемирная библиография
S   bibliografía universal

315-23 A 'bibliography' of *documents* with no limitation of subject or publishing place of the documents
DEF: 21-18

REF: bibliography 315-04 (BT), general b. 315-08 (RT), international b. 315-10 (RT)

4 Systems of information and documentation

41 Types of systems

adaptive system
adaptive control system;
self-adjusting system; self-aligning system
F système auto-adaptatif
D adaptives System;
anpassungsfähiges System
R самонастраивающая система;
самоприспосабливающаяся система;
адаптивная система
S sistema auto-adaptativo
41-01 An 'open system' which adapts itself to changes in its 'environment' by *feedback*
DEF: 17-23
REF: open system 41-30 (BT), cybernetic s. 41-08 (NT), self-organizing s. 41-35 (RT), adaptability 45-03 (RT)

centralized system
F système centralisé
D zentralisiertes System
R централизованная система
S sistema centralizado
41-02 A 'system' having one or few leading parts, the changes in which change the 'state' of the whole system
REF: system 41-40 (BT), decentralized s. 41-11 (OT)

closed system
F système fermé
D geschlossenes System
R замкнутая система
S sistema cerrado
41-03 (1) 'System' in which all controlling *elements* are integrated into this system
DEF: 12-12
REF: system 41-40 (BT), open s. 41-30/31 (OT)
41-04 (2) A 'system' without *input* or *output*.
DEF: 17-34/35, 17-49-50
REF: system 41-40 (BT), open s. 41-30/31 (OT)

communication system
F système de communication
D Kommunikationssystem
R система коммуникации
S sistema de comunicación
41-05 A 'system' for controlling *communication* processes according to given objectives
DEF: 17-08
REF: system 41-40 (BT), information s. 41-19/20 (NT), technical communication system 41-41 (NT), information transmission s. 41-21 (RT)

complex system
F système complexe
D komplexes System
R комплексная система;
сложная система
S sistema complejo
41-06 A 'system' that is composed of an interconnected set of 'subsystems'
REF: system 41-40 (BT), cybernetic s. 41-08 (NT), simple s. 41-38 (OT), complexity 45-06 (RT)

control system
F système de commande
D Kontrollsystem; Steuersystem
R система управления;
система регулирования
S sistema de control; sistema de mando
41-07 A 'system' used to control some processes or operations
REF: system 41-40 (BT), monitoring s. 41-25 (RT)

cybernetic system
F système cybernétique
D kybernetisches System
R кибернетическая система
S sistema cibernético
41-08 A 'complex, dynamic' and 'adaptive system'
REF: adaptive system 41-01 (BT), complex s. 41-06 (BT), dynamic s. 41-14 (BT)

data processing system
information processing system
F   système de traitement des données;
système de traitement des informations
D   Datenverarbeitungssystem;
Informationsverarbeitungssystem
R   система обработки данных;
система обработки информации
S   sistema de tratamiento de datos
41-09 A 'system' for data processing
DEF: 17-15
REF: system 41-40 (BT), electronic data
processing system 41-15 (NT), documentation s. 41-13 (NT), information s. 41-
19-20 (NT), information transmission s.
41-21 (NT), manual s. 41-24 (NT)

data retrieval system
fact retrieval system
F   système de recherche automatique des
données
D   Datenretrievalsystem;
Datenauffindungssystem
R   система поиска данных;
фактографическая
информационно-поисковая система
sistema de recuperación de datos
41-10 A 'system' whose purpose is *data
storage* and *retrieval*
DEF: 17-12, 312-28, 313-05
REF: information retrieval system 41-18
(BT), document r. s. 41-12 (RT), reference r. s. 41-33 (RT)

decentralized system
F   système décentralisé
D   dezentralisiertes System
R   децентрализованная система
S   sistema decentralizado
41-11 A 'system' having several leading
parts the changes in which do not necessarily change the 'state' of the whole
system
REF: system 41-40 (BT), centralized s.
41-02 (OT)

document retrieval system
F   système de recherche automatique des
documents
D   Dokumentretrievalsystem;
Dokumentauffindungssystem
R   система поиска документов;
документальная
информационно-поисковая система
S   sistema de recuperación de documentos
41-12 A 'system 'whose purpose is *docu-
ment storage* and *retrieval*
DEF: 21-18, 312-18, 313-07
REF: information retrieval system 41-18
(BT), data r. s. 41-10 (RT), reference r. s.
41-33 (RT)

documentation system
F   système documentaire

D   Dokumentationssystem
R   документационная система
S   sistema de documentación
41-13 A 'system' whose purpose is *documentation*
DEF: 31-19
REF: data processing system 41-09 (BT),
information retrieval s. 41-18 (NT),
indexing s. 41-17 (NT), storage and
retrieval s. 41-37 (NT), information s.
41-19/20 (RT), information transmission
s. 41-21 (RT)

dynamic system
F   système dynamique
D   dynamisches System
R   динамическая система
S   sistema dinámico
41-14 An 'open system' which changes its
'states'
REF: open system 41-30 (BT), cybernetic
s. 41-08 (NT)

electronic data processing system
automatic data processing system
F   système de traitement électronique des
données; système de traitement automatique des données
D   elektronisches Datenverarbeitungssystem;
automatisches Datenverarbeitungssystem
R   автоматическая система обработки
данных; электронная система
обработки данных
S   sistema para el tratamiento electrónico de
datos
41-15 A 'system' for *electronic data
processing*
DEF: 17-21
REF: data processing system 41-09 (BT),
multiple access s. 41-26 (NT), on-line
computer s. 41-29 (NT), real-time computer s. 41-32 (NT), manual s. 41-24 (OT)

environment (of the system)
negasystem
F   environnement du système
D   Systemumwelt; Umwelt des Systems
R   окружающая среда (системы)
S   medio circundante del sistema
41-16 All elements under consideration
not belonging to the 'system'
REF: system 41-40 (OT)

indexing system
F   système d'indexation
D   Indexierungssystem
R   система индексирования
S   sistema de indizado
41-17 An *indexing language* and the rules
of its application within a 'documentation
system'
DEF: 15-10
REF: documentation system 41-13 (BT),
information retrieval s. 41-18 (RT)

information retrieval system
  information selection system
F système de recherche automatique des informations
D Informationswiedergewinnungssystem; Informationsrückgewinnungssystem
R информационно-поисковая система
S sistema de recuperación de la información
  41-18 A 'system' whose purpose is *information storage* and *retrieval*
  DEF: 17-27/29, 312-18, 313-14
  REF: documentation system 41-13 (BT), retrieval s. 41-34 (BT), data r. s. 41-10 (NT), document r. s. 41-12 (NT), reference r. s. 41-33 (NT)

information system
F système d'information
D Informationssystem
R информационная система
F sistema de información
  41-19 (1) (in general) A 'system' enabling the *communication* and processing of *information*
  DEF: 17-04, 17-31
  REF: communication system 41-05 (BT), national information system 41-27 (NT), information transmission s. 41-21 (RT)
  41-20 (2) A 'communication system' intended to increase *knowledge*
  DEF: 12-23/24
  REF: communication system 41-05 (BT), management information system 41-23 (NT), technical i. s. 41-42 (NT), national i. s. 41-27 (NT), documentation s. 41-13 (RT)

information transmission system
F système de transmission de l'information
D Informationsübermittlungssystem
R система передачи информации
S sistema de transmisión de la información
  41-21 A 'system' that takes *input information* and delivers it at the *output* without change
  DEF: 17-34, 17-27/19, 17-49
  REF: data processing system 41-09 (BT), communication s. 41-05 (RT), documentation s. 41-13 (RT), information s. 41-19 (RT)

item entry system
F système d'entrée par sujets
D (Objekteingangssystem)
R информационно-поисковая система с подокументной организацией; информационно-поисковая система с прямой организацией
S sistema de entrada por materias
  41-22 A 'storage and retrieval system' where each *entry* constitutes one of the items of the *file*
  DEF: 33-08, 33-11

REF: storage and retrieval system 41-37 (BT), term entry s. 41-43 (OT)

management information system
F système d'information de gestion; système de gestion intégré
D Management-Informationssystem
R управленческая информационная система
S MIS; sistema de información para la gestión
  41-23 An 'information system (2)' to aid in the performance of management functions
  REF: information system 41-20 (BT)

manual system
F système manuel
D manuelles System
R система ручного типа
S sistema manual
  41-24 A 'data processing system' which does not make use of stored-program computing equipment
  REF: data processing system 41-09 (BT), electronic data processing s. 41-15 (OT)

monitoring system
F système de commande
D Monitorsystem; Überwachungssystem
R система контроля; система управления
S sistema de supervisión
  41-25 A 'subsystem' which observes, supervises, controls or verifies the operations of a 'system'
  REF: control system 41-07 (RT), monitoring program 42-26 (RT), real-time processing 42-38 (RT)

multiple-access system
F système à accès multiple
D Mehrfachzugriffsystem
R система с множественной (и дистанционной) выборкой
S sistema de acceso múltiple
  41-26 An 'electronic data processing system' which permits *multiple* and *remote access*
  DEF: 313-23, 313-30
  REF: electronic data processing system 41-15 (BT)

national information system
F système national d'information
D nationales Informationssystem
R национальная информационная система
S sistema nacional de información
  41-27 The national 'system' of *scientific* and *specialized information*
  DEF: 17-60, 17-64
  REF: information system 41-19/20 (BT), technical i. s. 41-42 (RT)

network
F   réseau
D   Netzwerk
R   сеть; система
S   red
41-28 A complex arrangement of inter-connected elements
REF: computer network 42-12 (NT), system 41-40 (RT)

on-line computer system
F   système en ligne
D   on-line-System
R   автоматическая информационно-поисковая система с прямым доступом; автоматическая система обработки данных параллельно с их поступлением
S   sistema en línea; sistema directo
41-29 An 'electronic data processing system' in which the *input data* enter the *computer* directly from their point of origin and/or *output* data are transmitted directly to where they are used
DEF: 17-34, 17-12, 42-10, 17-49
REF: electronic data processing system 41-15 (BT), real-time computer s. 41-32 (RT)

open system
F   système ouvert
D   offenes System
R   разомкнутая система
S   sistema abierto
41-30 (1) A 'system' with *input* and *output*
DEF: 17-34/35, 17-49/50
REF: system 41-40 (BT), adaptive s. 41-01 (NT), dynamic s. 41-14 (NT), self-organizing s. 41-35 (NT), closed s. 41-03/04 (OT)
41-31 (2) A 'system' in which some of the controlling *elements* are not integral parts of this system
DEF: 12-12
REF: system 41-40 (BT), closed s. 41-03/04 (OT)

real-time computer system
F   système automatique en temps réel
D   Echtzeit-Computersystem; Echtzeitsystem; Realzeitsystem
R   автоматическая информационно-поисковая система, действующая в реальном масштабе времени
S   sistema de tiempo real
41-32 An 'electronic data processing system' which controls an 'environment' by receiving *data*, processing them and returning the results sufficiently quickly to affect the functioning of the environment at that time
DEF: 17-12
REF: electronic data processing system 41-15 (BT), on-line computer s. 41-29 (RT) real time processing 42-38 (RT)

reference retrieval system
F   système de recherche automatique de références
D   Dokumentnachweissystem; Dokumentretrievalsystem
R   библиографическая информационно-поисковая система
S   sistema de recuperación de referencias
41-33 A 'system' whose purpose is *reference storage* and *retrieval*
DEF: 22-17, 312-28, 313-29
REF: information retrieval system 41-18 (BT), data r. s. 41-10 (RT), document r. s. 41-12 (RT)

retrieval system
F   système de recherche automatique
D   Retrievalsystem
R   поисковая система
S   sistema de recuperación
41-34 A 'system' whose purpose is *retrieval*
DEF: 313-31
REF: storage and retrieval system 41-37 (BT), information r. s. 41-18 (NT)

self-organizing system
F   système auto-adaptatif
D   selbstorganisierendes System
R   самоорганизующаяся система
S   sistema auto-organizado
41-35 A 'system' which modifies its behaviour according to a set of *inputs* representing the 'environment' within which it operates
DEF: 17-34
REF: open system 41-30 (BT), adaptive s. 41-01 (RT)

state (of a system)
F
D   Zustand (eines Systems)
R   состояние системы
S   estado (de un sistema)
41-36 Structure of *elements* of a 'system' and *relations* between the elements of this system at a certain time
DEF: 12-12, 38-27

storage and retrieval system
    data storage and retrieval system
F   système de mise en mémoire et de recherche automatique
D   Speicher- und Retrievalsystem
R   система накопления и поиска (информации)
S   sistema de almacenamiento y recuperación de datos
41-37 That subsystem of a 'documentation system' which permits *storage* and *retrieval*
DEF: 312-27, 313-31
REF: documentation system 41-13 (BT), retrieval s. 41-34 (NT)

simple system
F   système simple
D   einfaches System
R   простая система
S   sistema simple
41-38 A 'system' which has a single set of *input* devices and a single set of *output* devices
DEF: 17-34/35, 17-49/50
REF: system 41-40 (BT), complex s. 41-06 (OT)

subsystem
F   sous-système
D   Subsystem; Teilsystem
R   подсистема
S   subsistema
41-39 A series or group of elements of a 'system' which perform an operational function within the system and which may be looked at as a system by themselves
REF: system 41-40 (BT)

system
F   système
D   System
R   система
S   sistema
41-40 A set of *elements* with *relations* between the elements such that the set may be looked at as a whole
DEF: 12-12, 38-27
REF: element 38-27 (NT), component 44-05 (NT), for other (NT) and (RT) see section 41

technical communication system
F   système de communication spécialisée
D   fachliches Kommunikationssystem
R   специализированная система коммуникации
S   sistema de comunicación técnica
41-41 The 'communication system' controlling and performing *specialized communication*
DEF: 17-62
REF: communication system 41-05 (BT), technical information s. 41-42 (RT)

technical information system
F   système d'information spécialisé
D   Fachinformationssystem; fachliches Informationssystem
R   специализированная информационная система
S   sistema de información técnica
41-42 The 'communication system' aiming at *information* in one field of *knowledge*, consisting of *information services* providing facilities by which *information* and *data* are processed and transmitted from originator to *user*

DEF: 17-30/31, 12-24, 314-20, 17-27/28, 17-12, 46-30
REF: information system 41-20 (BT), national i. s. 41-26 (RT), technical communication s. 41-11 (RT)

term entry system
F   système à fichier inversé
D   (Merkmaleingangssystem)
R   информационно-поисковая система с инвертированной организацией; информационно-поисковая система со словарной организацией
S   sistema de términos por asientos
41-43 A 'storage and retrieval system' using an *inverted file*
DEF: 33-16
REF: storage and retrieval system 41-37 (BT), item entry s. 41-22 (OT)

uniterm system
F   système univoque
D   Unitermsystem
R   унитермовая система (индексирования)
S   sistema de unitérminos
41-44 An 'indexing system' allocating *uniterms* to the indexed items
DEF: 36-29
REF: indexing system 41-17 (BT)

42 Electronic data processing

accuracy
F   exactitude; précision
D   Genauigkeit; Fehlerfreiheit
R   точность
S   exactitud; precisión
42-01 A measure of the magnitude of 'error' expressed in such a way that the value of this measure increases as the magnitude of the error decreases
REF: error 42-19 (OT), check 42-08 (RT)

analog computer
F   calculateur analogique
D   Analogcomputer; Analogrechner
R   аналоговая вычислительная машина
S   computadora analógica
42-02 A 'computer' in which *data* are mainly represented by means of continuously variable physical quantities
DEF: 17-12
REF: computer 42-10 (BT) digital c. 42-16 (OT), hybrid c. 42-22 (RT)

arithmetic unit
    arithmetic and logic unit;
    operations unit; arithmetic unit
F   unité arithmétique;
    opérateur arithmétique
D   Recheneinheit; Rechenwerk
R   арифметическое устройство
S   unidad aritmética
    42-03 That part of a 'computer' that
    contains the circuits that perform arith-
    metic operations, logic operations, shifts
    and other operations
    REF: central processing unit 42-07 (BT),
    control u. 42-14 (RT)

assembler
    assembly program
F   assembleur; programme d'assemblage
D   Assembler; Assemblierer
R   компонующая программа;
    собирающая программа
S   ordenador
    42-04 A 'computer program' that is
    used to translate a program expressed
    in an *assembly language* into a *machine
    language* and perhaps to link 'sub-
    routines'
    DEF: 15-03, 15-15
    REF: computer program 42-13 (BT),
    compiler 42-09 (RT), translating program
    42-52 (RT)

automatic
F   automatique
D   automatisch
R   автоматический
S   automático
    42-05 The *characteristic* of a process or
    device that, under specified conditions,
    functions without intervention by a
    human operator
    DEF: 12-02

batch processing
    batch-bulk processing
F   traitement par lots
D   Stapelverarbeitung; Stapelbetrieb
R   периодическая обработка;
    обработка порциями
S   tratamiento por lotes
    42-06 Executing a set of 'computer
    programs' such that each is completed
    before the next program of the set is
    started
    REF: multiprocessing 42-27 (OT), multi-
    programming 42-28 (OT), real time
    p. 42-38 (OT), simultaneous operation
    42-42 (OT), time sharing 42-51 (OT),
    serial operation 42-41 (RT)

central processing unit
    central processor
F   unité centrale de traitement;
    unité centrale

D   Zentraleinheit
R   центральное устройство для
    обработки данных
S   unidad central de tratamiento
    42-07 A unit of a 'computer' that
    includes circuits controlling the inter-
    pretation and execution of computer
    'instructions'
    REF: hardware 42-21 (BT), arithmetic
    unit 42-03 (NT), control u. 42-14 (NT),
    peripheral equipment 42-35 (OT)

check
F   contrôle
D   Prüfung; Kontrolle
R   проверка; контроль
S   verificación; control
    42-08 A process for determining
    'accuracy'
    REF: duplication check 42-18 (NT),
    parity ch. 42-34 (NT), summation
    ch. 42-47 (NT), accuracy 42-01 (RT)

compiler
    compiling program
F   compilateur; programme de compilation
D   Compiler; Kompilierer
R   компилирующая программа;
    программирующая программа
S   compilador
    42-09 (1) A 'computer program' that
    is used to translate a program expressed
    in a *procedure-oriented language* into a
    machine-oriented language
    DEF: 15-21, 15-16
    REF: computer program 42-13 (BT),
    assembler 42-04 (RT), translating pro-
    gram 42-52 (RT)

computer
    computing machine
F   calculateur; ordinateur
D   elektronische Datenverarbeitungsanlage;
    elektronische Rechenanlage; Computer;
    programmgesteuerte Rechenanlage
R   вычислительная машина
S   computadora; computador
    42-10 A *data processing* device that can
    perform substantial computation, in-
    cluding numerous arithmetic operations
    or logic operations, without inter-
    vention by a human operator during
    a run
    DEF: 17-15
    REF: analog computer 42-02 (NT),
    digital c. 42-16 (NT), hybrid c. 42-22
    (NT), hardware 42-21 (RT), software
    42-43 (RT)

computer instruction
    machine instruction
F   instruction machine
D   (Computer-) Befehl; Maschinenbefehl
R   машинная команда

s   instrucción para computadora
42-11 An instruction that can be recognized and executed by the 'computer' for which it is designed
REF: computer program 42-13 (BT), instruction 42-24 (BT), routine 42-40 (BT), statement 42-45 (NT)

computer network
F   réseau de calculateurs;
     réseau d'ordinateurs
D   Computer-Verbundnetz
R   сеть вычислительных машин
s   red de computadoras
42-12 A complex consisting of two or more interconnected 'computers'
REF: network 41-28 (BT)

computer program
F   programme de calculateur
D   Computer-Programm;
     Rechnerprogramm; Programm (EDV)
R   программа (для вычислительной машины)
s   programa de computadora
42-13 A series of 'computer instructions' or 'statements' in a form acceptable to a 'computer' prepared in order to achieve a certain result
REF: program 42-36 (BT), software 42-43 (BT), assembler 42-04 (NT), compiler 42-09 (NT), computer instruction 42-11 (NT), monitoring p. 42-26 (NT), module 42-25 (NT), routine 42-40 (NT), source p. 42-34 (NT), sub-routine 42-46 (NT), supervisory p. 42-48 (NT), target p. 42-49 (NT), translating p. 42-52 (NT), programming 42-37 (RT), operating system 42-29 (RT)

control unit
F   unité de commande
D   Steuereinheit
R   устройство управления;
     блок управления
s   unidad de control
42-14 In a 'central processing unit' the part that retrieves 'computer instructions' in proper sequence, interprets each instruction and applies the proper *signals* to the 'arithmetic unit' and other parts in accordance with this interpretation
DEF: 17-57
REF: central processing unit 42-07(BT), arithmetic u. 42-03 (RT)

converter
F   convertisseur
D   Konverter; Umsetzer
R   преобразователь;
     перезаписывающее устройство
s   convertidor
42-15 A device for transferring *data* from one *data medium* to another

DEF: 17-12, 17-13/14
REF: peripheral equipment 42-35 (BT)

digital computer
F   calculateur numérique
D   Digital-Computer; Digital rechner
R   цифровая вычислительная машина
s   computadora digital
42-16 A 'computer' in which discrete representation of *data* is mainly used
DEF: 17-12
REF: computer 42-10 (BT), analog c. 42-02 (OT), hybrid c. 42-22 (RT)

display device
F   unité d'affichage
D   Bildschirmausgabegerät
R   устройство визуального вывода
s   terminal de pantalla
42-17 An 'output unit' that presents changeable *data* in the form of impermanent visual images
DEF: 17-12
REF: output unit 42-30 (BT)

duplication check
F   vérification par duplication
D   Duplizitätskontrolle
R   проверка повторением
s   verificación por duplicación
42-18 A check which requires that the results of two independent performances of the same operation be identical, either concurrently on duplicate equipment or at different times on the same equipment
REF: check 42-08 (BT)

error
F   erreur
D   Fehler
R   ошибка; погрешность
s   error
42-19 Any discrepancy between a computed, observed or measured quantity and the true, specified or theoretically correct value or condition
REF: accuracy 42-01 (OT)

format
F   disposition; format
D   Format; Datenformat
R   формат
s   formato
42-20 (3) (in data processing) The defined arrangement of *data* in or on a *data medium*
DEF: 17-12, 17-13/14

hardware
F   matériel (de traitement de l'information)
D   Maschinenausrüstung
R   техническое оснащение
     (информационных систем)

S equipo de computación; hardware
42-21 Physical equipment used in *data processing*
DEF: 17-15
REF: central processing unit 42-07 (NT), peripheral equipment 42-35 (NT), software 42-43 (OT), computer 42-10 (RT)

hybrid computer
F calculateur hybride
D Hybrid-Computer; Hybridrechner
R аналого-цифровая вычислительная машина; комбинированная вычислительная машина
S computadora híbrida
42-22 A 'computer' using both analog representation and discrete representation of *data*
DEF: 17-12
REF: computer 42-10 (BT), analog c. 42-02 (RT), digital c. 42-16 (RT)

input unit
input device
F unité d'entrée; dispositif d'entrée
D Eingabeeinheit; Eingabegerät
R устройство ввода
S unidad de entrada
42-23 A device in a *data processing system* by which *data* may be entered into the system
DEF: 41-09, 17-12
REF: peripheral equipment 42-35 (BT), terminal 42-50 (NT), output u. 42-30 (OT)

instruction
F instruction
D Instruktion; Befehl
R команда
S instrucción
42-24 A 'statement' that specifies one operation and the values or location of its operands, if any
REF: program 42-36 (BT), statement 42-45 (RT)

module
F module
D Modul; Programmbaustein
R модуль
S módulo
42-25 A 'computer program' unit that is discrete and identifiable with other units, and loading
REF: computer program 42-13 (BT), routine 42-40 (RT)

monitoring program
monitor program
F programme moniteur
D Überwachungsprogramm; Monitor-Programm

R управляющая программа
S programa de supervisión
42-26 A 'computer program' designed to observe, regulate, control or verify the operations of a *system*
DEF: 41-40
REF: computer program 42-13 (BT), supervisory p. 42-48 (RT), system 41-25 (RT)

multiprocessing
F multitraitement
D Mehrfachverarbeitung; Multiprocessing
R (одновременное выполнение двух или более программ несколькими блоками ЭВМ)
S multitratamiento
42-27 Simultaneous execution of two or more 'computer programs' or sequences of 'computer instructions' by several units 'computer'
REF: batch processing 42-06 (OT), serial operation 42-41 (OT), multiprogramming 42-28 (RT), parallel operation 42-32 (RT), simultaneous operation 42-42 (RT), time sharing 42-51 (RT)

multiprogramming
F programmation multiple
D Mehrfachverarbeitung; Multiprogramming
R мультипрограммирование (одновременное выполнение двух или более программ одним блоком ЭВМ)
S multiprogramación
42-28 Concurrent execution of two or more 'computer programs' by one unit of a 'computer'
REF: batch processing 42-06 (OT), serial operation 42-41 (OT), multiprocessing 42-27 (RT), parallel operation 42-32 (RT), simultaneous operation 42-42 (RT), time sharing 42-51 (RT)

operating system
F système d'exploitation
D Betriebsprogramm; Betriebssystem
R операционная программа
S sistema de operación
42-29 'Software' that controls the execution of 'computer programs' and that may provide scheduling, debugging, *input/output control*, accounting, compilation *storage allocation*, *data* management, and related services
DEF: 17-34, 17-49, 44-06, 312-28, 17-12
REF: software 42-43 (BT), computer program 42-13 (RT)

output unit
output device
F unité de sortie; dispositif de sortie
D Ausgabeeinheit; Ausgabegerät

R   устройство вывода
S   unidad de salida
42-30 A device in a *data processing system* by which *data* may be received from the system
DEF: 41-09, 17-12
REF: peripheral equipment 42-34 (BT), display device 42-17 (NT), terminal 42-50 (NT), input unit 42-23 (OT)

overflow
F   dépassement de capacité
D   Überlauf
R   переполнение;
      избыточная информация
S   excedente de capacidad
42-31 That portions of the result of an operation that exceeds the *storage capacity* of the intended *storage device*
DEF: 312-29, 312-31

parallel operation
F   fonctionnement en parallèle
D   Parallelbetrieb
R   параллельная работа
S   operación paralela
42-32 An operation where several units of a 'computer' work on portions of the same problem at the same time
REF: multiprocessing 42-27 (RT), multi-programming 42-28 (RT), simultaneous operation 42-42 (RT), time sharing 42-51 (RT)

parity bit
F   chiffre de parité
D   Paritätsbit
R   контрольный двоичный разряд
      при проверке на чётность
S   control de paridad
42-33 A check bit appended to an array of *binary digits* to make the sum of all the binary digits, including the check bit, always odd or even
DEF: 13-06
REF: check character 13-14 (BT), parity check 42-34 (RT)

parity check
      odd-even check
F   contrôle de parité
D   Paritätsprüfung
R   проверка на чётность;
      контроль по чётности
S   verificación de paridad
42-34 A 'check' whether an array of *binary digits* is either odd or even, to detect 'errors'
DEF: 13-06
REF: check 42-08 (BT), summation ch. 42-47 (RT), parity bit 42-33 (RT)

peripheral equipment
F   organe périphérique; unité périphérique

D   periphere Ausrüstung;
      periphere Ausstattung; periphere Geräte
R   внешние устройства;
      внешнее оборудование;
      периферийное оборудование
S   equipo periférico
42-35 In a *data processing system*, any unit of equipment, distinct from the 'central processing unit', which may provide the system with outside *communication*
DEF: 41-09, 17-04
REF: hardware 42-21 (BT), converter 42-15 (NT), input unit 42-23 (NT), output unit 42-30 (NT), central processing unit 42-07 (OT)

program
F   programme
D   Programm
R   программа
S   programa
42-36 A series of actions designed to achieve a certain result
REF: computer program 42-13 (NT), instruction 42-24 (NT)

programming
F   programmation
D   Programmieren; Programmierung
R   программирование
S   programación
42-37 The designing, writing and testing of 'computer programs'
REF: computer program 42-13 (RT)

real-time processing
F   traitement en temps réel
D   Echtzeitverarbeitung;
      Realzeitverarbeitung
R   обработка (информации)
      в реальном масштабе времени
S   tratamiento a tiempo real
42-38 *Data processing* in a sufficiently rapid manner so that the results of the processing are available in time to influence the process being monitored or controlled
DEF: 17-15
REF: batch processing 42-06 (OT), monitoring system 41-25 (RT), real time computer system 41-32 (RT)

register
F   registre
D   Register
R   регистр
S   registro
42-39 In a *data processing system*, a *storage device* usually intended for some special purpose or purposes and capable of storing a specified amount of *data* such as a *binary digit* or a *computer word*

DEF: 41-09, 312-31, 17-12, 13-06, 14-10/11
REF: internal storage 312-17 (BT)

routine
F   routine
D   Programmroutine; Routine
R   программа; подпрограмма
S   rutina
      42-40 An ordered set of 'computer in-
      structions' that may have some general
      or free use
      REF: computer program 42-13 (BT), com-
      puter instruction 42-11 (NT), sub-routine
      42-46 (RT)

serial operation
F   opération séquentielle
D   Serienbetrieb; serieller Betrieb
R   последовательная работа
S   operación en serie
      42-41 An operation where a 'computer'
      unit works on several problems or several
      parts of the same problem one after
      another
      REF: multiprocessing 42-27 (OT), multi-
      programming 42-28 (OT), simultaneous
      operation 42-42 (OT), time sharing 42-51
      (OT), batch processing 42-06 (RT)

simultaneous operation
F   opération simultanée
D   Simultanbetrieb
R   одновременная работа
S   operación simultánea
      42-42 An operation where a *system* of
      units works on several problems actually
      at the same time and/or apparently at
      the same time
      DEF: 41-40
      REF: batch processing 42-06 (OT), multi-
      processing 42-27 (RT), multiprogram-
      ming 42-28 (RT), parallel operation 42-
      32 (RT), time sharing 42-51 (RT)

software
F   programmétrie; programmes; software;
      "mentaille"
D   Software
R   математическое обеспечение
      (информационных систем)
S   software; sistemas de programación
      42-43 'Computer programmes', proce-
      dures, rules and any associated documen-
      tation concerned with the operations of
      a *data processing system*
      DEF: 41-09
      REF: computer programm 42-13 (NT),
      operating system 42-29 (NT), computer
      42-10 (RT)

source program
F   programme d'origine; programme source
D   Quellenprogramm

R   входная программа;
      исходная программа
S   programa fuente
      42-44 A 'computer program' expressed
      in a *source language*
      DEF: 15-25
      REF: computer program 42-13 (BT),
      target p. 42-49 (OT)

statement
F   énoncé
D   Anweisung
R   высказывание; утверждение
S   instrucción; enunciado
      42-45 A meaningful and interpretable
      arrangement of *symbols* that is complete
      in the context of its *programming lan-
      guage*
      DEF: 13-34, 15-22
      REF: computer instruction 42-11 (BT),
      instruction 42-34 (RT)

sub-routine
F   sous-programme; module
D   Subroutine; Unterprogramm
R   подпрограмма
S   subrutina; subprograma
      42-46 A sequence of 'statements' that
      may be used at more than one point in a
      particular 'computer program' or that
      is available for inclusion in other pro-
      grams
      REF: computer program 42-13 (BT), rou-
      tine 42-40 (RT)

summation check
F   contrôle par sommation
D   Summenkontrolle; Summenprobe
R   проверка суммированием
S   verificación por suma
      42-47 A 'check' based on the formation
      of the sum of the *digits* of a numeral,
      where usually the sum is compared with
      a precomputed value
      DEF: 13-18
      REF: check 42-08 (BT), parity ch. 42-34
      (RT)

supervisory program
      executive program; executive routine;
      supervisory routine
F   programme superviseur
D   Überwachungsprogramm;
      ausführendes Programm
R   программа-супервизор;
      исполнительная программа
S   programa
      42-48 A 'computer program' designed
      to control the execution of other com-
      puter programs and to regulate the flow
      of work in an 'automatic' *data processing
      system*
      DEF: 41-09

REF: computer program 42-13 (BT), monitoring p. 42-26 (RT)

target program
object program
F   programme résultant; programme-objet; programme généré; programme-cible
D   Maschinenprogramm; übersetztes Quellenprogramm
R   конечная программа
S   programa objeto
42-49 A 'computer program' in a *target language* that has been translated from a *source language*
DEF: 15-28, 15-25
REF: computer 42-13 (BT), source p. 42-44 (OT)

terminal
F   terminal
D   Terminal; Datenstation
R   оконечное устройство
S   terminal
42-50 An 'input-output unit' by which a user communicates with an *electronic data processing system*
DEF: 41-15
REF: input unit 42-23 (BT), output unit 42-30 (BT)

time sharing
F   temps partagé
D   Time-sharing
R   распределение времени
S   tiempo compartido
42-51 The apportionment of intervals of time availability of various items of equipment to complete the performance of several tasks by interlacing
REF: batch processing 42-06 (OT), serial operation 42-41 (OT), multiprocessing 42-27 (RT), multiprogramming 42-28 (RT), parallel operation 42-32 (RT), simultaneous operation 42-42 (RT)

translating program
F   programme de traduction
D   Übersetzungsprogramm
R   программа-транслятор
S   programa de traducción
42-52 A 'computer program' that translates from one *programming language* into another programming language
DEF: 15-22
REF: computer program 42-13 (BT), assembler 42-04 (RT), compiler 42-09 (RT)

43 Punched card systems

aperture card
unitized card; aperture punched card

F   carte perforée; carte à fenêtre
D   Filmlochkarte
R   апертурная карта; апертурная перфокарта
S   tarjeta perforada con ventana
43-01 A 'punched card' with an opening specifically prepared for the mounting of a frame or frames of *microfilm*
DEF: 110-31
REF: punched c. 43-20 (BT), combination c. 43-03 (RT)

body-punched aspect card
body-punched feature card; peep-hole card; peek-a-boo card; Batten card; coincidence hole card
F   carte à superposition par points de vue; carte à sélection visuelle
D   Sichtlochkarte
R   просветная перфокарта; суперпозиционная перфокарта
S   tarjeta perforada para selección visual; tarjeta peek-a-boo
43-02 An aspect card where the numbers of the *documents* are marked by holes in a prefixed position and combinations of *descriptors* may be found by optical matching of the cards
DEF: 21-18, 36-05
REF: hand-operated punched card 43-08 (BT), needle-operated punched c. 43-14 (OT)

combination card
F   carte combinée
D   Verbundkarte
R   комбинированная перфокарта
S   tarjeta combinada
43-03 A 'punched card' where additional *information* about the *document* may be given in verbal form
DEF: 17-28, 21-18
REF: punched c. 43-20 (BT), notched c. 43-17 (NT), slotted c. 43-25 (NT), aperture c. 43-01 (RT)

combination coding
F   codage combinatoire
D   Kombinationsverschlüsselung; Kombinationsschlüssel
R   комбинационное кодирование
S   codificación combinada; perforación marginal compuesta
43-04 *Coding* of a specific subject by the joint notching of two or more 'punch positions' in 'notched card systems'
DEF: 18-10
REF: coding 18-10 (BT)

double row coding
F   codages pour carte à préperforations marginales
D   mehrreihige Kerblochmarkierung

R (метод кодирования перфокарт
с двухрядной краевой перфорацией
с использованием трёх типов вырезок)
S codificación de tres muescas
43-05 A *coding* method for 'notched
cards' having a double row of holes on
the edge which permits to punch three
notches or slots at each position (deep,
shallow, intermediate)
DEF: 18-10
REF: coding 18-10 (BT)

dropping fraction
F jeu de cartes sélectionnées;
ensemble des cartes sélectionnées
D Auswurfmenge
R величина выборки
S conjunto seleccionado de tarjetas con
muesca
43-06 In *retrieval systems* using 'notched
cards', the fraction of the *file* delivered
after needle sorting
DEF: 41-34, 33-11
REF: output ratio 45-24 (RT)

guide holes
F trous-guide
D Fixierlöcher
R служебные перфорационные отверстия
S perforación guía
43-07 The prepunched holes in 'slotted
cards' allowing the fixation during
'needle sorting'

hand-operated punched card
F carte perforée à sélection manuelle
D Handlochkarte
R перфокарта ручного обращения;
ручная перфокарта
S tarjeta perforada para selección manual
43-08 A 'punched card' which is designed
to be used in a *retrieval system* which is
operated manually, e. g. by needles or
optical
DEF: 41-34
REF: punched card 43-20 (BT), body-
punched aspect c. 43-02 (NT), needle-
operated p. c. 43-14 (NT), machine-
operated p. c. 43-09 (OT)

machine-operated punched card
F carte perforée à tri mécanique
D Maschinenlochkarte
R перфокарта машинной сортировки;
машинная перфокарта
S tarjeta perforada para selección mecánica
43-09 A 'punched card' which is designed to be used in a *retrieval system* using
mechanical selection
DEF: 41-24, 313-20
REF: punched card 43-20 (BT), mark
sensing c. 43-11 (NT), hand-operated
p. c. 43-08 (OT)

mark-sensed punching
F perforation par marqueur électrosensible;
perforation à lecture optique
D Zeichenlochung
R перфорирование по графическим
меткам
S perforación por marcado electrosensible
43-10 *Automatic* punching of a card by
means of electrically conductive *marks*
made on the card with a special pencil
DEF: 42-05, 13-24
REF: mark sensing card 43-11 (RT)

mark sensing card
F carte perforée à lecture optique
D Zeichenlochkarte
R маркированная перфокарта
S tarjeta para marcado electrosensible
43-11 A 'machine-operated punched card'
which is punched automatically by
'mark-sensed punching'
REF: machine-operated punched card 43-
09 (BT), mark-sensed punching 43-10
(RT)

merging
F fusion
D Mischen; Zusammenmischen
R объединение; слияние (массивов
перфокарт)
S intercalación
43-12 The combining of two sets of
'punched cards' into one set of a given
sequence
REF: collating 34-06 (RT)

multiple punching
F perforation multiple
D Mehrfachlochung
R многократная пробивка
S perforación múltiple
43-13 The punching of two or more
holes in a column of a 'machine-operated
punched card'

needle-operated punched card
F carte perforée à sélection par aiguille
D Nadellochkarte
R ручная перфокарта для сортировки
спицами
S tarjeta perforada para la selección con
agujas
43-14 A *hand-operated punched card* with
prefixed holes which are slotted or
notched to indicate *descriptors* and the
file of which will be selected by *needle*
sorting.
DEF: 36-05, 33-11
REF: hand-operated punched card 43-08
(BT), notched c. 43-17 (NT), slotted
c. 43-25 (NT), body-punched aspect c.
43-02 (OT)

needle
F   aiguille
D   Nadel
R   смица (сортировоцная)
S   aguja de selección
43-15 A *selecting device* to be pushed through the pre-punched holes of 'punched cards' thereby selecting the cards containing the searched items being punched at this hole when turning the pile
DEF: 313-40

notch
F   encoche; perforation marginale
D   Kerbe
R   наружный вырез; открытый вырез
S   muesca
43-16 The opening of a hole a 'notched card'
REF: slot 43-24 (RT)

notched card
    edge-notched card;
    marginal punched card;
    edge-punched card; border-punched card
F   carte à encoches;
    carte à perforations marginales
D   Kerblochkarte; Randlochkarte
R   перфокарта с краевой перфорацией
S   tarjeta con muescas
43-17 A 'needle-operated punched card' the holes of which are opened to the border of the card to indicate *descriptors*
DEF: 36-05
REF: combination card 43-03 (BT), needle-operated punched c. 43-14 (BT), slotted c. 43-25 (RT)

punch position
    punching position
F   emplacement d'une perforation
D   Lochstelle
R   перфорационная позиция; положение пробивки
S   posición de perforación
43-18 A defined location on a 'punched card' or a 'punched tape' where a hole may be punched
REF: storage location 312-33 (RT)

punch tape code
    punched tape code
F   code de ruban perforé
D   Lochstreifencode
R   код перфоленты
S   código de cinta perforada
43-19 A *code* used to represent *data* on 'punched tape'
DEF: 18-06, 17-12
REF: code 18-06 (BT)

punched card
    punch card
F   carte perforée
D   Lochkarte
R   перфокарта; перфорационная карта
S   tarjeta perforada
43-20 A card with holes to be punched, notched or slotted in particular 'punch positions', each positioned hole having a particularly assigned *meaning* to represent *data*
DEF: 14-27, 17-12
REF: punched tape 43-22 (BT), verge perforated card 43-27 (RT), storage device 312-32 (BT), aperture c. 43-01 (NT), combination c. 43-03 (NT), hand-operated punched card 43-08 (NT), machine-operated p. c. 43-09 (NT)

punched-card field
F   zone de carte perforée
D   Lochfeld
R   поле (машинной) перфокарты
S   campo de tarjeta perforada
43-21 A set of columns and/or rows on a 'punched card' fixed as to number and position into which the same item or items of *data* are regularly entered
DEF: 17-12
REF: field 312-13 (BT)

punched tape
    punched paper tape
F   bande perforée
D   Lochstreifen
R   перфолента; перфорационная лента
S   cinta perforada
43-22 A tape, usually paper, upon which *data* may be represented in the form of punched holes
DEF: 17-12
REF: storage device 312-32 (BT), punched card 43-20 (OT), verge perforated card 43-27 (RT)

punching field
    selection field
F   zone de perforation
D   Lochfläche
R   кодовое поле перфокарты; поле перфорации
S   campo de perforación
43-23 The area on a 'punched card' or 'vergeperforated card' where 'punch positions' are possible
REF: writing field 43-28 (OT)

slot
F   fente
D   Schlitz
R   щелевой вырез; щель
S   ranura

43-24 The punched-out areas of 'slotted cards' to connect two or more 'guide holes'
REF: notch 43-16 (RT)

slotted card
F   carte à fentes
D   Schlitzlochkarte
R   щелевая перфокарта
S   tarjeta con ranuras
43-25 A 'needle-operated punched card' in which prefixed 'guide holes' are connected to represent *data* and the *file* of which may be selected by 'needle sorting'
DEF: 17-12, 33-11
REF: combination card 43-03 (BT), needle-operated punched c. 43-14 (BT), notched c. 43-17 (RT)

triangular code
F   code triangulaire
D   Dreiecksschlüssel
R   треугольный код
S   código triangular
43-26 A *code* for 'needle-operated punched cards' in the form of an auxiliary triangle of *symbols*
DEF: 18-06, 13-34
REF: code 18-06 (BT)

verge-perforated card
     verge-punched card
F   carte à perforations centrales
D   Streifenlochkarte
R   перфоленточная карта
S   tarjeta perforada al margen
43-27 A card in which holes, similar to those for punched 'tape', are punched near one edge
REF: storage device 312-32 (BT), punched card 43-20 (RT), punched tape 43-22 (RT)

writing field
F   zone réservée pour des indications en clair
D   Schreibfläche
R   свободное поле перфокарты
S   campo para datos escritos
43-28 The area of a 'punched card' where *data* may be represented by writing
DEF: 17-12
REF: punching field 43-23 (OT)

44 Systems analysis and design

alternatives
F   alternatives
D   Alternativen
R   альтернативы
S   alternativas

44-01 Competitive means for achieving 'goals'

black box
F   boîte noire
     black box
D   black Box;
     "schwarzer Kasten"
R   "чёрный ящик"
S   caja negra
44-02 A *system* whose actual workings are not disclosed and whose behaviour can only be studied through *input* and *output* values
DEF: 41-40, 17-34/35, 17-49/50

block diagram
F   schéma fonctionnel
D   Blockdiagramm
R   блок-схема; принципиальная схема; структурная схема
S   diagrama de bloques
44-03 A 'diagram' of a *system* in which the principal parts are represented by suitably associated geometrical figures to show both the basic functions and functional relationship between the parts
DEF: 41-40
REF: diagram 44-08 (BT), flow chart 44-10 (RT), logical d. 44-16 (RT)

component
F   élément constitutif; composant
D   Systemkomponente
R   компонент; элемент
S   componente
44-04 A somewhat standardized *element* of *systems*
DEF: 12-12, 41-40
REF: system 41-40 (BT)

constraint
F   contrainte
D   Einschränkung; Begrenzung
R   ограничение; условие
S   restricción
44-05 A condition imposed on a *system* which limits the freedom of behaviour of the system
DEF: 41-40

control
F   commande
D   Kontrolle; Steuerung; Regelung
R   управление; регулирование; контроль
S   control
44-06 To exercise such an influence over something as to guide, correct, manage, or restrain it
REF: system engineering 44-36 (NT)

criterion
F critère
D Entscheidungskriterium
R критерий
S criterio
44-07 A rule or standard for choosing 'alternatives'

diagram
F diagramme
D Diagramm
R диаграмма; схема; график
S diagrama
44-08 A schematic graphical representation of a sequence of operations or the 'structure' of a system
DEF: 41-40
REF: block diagram 44-03 (NT), flow chart 44-10 (NT), flow d. 41-11 (NT), logical d. 44-16 (NT), Venn d. 44-38 (NT)

feasibility study
F étude de possibilité de réalisation; étude de faisabilité
D Brauchbarkeitsuntersuchung; Durchführbarkeitsstudie
R изучение возможности реализации; изучение осуществимости
S estudio de factibilidad
44-09 A study projecting how a proposed *system* might operate in a particular organization
DEF: 41-40
REF: pilot study 44-27 (RT)

flow chart
F organigramme
D Flußdiagramm
R блок-схема; схема последовательности; схема потоков
S diagrama de flujo; flujograma
44-10 A graphical representation for the definition, analysis or solution of a problem, in which *symbols* are used to represent operations, *data*, flow, equipment, etc.
DEF: 13-34, 17-12
REF: diagram 44-08 (BT), logical flow chart 44-17 (NT), block diagram 44-03 (RT), flow diagram 44-11 (RT), logical diagram 44-16 (RT)

flow diagram
F ordinogramme; diagramme de calcul
D Ablaufdiagramm; Programmablaufdiagramm
R блок-схема программы; графическое изображение программы
S diagrama de flujo; diagrama de operaciones
44-11 A graphic representation of a *program* or a *routine*

REF: 42-36, 42-40
REF: diagram 44-08 (BT), block d. 44-03 (RT), flow chart 44-10 (RT), logical d. 44-16 (RT)

flow direction
F direction de flux
D Flußrichtung
R направление (последовательности или потока)
S dirección de flujo
44-12 The antecedent-to-successor relation in 'flow charts', indicated by arrows or other conventions

functional unit
F unité fonctionnelle
D funktionelle Einheit
R функциональное устройство; функциональный элемент
S unidad funcional
44-13 A 'component' element, or *subsystem* of a *system* performing a particular function for that system
DEF: 41-39, 41-40

goal
F but
D Ziel; Zielstruktur
R цель
S meta
44-14 The general 'structure' of the state of the *system* which should be achieved
DEF: 41-40
REF: sub-goal 44-31 (NT), mission 44-18 (RT), objectives 44-22 (RT), requirement 44-28 (RT)

logic design
   logical design
F conception logique
D logischer Entwurf
R синтез логических схем; составление логических схем
S diseño lógico
44-15 The specification of the working relations between the 'components' of a *system* in terms of symbolic logic and without primary regard for hardware implementation
DEF: 41-40
REF: systems design 44-35 (BT), operational d. 44-23 (RT), pilot model 44-25 (RT)

logic diagram
F diagramme logique
D logisches Diagramm
R логическая схема; схема выполнения логических операций
S diagrama lógico
44-16 A 'diagram' which represents the 'functional units' of a *system* and their interconnexion without necessarily ex-

pressing construction, engineering or electrical schematic circuit details
DEF: 41-40
REF: diagram 44-08 (BT), block d. 44-03 (RT), flow chart 44-10 (RT)

logical flow chart
F organigramme logique
D logisches Flußdiagramm
R схема последовательности логических операций
S flujograma lógico; diagrama lógico de flujo
44-17 A detailed solution of the work order in terms of the logic, or built-in *characteristics* of a specific *computer*
DEF: 12-02, 42-11
REF: flow chart 44-10 (BT)

mission
F mission
D Aufgabe
R (рабочее) задание
S misión
44-18 A *statement* of what a *system* or a group is to do to solve a given problem and when and where
DEF: 41-40, 42-45
REF: goal 44-14 (RT), objectives 44-22 (RT), requirement 44-28 (RT)

model
F modèle
D Modell
R модель
S modelo
44-19 A representation of something which abstracts the features of the represented relevant to the question being studied
REF: pilot m. 44-25 (NT)

network analysis
network techniques; critical path scheduling
F analyse en réseau; analyse en graphe
D Netzplantechnik; Methode der kritischen Wege
R метод сетевого планирования и управления; метод критического пути
S análisis de redes
44-20 A method for planning and 'control' of projects by representing the different stages of development by 'nodes' and arrows between them to find out the optimal procedure (critical path)
REF: systems analysis 44-33 (RT)

node
F nœud
D Knoten

R узел; узловая точка
S nodo
44-21 The representation of a state or an event by means of a point on a 'diagram'

objectives
F objectifs
D Zielvorgaben
R (конечные) задачи
S objetivos
44-22 The end results that have to be achieved by a *system* or organization
DEF: 41-40
REF: goal 44-14 (RT), mission 44-18 (RT), requirement 44-28 (RT)

operational design
F conception opérationnelle
D operationaler Entwurf
R операционное проектирование
S diseño operacional
44-23 The detailed description of how *system* tasks are to be accomplished
DEF: 41-40
REF: systems design 44-35 (BT), logic d. 44-15 (RT), pilot model 44-25 (RT)

organic structure
F structure organique
D organische Struktur
R гибкая структура
S estructura orgánica
44-24 A flexible organization of a *system* that is structured to meet a situation of rapid or continual change
DEF: 41-40
REF: structure 44-30 (RT)

pilot model
F modèle pilote
D Testmodell; Vorausmodell
R опытная модель; экспериментальная модель
S modelo piloto
44-25 A 'model' of a *system* used for purposes of testing which is less complex than the complete model
DEF: 41-40
REF: model 44-19 (BT), systems design 44-35 (NT), operational design 44-23 (RT)

pilot run
F test; essai en conditions réelles
D Testlauf; Probelauf
R опытный прогон; пробное испытание
S ensayo piloto
44-26 A first testing of a designed *system* under operational conditions
DEF: 41-40
REF: system testing 45-43 (RT)

pilot study
F   étude pilote
D   Vorstudie
R   предварительное изучение
S   estudio piloto
44-27 A first analysis of a problem used to show broad possibilities of solution
REF: feasibility study 44-09 (RT)

requirement
F   impératif
D   Anforderung; Auflage
R   требование; необходимое условие
S   requisito; condición
44-28 A *statement* of an obligation the *system* must fulfil to effect the 'mission'
DEF: 42-45, 41-40
REF: goal 44-14 (RT), mission 44-18 (RT), objectives 44-22 (RT)

simulation
F   simulation
D   Simulation
R   моделирование
S   simulación
44-29 The representation of certain features of the behaviour of a physical or abstract *system* by the behaviour of another system
DEF: 41-40

structure
F   structure
D   Struktur
R   структура системы
S   estructura
44-30 The interrelationship of *elements* of a *system*
DEF: 12-12, 41-40
REF: organic structure 44-24 (NT)

sub-goals
F   objectif limité; objectif partiel
D   Unterziele; Nebenziele
R   ограниченные цели; частные цели
S   metas parciales
44-31 'Goals' of a *system* or organization which are assigned to particular elements, *subsystems* or individual groups
DEF: 41-40, 41-39
REF: goal 44-14 (BT)

synthesis
F   synthèse
D   Synthese
R   синтез
S   síntesis
44-32 Bringing together the solutions of all tasks into a *system*
DEF: 41-40
REF: systems design 44-35 (BT)

systems analysis
F   analyse de systèmes
D   Systemanalyse
R   анализ систем; системный анализ
S   análisis de sistemas
44-33 The analysis of an existing or proposed *system* in order to find optimal solutions for achieving the 'objectives' of the system
DEF: 41-40
REF: systems design 44-35 (OT), systems engineering 44-36 (OT), system testing 45-43 (OT), network analysis 44-20 (RT), systems approach 44-34 (RT)

systems approach
F   approche des systèmes
D   Systemansatz
R   системный подход
S   enfoque de sistemas
44-34 The methodology of solving problems by looking at the problem under the viewpoint of *system*
DEF: 41-40
REF: systems analysis 44-33 (RT)

systems design
F   conception des systèmes
D   Systementwurf
R   проектирование систем
S   diseño de sistemas
44-35 The design of a proposed *system* or a new system which will supplant or improve upon an existing system
DEF: 41-40
REF: logic design 44-15 (NT), operational d. 44-23 (NT), pilot model 44-25 (NT), synthesis 44-32 (NT), systems analysis 44-33 (OT), systems engineering 44-36 (OT), system testing 45-43 (OT)

systems engineering
    systems management
F   gestion des systèmes
D   Systemsteuerung
R   системотехника;
    комплексная техника систем
S   ingeniería de sistemas;
    gestión de sistemas
44-36 Methods to ensure realization of 'systems design, objectives, reliability' and *performance*
DEF: 45-34
REF: systems analysis 44-33 (OT), systems design 44-35 (OT), system testing 45-43 (OT)

variable
F   variable
D   Variable
R   переменная (величина)
S   variable

44-37 A single measurable factor which influences the behaviour of the *system*
DEF: 41-40

Venn diagram
F　diagramme de Venn
D　Venn-Diagramm
R　диаграмма Венна
S　diagrama de Venn
S　**44-38** A 'diagram' in which sets are represented by closed regions
REF: diagram 44-08 (BT)

45 Systems testing and evaluation

acceptance rate
F
D　Benutzer-Relevanzquote
R　(отношение числа релевантных документов в выдаче, по оценке потребителя, к общему объему выдачи)
S　tasa de aceptación
　45-01 Proportions of items accepted as relevant by the *user* to the number of items supplied by the *system*
DEF: 46-30, 41-40
REF: relevance ratio 45-34 (RT)

activity ratio
F　taux d'activité
D　Aktivitätsquote
R　показатель активности (использования информации в массиве)
S　tasa de actividad
　45-02 The ratio of the number of *records* in a *file* which have activity to the total number of records in that file
DEF: 21-44, 33-11
REF: effectiveness indicators 45-15 (BT)

adaptability
F　faculté d'adaptation; adaptabilité
D　Anpassungsfähigkeit
R　гибкость; способность к адаптации
S　adaptabilidad
　45-03 The quality of a *system* to adapt to changes in the *environment* or of internal *structure*
DEF: 41-40, 41-16, 44-30
REF: adaptive s. 41-01 (RT), compatibility 45-05 (RT)

benefit
F　bénéfice
D　Nutzen
R　полезность; эффективность
S　beneficio
　45-04 The fulfilment of the objectives of a *system* by its *output*

DEF: 41-40, 17-49/50
REF: user benefit 45-46 (NT), effort 45-18 (OT)

compatibility
F　compatibilité
D　Kompatibilität
R　совместимость
S　compatibilidad
　45-05 The quality of a *system* to use the *inputs* or *outputs* of another system as its inputs
DEF: 41-40, 17-34, 17-49
REF: adaptability 45-03 (RT)

complexity
F　complexité
D　Komplexität
R　сложность
S　complejidad
　45-06 The degree to which the *elements* of a *system* are interrelated with each other
DEF: 12-12, 41-40
REF: complex system 41-06 (RT)

concentration ratio
　generality of question
F　taux de références pertinentes
D　Konzentrationsquote
R　плотность (массива)
S　tasa de relevancia
　45-07 The ratio of the number of relevant items recovered by a *retrieval system* to the total number of items in the *file*
DEF: 41-34, 33-11
REF: effectiveness indicators 45-15 (BT), output 45-24 (RT)

cost-benefit analysis
F　analyse de coût-bénéfice
D　Kosten-Nutzen-Analyse
R　анализ соотношения "стоимость–польза"
S　análisis beneficio-costo
　45-08 The analysis of the ratio of 'costs' of a *system* to the 'benefits' of the system
DEF: 41-40
REF: efficiency control 45-17 (BT), cost-effectiveness analysis 45-09 (NT)

cost-effectiveness analysis
F　analyse de coût-efficacité
D　Kosten-Leistungs-Analyse
R　анализ соотношения "стоимость–эффективность"
S　análisis eficiencia-costo
　45-09 The analysis of the ratio of the 'costs' of a *system* to the 'effectiveness' of the system
DEF: 41-40

REF: cost-benefit analysis 45-08 (BT),
efficiency control 45-17 (RT)

costs
F   coûts
D   Kosten
R   затраты (денежные)
S   costos
45-10 The 'effort' a *system* needs to
produce 'effectiveness', expressed in
terms of money
DEF: 41-40
REF: effort 45-18 (BT), system costs
45-39 (NT), user c. 45-47 (NT), profit
45-29 (OT)

cost-sensivity analysis
F   analyse des incidences financières
D   Kosten-Sensivitäts-Analyse
R   (анализ соотношения между
     изменениями в характеристиках
     системы и в необходимых затратах)
S   análisis de sensibilidad económica
45-11 The analysis how variations in
the specifications of a *system* affect
the *requirements* of that system for
resources
DEF: 41-40, 44-28
REF: expandability 45-19 (RT)

coverage ratio
F   taux de couverture
D   Abdeckungsquote
R   показатель полноты охвата
S   tasa de exhaución
45-12 The ratio of all items concerning
a particular *subject field* to be retrieved
in a *documentation system* during a
specific period of time to the whole
amount of items existing in this subject
field
DEF: 12-31, 41-13
REF: effectiveness indicators 45-15 (BT),
relative coverage ratio 45-31 (RT),
retrieval r. 45-36 (RT)

economic efficiency
F   efficacité économique; économicité
D   Wirtschaftlichkeit
R   экономическая эффективность
S   eficiencia económica
45-13 The confrontation of 'costs' and
'profits' of a *system*
DEF: 41-40
REF: efficiency 45-16 (BT)

effectiveness
     performance
F   efficacité; résultats
D   Leistung; Leistungsfähigkeit
R   эффективность; производительность
S   eficacia

45-14 The *outputs* of a *system* intended
to cause 'benefit'
DEF: 17-49/50, 41-40
REF: effort 45-18 (OT), benefit 45-04
(RT), efficiency 45-16 (RT), system
effectiveness 45-40 (RT)

effectiveness indicators
     efficiency factors; performance factors
F   indicateurs d'efficacité
D   Leistungsindikatoren
R   показатели эффективности
S   indicadores de eficacia
45-15 Factors indicating the 'effectiveness' of a *system*
DEF: 41-40
REF: activity ratio 45-02 (NT), coverage
ratio 45-12 (NT), concentration ratio
45-07 (NT), fallout ratio 45-20 (NT),
miss ratio 45-21 (NT), noise ratio
45-22 (NT), novelty ratio 45-23 (NT),
output ratio 45-24 (NT), pertinency
ratio 45-27 (NT), practile 45-28 (NT),
recall ratio 45-34 (NT), relative recall
ratio 45-32 (NT), relative coverage ratio
45-31 (NT), relevance ratio 45-34 (NT),
retrieval ratio 45-36 (NT), specificity
45-38 (NT), usage frequency 45-45 (NT),
efficiency control 45-17 (RT)

efficiency
F   efficacité
D   Effizienz; Wirkungsgrad
R   эффективность; экономичность
S   eficiencia
45-16 The confrontation of measurable
'effort' of a *system* to measurable
'effectiveness'
DEF: 41-40
REF: economic efficiency 45-13 (NT),
effectiveness 45-14 (RT), efficiency con-
trol 45-17 (RT)

efficiency control
F   contrôle de l'efficacité
D   Effizienzkontrolle
R   контроль эффективности
S   control de eficiencia
45-17 The application of tests and
measures to control the 'efficiency' of
a *system*
DEF: 41-40
REF: cost-benefit analysis 45-08 (NT),
effectiveness indicators 45-15 (RT), efficiency 45-16 (RT), performance evaluation 45-25 (RT), system testing
45-44 (RT)

effort
F   effort
D   Aufwand
R   затраты (в усилиях)
S   ritmo de inversión de recursos

45-18 The means used for planning, implementation, management and usage of a *system* in a specific period of time
DEF: 41-40
REF: system effort 45-41 (NT), user e. 45-48 (NT), benefit 45-04 (OT)

expandability
F faculté d'expansion; faculté d'adaptation
D Ausweitungsfähigkeit
R возможность расширения системы
S capacidad de expansión
45-19 The quality of a *system* that it can be expanded at a later date to accommodate problem areas not covered by it at present
DEF: 41-40
REF: cost-sensitivity-analysis 45-11 (RT)

fallout ratio
F taux de déchets
D Abfallquote
R (соотношение числа нерелевантных документов в выдаче и их общего числа в массиве)
S tasa de irrelevancia
45-20 The ratio of the number of non-relevant items recovered by a *retrieval system* to the total number of non-relevant items in the *file*
DEF: 41-40
REF: effectiveness indicators 45-15 (BT), specificity 45-38 (OT), noise ratio 45-22 (RT)

miss ratio
   omission; omission factor
F taux d'omission
D Fehlquote
R коэффициент потерь
S tasa de omisión
45-21 The ratio of the number of non-relevant items recovered by a *retrieval system* to the total number of relevant items in the *file*
DEF: 41-34, 33-11
REF: effectiveness indicators 45-15 (BT), recall ratio 45-30 (OT)

noise ratio
   noise factor
F taux de bruit;
   taux de réponse non pertinent
D Ballastquote
R коэффициент поискового шума
S tasa de ruido
45-22 The ratio of the number of relevant items recovered by a *retrieval system* to the total number of items retrieved
DEF: 41-34
REF: effectiveness indicators 45-15 (BT), relevance ratio 45-34 (OT)

novelty ratio
F taux de nouveauté
D Neuheitsquote
R коэффициент новизны
S tasa de novedad
45-23 The ratio of the number of items recovered by a *retrieval system* which are new to the user to the total number of relevant items in the *file*, the total number of items retrieved, or the total number of relevant items retrieved
DEF: 41-34, 33-11
REF: effectiveness indicators 45-15 (BT)

output ratio
   resolution factor
F taux de références retrouvées
D Ausstoßquote
R коэффициент выдачи
S tasa de recuperación
45-24 The ratio of the number of items recovered by a *retrieval system* to the total number of items in the *file*
DEF: 41-34, 33-11
REF: effectiveness indicators 45-15 (BT), concentration ratio 45-07 (RT)

performance evaluation
F analyse des performances
D Leistungskontrolle
R оценка работы (системы);
   оценка эффективности
S evaluación de funcionamiento
45-25 The analysis of an operating *system* in terms of initial *objectives* and estimates to provide *information* about operating experience and to identify corrective actions required if any
DEF: 21-18
REF: efficiency control 45-17 (RT), system testing 45-44 (RT), system evaluation 45-42 (RT)

pertinency
   pertinence
F pertinence
D Pertinenz; benutzerspezifische Relevanz
R пертинентность
S pertinencia
45-26 The usefulness of a relevant *document* at a particular time to a particular inquirer
DEF: 21-18
REF: relevance 45-33 (BT), pertinency ratio 45-27 (RT), user-relevance response 45-49 (RT)

pertinency ratio
   pertinency factor
F taux de pertinence
D Pertinenzquote
R коэффициент пертинентности
S tasa de pertinencia

45-27 The ratio of the number of items recovered by a *retrieval system* found to be pertinent to the total number of items retrieved
DEF: 41-34
REF: effectiveness indicators 45-15 (BT), relevance ratio 45-34 (RT)

practile
F   taux de références retrouvées par recherche
D   suchgangsbezogene Relevanzquote (Praktikel)
R   (доля релевантной информации), выдаваемой за один поисковый цикл
S   porcentaje de recuperación por corrida
45-28 The percentage of relevant items recovered by a *retrieval system* per *retrieval run*
DEF: 41-34, 313-32
REF: effectiveness indicators 45-15 (BT), relevance ratio 45-34 (RT)

profit
F   profit
D   Ertrag; Profit
R   выгода; польза
S   ganancia
45-29 The economic realization of *outputs* of a system
DEF: 17-49/50, 41-40
REF: costs 45-10 (OT)

recall ratio
   recall factor; hit rate; sensitivity; completeness
F   taux de rappel
D   Trefferquote
R   коэффициент полноты выдачи
S   tasa de acierto
45-30 The ratio of the number of relevant items recovered by a *retrieval system* to the total number of relevant items in the *file*
DEF: 41-34, 33-11
REF: effectiveness indicators 45-15 (BT), miss ratio 45-21 (OT), relative recall r. 45-32 (RT), retrieval r. 45-36 (RT)

relative coverage ratio
F   taux de couverture relatif
D   relative Abdeckungsquote
R   коэффициент относительной полноты выдачи
S   tasa relativa de exhaución
45-31 The ratio of the number of items concerning a particular subject field to be retrieved by a *documentation system* in a certain period of time to the total number of items existing in this subject field
DEF: 41-13
REF: effectiveness indicators 45-15 (BT), coverage ratio 45-12

relative recall ratio
F   taux de rappel subjectif
D   subjektive Trefferquote
R   показатель относительной полноты охвата
S   tasa de acierto relativo
45-32 The ratio of the number of relevant items recovered by a *retrieval system* to the number of relevant items which the user thinks to be necessary for satisfying his needs
DEF: 41-34
REF: effectiveness indicators 45-15 (BT), recall ratio 45-30 (RT)

relevance
   precision
F   relevance
D   Relevanz
R   релевантность
S   relevancia
45-33 The quality of items recovered by a *retrieval system* to fulfil the needs of the *users*
DEF: 41-34
REF: pertinency 45-26 (RT), system relevance response 45-43 (RT), user-relevance response 45-49 (RT)

relevance ratio
   relevance factor; precision ratio; accuracy
F   taux de relevance
D   Relevanzquote
R   коэффициент точности выдачи
S   tasa de relevancia
45-34 The ratio of the number of all relevant items recovered by a *retrieval system* to the total number of items retrieved, regardless of how 'relevance' is measured
DEF: 41-34
REF: effectiveness indicators 45-15 (BT), acceptance rate 45-01 (RT), noise r. 45-22 (RT), pertinency r. 45-27 (RT)

reliability
F   fiabilité
D   Zuverlässigkeit
R   надёжность
S   confiabilidad
45-35 The probability of a *system* or equipment performing its purpose adequately over the period of time intended under the operating conditions encountered
DEF: 41-40

retrieval ratio
F   taux de références pertinentes retrouvées
D   Nachweisquote
R   коэффициент абсолютной полноты выдачи
S   tasa de recuperación

45-36 The ratio of the number of relevant items recovered by a *retrieval system* to the total number of all existing relevant items
DEF: 41-34
REF: effectiveness indicators 45-15 (BT), coverage ratio 45-12 (RT), recall r. 45-30 (RT)

selectivity
F sélectivité
D Selektionsgüte
R избирательность; селективность
S selectividad
45-37 The degree to which a *retrieval system* is able to recover relevant items and to suppress non-relevant items
DEF: 41-34

specificity
F spécificité
D Exaktheitsquote
R специфичность (отношение числа невыданных нерелевантных документов к общему числу нерелевантных документов в массиве)
S especificidad
45-38 The ratio of the number of non-relevant and non-retrieved items to the total number of non-relevant items in the *file*
DEF: 33-11
REF: effectiveness indicators 45-15 (BT), fallout ratio 45-20 (OT)

system costs
F coût d'un système
D Systemkosten
R затраты на систему (денежные)
S costos de un sistema
45-39 The 'costs' which are needed for planning, implementation and management of an *information* or *documentation system*
DEF: 41-19/20, 41-13
REF: costs 45-10 (BT), user c. 45-47 (OT)

system effectiveness
F performance d'un système
D Leistungsfähigkeit des Systems
R эффективность системы
S eficacia del sistema
45-40 The probability that a *system* can successfully meet an operational demand within a given time when operated under specific conditions
DEF: 41-40
REF: effectiveness 45-14 (RT)

system effort
F exigences d'un système
D Systemaufwand
R затраты на систему (в усилиях)

S ritmo de inversión de recursos en un sistema
45-41 The 'effort' necessary for planning, implementation and management of an *information* or *documentation system*
DEF: 41-19/20, 41-13
REF: effort 45-18 (BT), user e. 45-48 (OT)

system evaluation
F évaluation d'un système
D Bewertung von Systemen
R оценка систем
S evaluación de un sistema
45-42 The estimation and analysis of the work of a *system* in comparison to other systems or fixed standards
DEF: 41-40
REF: performance evaluation 45-25 (RT), system testing 45-34 (RT)

system relevance response
F cohérence d'un système
D Systemrelevanz
R (степень формального соответствия запроса и информации в массиве)
S coherencia de un sistema
45-43 The degree of formal correspondence of *encoded question* and *entries* into the *file*
DEF: 313-08, 33-08, 33-11
REF: user-relevance response 45-49 (OT), relevance 45-33 (RT)

system testing
F contrôle d'un système
D Systemtest
R испытание систем
S prueba de un sistema
45-44 The experimental measurement of the performance of a *system*
DEF: 41-40
REF: systems analysis 44-34 (OT), systems design 44-36 (OT), systems engineering 44-37 (OT), efficiency control 45-17 (RT), performance evaluation 45-25 (RT), system evaluation 45-42 (RT)

usage frequency
F fréquence d'utilisation
D Benutzungsfrequenz
R частота использования
S frecuencia de utilización
45-45 The frequency of *use* of a *system* or *outputs* of a system in a given period of time
DEF: 46-27, 41-40, 17-49
REF: effectiveness indicators 45-15 (BT)

user benefit
F bénéfice de l'utilisateur
  bénéfice individuel
D Benutzernutzen; individueller Nutzen
R полезность для потребителя

s   beneficio del usuario
45-46 The 'benefit' a *user* has by using an
information or *documentation system*
DEF: 46-30, 41-19/20, 41-13
REF: benefit 45-04 (BT), user effort
45-48 (OT)

user costs
F   coût pour l'utilisateur
D   Benutzerkosten
R   затраты потребителя (денежные)
s   costos por usuario
45-47 The 'costs' a *user* has to meet by
using an *information* or *documentation
system*
DEF: 46-30, 41-19/20, 41-13
REF: costs 45-10 (BT), user effort 45-48
(BT), system costs 45-39 (OT)

user effort
F   servitudes pour l'utilisateur
D   Benutzeraufwand
R   затраты потребителя (во времени,
деньгах и пр.)
s   recursos invertidos por el usuario
45-48 The 'effort' (of time, money, etc.) a
user has to afford by using an *information*
or *documentation system*
DEF: 46-30, 41-19/20, 41-13
REF: effort 45-18 (BT), user costs 45-47
(NT), system effort 45-41 (OT), user
benefit 45-46 (OT)

user relevance response
F   appréciation de la relevance par
l'utilisateur
D   Benutzerrelevanz
R   (степень соответствия выдачи
и информационной потребности,
выраженной потребителем)
s   coherencia relativa de un sistema
45-49 The degree of correspondence of
the *outputs* of an *information* or *documentation system* and the needs of the *user*
expressed by the user
DEF: 17-49, 41-19/20, 41-13, 46-30
REF: system relevance response 45-43
(OT), pertinency 45-26 (RT), relevance
45-33 (RT)

46 Usage and user analysis

benefit analysis
F   analyse de bénéfices
D   Nutzungsforschung; Nutzungsanalyse
R   анализ полезности
s   análisis de beneficios
46-01 The scientific analysis of the *benefit*
a *user* or a group of users have by using a
particular *information service* or *information* or *documentation system*

DEF: 45-04, 314-20, 41-19/20, 41-13
REF: use a. 46-28 (RT), user a. 46-31 (RT)

channel study
F   étude des voies de communication
D   Informationskanaluntersuchung
R   изучение информационного канала
s   estudios de los canales de comunicación
46-02 A study of the 'use a user' or a
group of users make of a particular *communication channel* for *information*
DEF: 17-05, 17-31
REF: use study 46-29 (BT), critical incident
s. 46-04 (RT), dissemination s. 46-07 (RT)

critical-incident-decision study
F   étude des cas impliquant une décision
D   entscheidungsbezogene Benutzerstudie
R   анализ ситуаций для принятия
решений
s   análisis de hábitos de información
con toma de decisiones
46-03 A 'critical-incident study' analysing only decision situations
REF: critical-incident study 46-04 (BT)

critical-incident study
F   étude de cas typiques
D   ereignisbezogene Benutzerstudie
R   анализ ситуаций (при изучении
информационных потребностей)
s   análisis de hábitos de información
46-04 A 'user study' analysing 'information-seeking behaviour' of a 'user' or a
group of users in specific *information*-
receiving events
DEF: 17-28
REF: user study 46-36 (BT), critical-
incident decision s. 46-03 (NT), channel s.
46-02 (RT), dissemination s. 46-07 (RT)

demand study
F   étude de demande
D   Bedarfsuntersuchung
R   изучение информационных
потребностей
s   estudio de la demanda
46-05 A study of the 'information
demands, needs' and/or 'interests' of a
particular group of 'users'
REF: user study 46-36 (BT), evaluation s.
46-08 (RT)

diary technique
F   analyse par enregistrement quotidien
D   Tagebuchtechnik
R   метод изучения на основе записей
в дневнике
s   análisis por registro diario
46-06 A research technique where the
subject of the study is asked to record the
time spent on particular activities or
during a period of time by means of a
diary

dissemination study
F étude de la diffusion des informations
D Verbreitungsuntersuchung
R изучение распространения
информации
S estudio de la difusión de la información
46-07 A study of the *dissemination* of
information in a particular *subject field*
or organization
DEF: 19-04, 12-31
REF: use s. 46-29 (BT), channel s. 42-02
(RT), critical-incident s. 46-04 (RT)

evaluation study
F étude d'évaluation
D Bewertungsuntersuchung
R изучение оценок
S estudio de evaluación
46-08 A 'user study' analysing the evaluations a 'user' or a group of users make of
a particular *information service* or of a
particular *information* or *documentation
system*
DEF: 314-20, 41-19/20, 41-13
REF: user study 46-36 (BT), demand s.
46-05 (RT), preference s. 46-23 (RT)

experimental study
F étude expérimentale
D Experimentaluntersuchung
R экспериментальное изучение
S estudio experimental
46-09 A 'user' or 'use study' where some
variables in the *information* situation are
altered experimentally and the reactions
of the 'users' were analysed
DEF: 44-37, 17-31

indirect study
F étude indirecte
D indirekte Benutzeruntersuchung;
indirekte Benutzungsstudie
R непрямое изучение;
косвенное изучение
S estudio indirecto de usuarios
46-10 A 'user' or 'use study' where users
were not asked directly but where their
behaviour is observed indiretrly (e.g.
by means of loan statistics or *contents
analysis*)
DEF: 17-11
REF: diary technique 46-06 (OT), interview survey 46-20 (OT), panel technique
46-22 (OT), questionnaire survey 46-25
(OT)

information demand
F demande d'information
D Informationsbedarf
R потребность в информации
(коллективная)
S demanda de información
46-11 The demand for *information* existing at a specific time in a particular
subject field or organization, i.e. the sum
of all individual 'information needs' of
the persons working in this subject field
or organization
DEF: 17-27/28, 12-31
REF: user demand 46-32 (NT), information interest 46-12 (RT), information
needs 46-13 (RT), information requirements 46-14 (RT)

information interest
F intérêt subjectif pour l'information
D Informationsinteresse
R заинтересованность в информации
S interés individual por la información
46-12 The subjective interest for different
kinds of *information* of an individual
DEF: 17-27/28
REF: user interest 46-33 (NT), informa-
tion demand 46-11 (RT), information
needs 46-13 (RT), information require-
ments 46-14 (RT)

information needs
F besoins d'information; besoin
D Informationsbedürfnisse
R потребность в информации
(индивидуальная)
S necesidades de información
46-13 The needs for *information* an individual 'user' or potential user has, whether
they may be conscious or not
DEF: 17-27/28, 31
REF: user needs 46-34 (NT), information
demand 46-11 (RT), information interest
46-12 (RT), information requirements 46-
14 (RT)

information requirements
F exigences en matière d'information
D Informationsanforderungen
R информационные запросы;
потребность в информации
S solicitudes de información
46-14 The conscious and expressed 'information needs' of a 'user'
REF: information demand 46-11 (RT),
information interest 46-12 (RT), information needs 46-13 (RT)

information source
F source d'information
D Informationsquelle
R источник информации
S fuentes de información
46-15 The source from which an individ-
ual gets *information* fulfilling his 'infor-
mation needs'
DEF: 17-27/28, 31
REF: source material 21-57 (RT)

information utilization
F utilisation de l'information
D Informationsnutzung
R использование информации

S utilización de la información
46-16 To get *information* from 'information sources'
DEF: 17-31
REF: information-gathering patterns 46-17 (RT), utilization 46-39 (RT)

information-gathering patterns
F modèle de collecte de l'information
D Strukturen der Informationsbeschaffung
R схемы сбора информации;
   схемы получения информации
S pautas de acopio de información
46-17 The patterns of the 'use' a 'user' or a group of users make of the different potential 'information sources' within a *subject field* or organization
DEF: 12-31
REF: information utilization 46-16 (RT), information-seeking behaviour 46-18 (RT)

information-seeking behaviour
F comportement dans la recherche de l'information
D Informationsbeschaffungsverhalten; Informationsverhalten
R поведение потребителя в процессе поиска информации
S hábitos de información
46-18 The behaviour of an individual to get some *information* fulfilling his subjective 'information needs'
DEF: 17-27/28, 31
REF: information-gathering patterns 46-17 (RT)

interest profile
F profil d'intérêt
D Interessenprofil
R "профиль интересов";
   набор дескрипторов, отражающих заинтересованность в информации
S perfil de interés
46-19 The profile of *descriptors* characterizing 'information interests'
DEF: 36-05
REF: user profile 46-35 (NT)

interview survey
F enquête par interview
D Umfrage
R изучение на основе интервьюирования
S encuesta por entrevista
46-20 A survey in which a group of persons, normally a 'sample', is asked subsequently personally, according to a somewhat prefixed scheme of questions, usually a 'questionnaire'
REF: indirect study 46-10 (OT), panel technique 46-22 (RT), questionnaire survey 46-25 (RT)

mail questionnaire
F questionnaire par poste

D Postwurfumfrage; schriftliche Umfrage; schriftliche Befragung
R анкета, распространяемая по почте
S cuestionario por correo
46-21 A 'questionnaire' being sent out and returned by the respondent by mail
REF: questionnaire survey 46-25 (BT)

panel-technique
F méthode de panel
D Panel-Verfahren; Panel-Technik
R метод изучения с участием представительной группы лиц
S encuesta múltiple a un grupo
46-22 A research technique where a group of persons is interviewed or questionnaired several times
REF: indirect study 46-10 (OT), interview survey 46-20 (RT), questionnaire survey 46-25 (RT)

preference study
F étude préférentielle
D Präferenzuntersuchung
R изучение на основе показателей предпочтительности
S estudio de preferencias
46-23 A 'user study' where the users are asked to express their preferences of *information services* or modes of *information*
DEF: 314-20, 17-30/31
REF: user study 46-36 (BT), evaluation s. 46-08 (BT)

questionnaire
F questionnaire
D Fragebogen
R анкета; вопросник
S cuestionario
46-24 A detailed list of questions with alternatives for answering used to interview or question a group of people in a comparable and computable way
REF: interview survey 46-20 (RT), questionnaire survey 46-25 (RT)

questionnaire survey
F étude par questionnaire
D Fragebogenuntersuchung
R изучение методов анкетирования; анкетный опрос
S encuesta por cuestionario
46-25 A survey using 'questionnaires' which are filled in by the respondents themselves and not by an interviewer
REF: mail questionnaire 46-21 (NT), indirect study 46-10 (OT), interview survey 46-20 (RT), panel-technique 46-22 (RT), sample 46-26 (RT)

sample
F échantillon
D Sample; Stichprobe

R   выборка; образец
S   muestra
46-26 A subset of the population to be studied, chosen in a way that every member of the population has an equal or nearly equal chance to become a member of the subset
REF: interview survey 46-20 (RT), questionnaire survey 46-25 (RT)

use
   usage
F   utilisation
D   Benutzung
R   использование
S   utilización
46-27 To frequent the services of *information* or *documentation systems*
DEF: 41-19/20, 41-13
REF: utilization 41-42 (RT)

use analysis
   usage analysis
F   analyse des modes d'utilisation
D   Benutzungsforschung
R   анализ использования
S   análisis de utilización
46-28 The analysis of patterns of 'use' of *information services* or *information* or *documentation systems*
DEF: 314-20, 41-19/20, 41-13
REF: use study 46-29 (NT), benefit analysis 46-01 (RT), user a. 46-31 (RT)

use study
F   étude des modes d'utilisation
D   Benutzungsuntersuchung
R   изучение использования
S   estudio de utilización
46-29 A study of the patterns of use of *information services* or *information* or *documentation systems*
DEF: 314-20, 41-19/20, 41-13
REF: use analysis 46-28 (BT), channel study 46-02 (NT), dissemination s. 46-07 (NT), user s. 46-36 (RT)

user
F   utilisateur; usager
D   Benutzer
R   потребитель; пользователь
S   usuario
46-30 A person or an organization needing *specialized information* from an existing or planned *information service* or *information* or *documentation system*
DEF: 17-63/65, 314-20, 41-19/20, 41-13

user analysis
F   analyse des utilisateurs
D   Benutzerforschung
R   изучение потребителей
S   análisis de usuarios

46-31 The analysis of *characteristics* of 'users' and their behaviour related to *information*
DEF: 12-01, 17-27/31
REF: user study 46-36 (NT), benefit analysis 46-01 (RT), use a. 46-28 (RT)

user demand
F   demande des utilisateurs
D   Benutzerbedarf
R   потребность в информации (групповая)
S   demanda de los usuarios
46-32 The demand for *information* of a group of existing 'users', i. e. the sum of all individual 'user needs' of these users
DEF: 17-27/28, 31
REF: information demand 46-11 (BT), user interest 46-33 (RT), user needs 46-34 (RT)
REF: information demand 46-11 (BT), user interest 46-33 (RT), user needs 46-34 (RT)

user interest
F   intérêt des utilisateurs
D   Benutzerinteresse
R   заинтересованность в информации (субъективная)
S   interés de los usuarios
46-33 The subjective interest on different kinds of *information* of a 'user'
DEF: 17-27/28, 31
REF: information interest 46-12 (BT), user demand 46-32 (RT), user needs 46-34 (RT)

user needs
F   besoins des utilisateurs
D   Benutzerbedürfnisse
R   потребность в информации (индивидуальная)
S   necesidades de los usuarios
46-34 The 'information needs' an individual 'user' or potential user has, whether they may be fulfilled by an *information service* or *information* or *documenation system*
DEF: 314-20, 41-19/20, 41-13
REF: information needs 46-13 (BT), user demand 46-32 (RT), user interest 46-33 (RT)

user profile
F   profil des utilisateurs
D   Benutzerprofil
R   "профиль потребителя"
S   perfiles de interés de usuarios
46-35 A list of *index terms* selected to indicate the area of interest of a 'user' of an *information service*, used in the selection of *documents* in *selective dissemination of information*
DEF: 36-10, 314-20, 21-18, 314-25
REF: interest profile 46-19 (BT)

user study
F   étude des utilisateurs
D   Benutzeruntersuchung; Benutzerstudie
R   изучение потребителей
S   estudio de usuarios
46-36 A study of the *characteristics* of 'users' and their behaviour related to *information*
DEF: 12-01, 17-27/31
REF: user analysis 46-31 (BT), critical-incident study 46-04 (NT), demand s. 46-05 (NT), evaluation s. 46-08 (NT), preference s. 46-23 (NT), use s. 46-29 (RT)

user types
F   types d'utilisateurs
D   Benutzertypen
R   типы потребителей
S   tipos de usuarios
46-37 Types of 'users' which are defined by similar 'user needs'

user-administered records
F
D   (Erhebung durch den Benutzer)
R   (регистрационные записи, осуществляемые потребителями информации)
S   auto-registro de características de usuarios
46-38 Records of the behaviour of 'users' which are recorded with the help of the users themselves
REF: diary technique 46-06 (RT)

utilization
F   utilisation
D   Nutzung
R   использование
S   aprovechamiento
46-39 To gain benefit form *information* or *documentation systems* by using their services
DEF: 41-19/20, 41-13
REF: information utilization 46-16 (RT), use 46-27 (RT)

5 Organizations and professions in information and documentation

51 Organizations

archives
F   archives
D   Archiv
R   архивный фонд (1); архив (2)
S   archivos
51-01 (1) *Records* which have been preserved by the persons responsible for the transactions to which they relate, or by their successors, in their own custody, and normally in the arrangement in which they were created or received during the business in question
DEF: 21-44
51-02 (2) Organization for collecting 'archives' (1), to store them and place them at the disposal of 'users'
DEF: 46-30
51-03 REF: film library 51-16 (NT), phonographic records library 51-29 (NT), photograph library 51-30 (NT), library 51-25 (RT)
(3) Buildings in which 'archives' (1) are preserved and made available for 'use'
DEF: 46-27

centre (Brit.)
center (U.S.A.)
F   centre
D   Zentrum; Zentralstelle
R   центр
S   centro
51-04 An organization that makes available at one central point a pool of specialized personnel or services for the *benefit* of other activities or individuals
DEF: 45-04
REF: clearing house 51-06 (NT), data centre 51-09 (NT), document c. 51-13 (NT), documentation c. 51-14 (NT), information analysis c. 51-18/19 (NT), information c. 51-20 (NT), information evaluation c. 51-22 (NT), national library 51-28 (NT), referral c. 51-34 (NT), technical information c. 51-41 (NT)

city library
    municipal library
F   bibliothèque municipale
D   Stadtbücherei; Stadtbibliothek
R   городская библиотека
S   biblioteca municipal; biblioteca urbana
51-05 A 'library' acting under the re-

sponsibility of the government of the city, serving as a main library of the city. REF: library 51-25 (BT), national 1. 51-28 (OT), district 1. 51-12 (RT)

clearing house
F   centre d'échange et de compensation
D   Clearinghaus
R   координационный информационный центр; справочно-информационный центр (по научным исследованиям и разработкам)
S   centro de referencia
51-06 An organization that collects and maintains *records*, particularly of research and development being planned, currently in progress, or completed, provides *documents* derived from these activities, and may provide referral services to other sources for *information* relating to these activities
DEF: 21-44, 21-18, 17-27/28
REF: centre 51-04 (BT), document c. 51-13 (RT), information c. 51-20 (RT), referral c. 51-34 (RT)

data bank
    library of data (1)
F   banque de données
D   Datenbank
R   банк данных
S   banco de datos
51-07 (1) A *collection* of related *files* which stores and organizes *data* so that they and new data generated from them are made available under a multiplicity of aspects using *electronic data processing* equipment
DEF: 312-05, 33-11, 17-12, 17-21
REF: data base 312-07 (RT)
51-08 (2) An organization which stores and organizes related *data* and makes them available under a multiplicity of aspects using *electronic data processing* equipment
DEF: 17-12, 17-21
REF: documentation centre 51-14/15 (RT), information analysis c. 51-18/19 (RT), data c. 51-09 (RT)

data centre
F   centre de données
D   Datenzentrum
R   центр данных
S   centro de datos
51-09 An organization handling and providing mainly *numeric data* usually without evaluation
DEF: 17-48
REF: centre 51-04 (BT), data bank 51-08 (RT), information analysis 51-19 (RT)

department library
F
D   Abteilungsbibliothek; Fakultätsbibliothek; Institutsbibliothek
R   библиотека отдела; факультетская библиотека
S   bibliotheca departemental
51-10 The 'library' of a department of a university or business organization, not being the main library of the university or organization
REF: library 51-25 (BT)

deposit library
F   bibliothèque de dépôt
D   Depot-Bibliothek
R   библиотека-хранилище; библиотека, получающая обязательный экземпляр
S   biblioteca de depósito
51-11 A 'library' in which *documents* are deposited continually under special conditions
DEF: 21-18
REF: library 51-25 (BT), legal deposit 1. 51-23 (RT)

district library
    regional library
F   bibliothèque régionale
D   Bezirksbibliothek; Kreisbibliothek
R   районная библиотека
S   biblioteca regional
51-12 A 'public library' acting under the responsibility of the government of a district, serving as the main library of the district
REF: public library 51-31 (BT), city 1. 51-05 (RT)

document centre
F   centre des documents
D   Dokumentenzentrale
R   центр (сбора, накопления и поиска) документов
S   centro de documentos
51-13 An organization primarily limited to selecting, acquiring, storing and retrieving specific *documents*, disseminating them only in response to requests expressed as unique numbers
DEF: 21-18
REF: centre 51-04 (BT), clearing house 51-06 (RT), documentation c. 51-14/15 (RT), library 51-25 (BT)

documentation centre
F   centre de documentation
D   Informations- und Dokumentationsstelle; Dokumentationsstelle; Informations- und Dokumentationszentrum; Dokumentationszentrum

R   документационный центр;
    информационный центр
S   centro de documentación
    51-14 (1) An organization that performs
    all the functions of a 'document centre'
    and in addition, announces, abstracts,
    extracts, indexes, and disseminates *docu-
    ments* in response to demands for *content*
    DEF: 21-18, 17-10
    REF: centre 51-04 (BT), clearing house
    51-06 (RT), document c. 51-13 (RT), in-
    formation analysis c. 51-18/19 (RT),
    information c. 51-20 (RT), information
    evaluation c. 51-22 (RT), technical infor-
    mation c. 51-41 (RT)
    51-15 (2) An organization which carries
    out functions of *documentation* and *infor-
    mation* in varying degrees. Note: accord-
    ing to its organizational status it can be
    called 'unit', 'department', 'service', etc.,
    too
    DEF: 31-19, 17-30
    REF: see 51-14

film library
    film archives
F   cinémathèque;
    archives cinématographiques
D   Filmarchiv; Filmothek
R   фильмотека
S   filmoteca; cinemateca, cineteca
    51-16 An organization which collects,
    stores, and makes available for *use*
    cinema, films and filmstrips
    DEF: 46-27
    REF: archives 51-02 (BT), special library
    51-40 (BT), photograph 1. 51-30 (RT)

government library
F
D   Behördenbibliothek;
    Regierungsbibliothek
R   ведомственная библиотека
S   biblioteca gubernamental
    51-17 A 'special library' serving a spe-
    cific government
    REF: special library 51-39 (BT)

information analysis centre
F   centre d'analyse de l'information
D   Informationsanalysezentrum;
    Informationsanalysestelle
R   центр анализа информации
S   centro de análisis de la información
    51-18 (1) An organization analysing,
    condensing, synthesizing, repackaging
    and disseminating *contents* of *documents*
    DEF: 17-10, 21-18
    REF: centre 51-04 (BT), clearing house
    51-06 (RT), data bank 51-08 (RT), docu-
    mentation c. 51-14/15 (RT), information
    c. 51-20 (RT), information evaluation c.
    51-22 (RT), technical information c. 51-
    41 (RT)

    51-19 (2) An organization primarily for
    judging, condensing and disseminating
    the values of *information* derived from
    experiments, research, development, test
    and engineering and for summarizing
    and reporting such evaluation
    DEF: 17-27/28
    REF: centre 51-04 (BT), data c. 51-09
    (RT), data bank 51-08 (RT), information
    c. 51-20 (RT), technical information c.
    51-41 (RT)

information centre
F   centre d'information
D   Informationsstelle; Informationszentrum
R   информационный центр
S   centro de información
    51-20 An organization conveying *infor-
    mation* or substantive responses to *in-
    quiries*
    DEF: 17-28, 313-15
    REF: information department 51-21 (NT),
    centre 51-04 (BT), clearing house 51-06
    (RT), documentation c. 51-14/15 (RT),
    information analysis c. 51-18/19 (RT),
    information evaluation c. 51-22 (RT),
    referral c. 51-34 (RT), technical c. 51-41
    (RT)

information department
F   département d'information
D   Informationsabteilung
R   информационное подразделение;
    отдел информации
S   departamento de información
    51-21 That part of an organization serv-
    ing as an 'information centre' for that
    organization
    REF: information centre 51-20 (BT)

information evaluation centre
F   centre d'évaluation de l'information
D   Informationsbewertungsstelle;
    Informationsbewertungszentrum
R   центр оценки информации
S   centro de evaluación de la informacion
    51-22 An organization which analyses,
    synthesizes and repackages the *contents*
    of *documents*
    DEF: 17-10, 21-18
    REF: centre 51-04 (BT), clearing house
    51-06 (RT), documentation c. 51-14/15
    (RT), information analysis c. 51-18 (RT),
    information c. 51-20 (RT), technical
    information c. 51-41 (RT)

legal deposit library
    copyright library
F   bibliothèque bénéficiant du dépôt légal
D   Pflichtexemplar-Bibliothek
R   библиотека, получающая
    обязательный экземпляр
S   biblioteca de depósito legal

51-23 A 'library' receiving by law or under other arrangements free *copies* of all or all required national *publications*
DEF: 110-05, 19-14
REF: library 51-25 (BT), deposit 1. 51-11 (RT), national 1. 51-28 (RT)

leihing library
F   bibliothèque de prêt
D   Ausleihbibliothek
R   библиотека, выдающая литературу на дом
S   biblioteca de préstamo
51-24 A 'library' which lends *documents* to *users*
DEF: 21-18, 46-30
REF: library 51-25 (BT), reference 1. 51-33 (OT), rental 1. 51-35 (RT)

library
F   bibliothèque
D   Bibliothek
R   библиотека
S   biblioteca
51-25 Any organized *collection* of printed *books* and *periodicals* or of any other graphic or audio-visual materials and the service of a staff to provide and facilitate the *use* of such materials as are required to meet the informational, research, educational or recreational *needs* of its *users*
DEF: 312-05, 21-09, 21-38, 46-27, 46-34
REF: city library 51-04 (NT), departmental 1. 51-10 (NT), district 1. 51-12 (NT), deposit 1. 51-11 (NT), lending 1. 51-24 (NT), legal deposit 1. 51-23 (NT), national 1. 51-28 (NT), public 1. 51-31 (NT), reference 1. 51-33 (NT), rental 1. 51-35 (NT), research 1. 51-37 (NT), special 1. 51-38/40 (NT), technical 1. 51-42 (NT), universal 1. 51-43 (NT), university 1. 51-44 (NT), archives 51-02 (RT), document centre 51-13 (RT)

library of programs
F
D   Programmbibliothek
R   библиотека (стандартных) программ
S   biblioteca de programas para computadora; programoteca
51-26 A *collection* of standard and fully tested *computer programs*, *routines* and *subroutines*
DEF: 312-05, 42-13, 42-40, 42-46
REF: special library 51-40 (BT)

mobile library
    travelling library; book mobile library
F   bibliobus
D   Autobücherei
R   передвижная библиотека
S   biblioteca ambulante; bibliobus

51-27 A service of a 'public lending library' using a vehicle specially equipped and furnished to provide *documents* direct to the *users*
DEF: 21-18, 46-30
REF: public library 51-31 (BT), lending 1. 51-24 (BT)

national library
F   bibliothèque nationale
D   Nationalbibliothek
R   национальная библиотека; государственная библиотека
S   biblioteca nacional
51-28 A 'library' which is responsible for acquiring and conserving *copies* of all significant *publications* published in the country and may function as a 'legal deposit library'. Note: It will normally perform some of the following functions: produce a national bibliography, hold and keep up to date a large and representative collection of foreign literature including books about the country, act as a national bibliographical information centre, compile union catalogues, publish the retrospective national bibliography
DEF: 110-05, 19-14
REF: library 51-25 (BT), city 1. 51-05 (OT), district 1. 51-12 (OT), legal deposit 1. 51-23 (RT)

phonograph records library (U.S.A.)
    gramophone records library (Brit.)
F   phonothèque
D   Lautarchiv; Phonothek; Schallplattenarchiv
R   дискотека; фонотека
S   fonoteca; discoteca
51-29 An organization which collects, stores and makes available for use phonographic *recorde*
DEF: 21-44
REF: archives 51-02 (BT), special library 51-40 (BT)

photograph library
    picture archive
F   archives photographiques; photothèque; diathèque
D   Bildarchiv
R   фототека
S   archivos fotográficos; fototeca
51-30 An organization which collects, stores and makes available for use photographs
REF: archives 51-02 (BT), special library 51-40 (BT)

public library
F   bibliothèque publique
D   öffentliche Bibliothek; öffentliche Bücherei

allgemeinbildende Bibliothek (GDR);
Volksbücherei
R   публичная библиотека;
общедоступная библиотека;
массовая библиотека
S   biblioteca pública
51-31 A 'library' which serves the population of a community or region free of charge or for a nominal fee
REF: library 51-25 (BT), district 1. 51-12 (NT)

publishing house
F   maison d'édition
D   Verlag
R   издательство
S   casa editora; editorial
51-32 An organization which produces *publications*
DEF: 19-14

reference library
reference collection
F
D   Präsenzbibliothek; Präsenzsammlung
R   справочная библиотека
S   colección de referencia;
biblioteca de referencia
51-33 A 'library' or part of it from which *documents* may not be borrowed, usually containing *reference works* and providing *information* with the help of trained personnel
DEF: 21-18, 21-45, 17-30
REF: library 51-25 (BT), lending 1. 51-24 (OT), rental 1. 51-35 (OT)

referral centre
F   centre d'orientation
D   Referral-Center;
Informationsvermittlungsstelle
R   справочно-информационный центр
S   centro de referencia;
centro de orientación
51-34 An organization that refers inquirers to the source which is most likely to be able to supply a suitable reply
REF: centre 51-04 (BT), clearing house 51-06 (RT), documentation c. 51-14/15 (RT), information c. 51-20 (RT), technical information c. 51-41 (RT)

rental library
rental collection;
subscription library
F   bibliothèque de prêt payant
D   Leihbibliothek;
gewerbliche Leihbibliothek
R   платная библиотека
S   biblioteca de alquiler de libros
51-35 A 'library' the *documents*' of which are available on loan for a fee

DEF: 21-18
REF: library 51-25 (BT), reference l. 51-33 (OT), lending l. 51-24 (RT)

repository
storage library
F   centrale de dépôt
D   Aussenmagazin; Speicherbibliothek
R   библиотека-хранилище (склад)
S   central de depósito
51-36 A warehouse used by one or more 'libraries' with storage for little used library materials, the ownership of which is retained by the depositing library

research library
scholarly library; learned library
F   bibliothèque de recherche;
bibliothèque d'étude
D   Forschungsbibliothek; Spezialbibliothek
R   научная библиотека
S   biblioteca de investigación
51-37 A 'library' provided with specialized *documents* where exhaustive investigation can be carried on
DEF: 21-18
REF: library 51-25 (BT), universal l. 51-43 (OT), special l. 51-38/39 (RT), technical l. 51-42 (RT)

special library
F   bibliothèque spécialisée
D   Spezialbibliothek
R   специальная библиотека;
отраслевая библиотека
S   biblioteca especializada
51-38 (1) A 'library' primarily serving one discipline or particular field
REF: library 51-25 (BT), universal l. 51-43 (OT), research l. 51-37 (RT), technical l. 51-42 (RT)
51-39 (2) A 'library' primarily serving a specific category of *users*
DEF: 46-30
REF: see 51-38, government library 51-17 (NT)
51-40 (3) A 'library' primarily devoted to a specific form of *document*
DEF: 21-18
REF: library 51-25 (BT), film l. 51-16 (NT), library of programs 51-26 (NT), phonograph records l. 51-29 (NT), photograph l. 51-30 (NT), universal l. 51-43 (OT)

technical information centre
F   centre d'information technique
D   Fachinformationsstelle;
Fachinformationszentrum
R   центр технической информации
S   centro de información técnica

51-41 An organization for acquiring, processing, and disseminating *specialited information*
DEF: 17-62
REF: centre 51-04 (BT), clearing house 51-06 (RT), documentation c. 51-14/15 (RT), information analysis c. 51-18/19 (RT), information c. 51-20 (RT), information evaluation c. 51-22 (RT), referral c. 51-34 (RT)

technical library
F   bibliothèque technique
D   Fachbibliothek
R   техническая библиотека;
     отраслевая библиотека
S   biblioteca técnica
51-42 A 'library' predominantly devoted to science and engineering in more than one discipline or speciality
REF: library 51-25 (BT), universal l. 51-43 (OT), research l. 51-37 (RT), special l. 51-38/39 (RT)

universal library
     general library
F   bibliothèque encyclopédienne
D   Universalbibliothek;
     Allgemeinbibliothek
R   универсальная библиотека
S   biblioteca general
51-43 A 'library' covering in principle all fields of *knowledge*
DEF: 12-24
REF: library 51-25 (BT), research l. 51-37 (OT), special l. 51-38/40 (OT), technical l. 51-42 (OT), university l. 51-44 (RT)

university library
F   bibliothèque universitaire
D   Universitätsbibliothek
R   университетская библиотека
S   biblioteca universitaria
51-44 A 'library' serving universities or any other equivalent institution of higher education
REF: library 51-25 (BT), universal l. 51-43 (RT)

52 Professions and occupations

abstractor
F   analyste
D   Referent
R   референт; составитель реферата
S   analista; extractador
52-01 A person who analyses scientific or technical *documents* and makes *abstracts* of them
DEF: 21-18, 314-01

archivist
F   archiviste
D   Archivar
R   архивариус; архивист
S   archivista
52-02 A person who is occupied in the preservation and organization of *archives*
DEF: 51-01/02
REF: librarian 52-17 (RT)

author
F   auteur
D   Autor
R   автор
S   autor
52-03 A person chiefly responsible for the creation of the intellectual or artistic *content* of a *document*
DEF: 17-10, 21-18
REF: compiler 52-09 (RT), editor 52-11 (RT), publisher 52-20 (RT)

bibliographer
F   bibliographe
D   Bibliograph
R   библиограф
S   bibliógrafo
52-04 A person who compiles a *bibliography*
DEF: 315-04
REF: compiler 52-09 (RT)

cataloguer (Brit.)
     cataloger (U.S.A.)
F   catalographe
D   Katalogisierer; Katalogführer
R   каталогизатор
S   catalogador
52-05 A person who builds up or maintains a *catalogue*
DEF: 32-07
REF: classifier 52-08 (RT), indexer 52-12 (RT)

classificationist
F   spécialiste de la classification
D   Klassifikator
R   составитель классификации
S   especialista en clasificación
52-06 A person who designs a *classification*
DEF: 311-05
REF: documentalist 52-08 (RT), information scientist 52-15 (RT), terminologist 52-24 (RT)

classifier
F   classificateur
D   Klassifizierer
R   классификатор
S   clasificador
52-07 A person who indexes by using a *classification*
DEF: 311-05

REF: indexer 52-12 (BT), cataloguer 52-05 (RT)

documentalist
F documentaliste
D Dokumentar (FRG);
   Dokumentalist (GDR)
R документалист
S documentalista
   52-08 A person who carries out responsible work in the field of *documentation*
   DEF: 31-19
   REF: indexer 52-12 (NT), abstracter 52-01 (RT), classificationist 52-06 (RT), information analyst 52-13 (RT), information specialist 52-16 (RT), special librarian 52-22 (RT)

compiler
F compilateur
D Kompilator; Sammler
R составитель
S compilador
   52-09 (2) A person who produces a single *document* by collecting and arranging written or printed material from various sources.
   DEF: 21-18
   REF: author 52-03 (RT), editor 52-11 (RT), publisher 52-20 (RT), bibliographer 52-04 (RT)

computer scientist
F informaticien
D Computerwissenschaftler;
   Informatiker (FRG)
R специалист в области теории математических машин
S especialista en computación
   52-10 A person who is engaged in the field of *computer science*
   DEF: 11-05
   REF: information scientist 52-15 (RT)

editor
F éditeur
D Redakteur; Bearbeiter
R редактор
S redactor
   52-11 A person who is responsible for, or prepares for *publication*, the *contents* of a *document* to which he may or may not have contributed
   DEF: 19-13, 17-10, 21-18
   REF: author 52-11 (RT), compiler 52-09 (RT), publisher 52-20 (RT)

indexer
F indexeur
D Indexierer; Indizierer (GDR)
R индексатор
S indizador

52-12 A person who indexes *documents*
DEF: 21-18
REF: documentalist 52-08 (BT), information specialist 52-16 (BT), classifier 52-07 (NT), cataloguer 52-05 (RT)

information analyst
F analyste (de l'information)
D Datenauswerter;
   (Informationsanalytiker)
R специалист, занимающийся анализом и оценкой информации
S analista de la información
   52-13 A person who analyses and/or evaluates *data* for the purpose of an *information analysis centre* or *information evaluation centre*
   DEF: 17-12, 51-18/19, 51-22
   REF: documentalist 52-08 (RT), information specialist 52-16 (RT)

information officer
F documentaliste
D Informationsbeauftragter
R информационный работник
S documentalista;
   técnico de la información
   52-14 A person who is responsible for the collection, searching for, and *dissemination* of *specialized information* within an organization
   DEF: 19-04, 17-62

information scientist
F documentaliste
D Informationswissenschaftler
R информатик
S científico de la información
   52-15 A person who works on the theory or application of *informatics* or *information science*; i.e. analyses, designs, implements, etc., *information systems*
   DEF: 11-08, 11-09/10, 41-19/20
   REF: classificationist 52-06 (RT), computer scientist 52-10 (RT), systems analyst 52-23 (RT)

information specialist
F documentaliste spécialisé
D Fachdokumentar;
   wissenschaftlicher Dokumentar;
   Fachinformator (GDR)
R информатор;
   информационный работник
S documentalista especializado
   52-16 A person who is specialized in exploitation of *document contents*, with strong competence in the subject-matter being analysed
   DEF: 21-18, 17-10
   REF: abstracter 52-01 (RT), documentalist 52-08 (RT), indexer 52-12 (RT), information analyst 52-13 (RT), special librarian 52-22 (RT)

librarian
F   bibliothécaire
D   Bibliothekar
R   библиотекарь
S   bibliotecario
52-17 A person who is occupied in the collection, conservation and organization for use of *documents* in a *library*
DEF: 21-18, 51-25
REF: public librarian 52-19 (NT), science l. 52-21 (NT), archivist 52-02 (RT)

programmer
F   programmeur
D   Programmierer
R   программист
S   programador
52-18 A person who writes *computer programs*
DEF: 42-13
REF: systems analyst 52-23 (RT)

public librarian
F   bibliothécaire de lecture publique
D   öffentlicher Bibliothekar; Volksbibliothekar
R   библиотекарь публичной библиотеки
S   bibliotecario especializado de bibliotecas públicas
52-19 A 'librarian' who is trained for work in *public libraries*
DEF: 51-31
REF: librarian 52-17 (BT), science l. 52-21 (OT)

publisher
F   éditeur
D   Verleger; Herausgeber
R   издатель; издающая организация
S   editor
52-20 A person or an organization who or which prints and issues *publications*
DEF: 19-14
REF: author 52-03 (RT), compiler 52-03 (RT), editor 52-11 (RT)

science librarian
F
D   wissenschaftlicher Bibliothekar
R   библиотекарь научной библиотеки
S   bibliotecario de bibliotecas científicas

52-21 A 'librarian' who is trained for work in scientific *libraries*
DEF: 51-25
REF: librarian 52-17 (BT), public l. 52-19 (OT), special l. 52-22 (NT)

special librarian
F   bibliothécaire spécialisé
D   Spezialbibliothekar
R   библиотекарь специальной библиотеки; библиотекарь отраслевой библиотеки
S   bibliotecario especializado
52-22 A 'librarian' who is operating in a special discipline and for that purpose requires a broadened and intensified knowledge of his selected field
REF: scientific librarian 52-21 (BT), documentalist 52-08 (RT), information specialist 52-16 (RT)

systems analyst
F   analyste de systèmes
D   Systemanalysator; Systemanalytiker
R   системоаналитик
S   analista de sistemas
52-23 A person who analyses, designs, implements and controls *systems*, especially computerized *information systems*
DEF: 41-40, 41-19/20
REF: information scientist 52-15 (RT), programmer 52-18 (RT)

terminologist
F   terminologiste
D   Terminologe
R   терминолог
S   especialista en terminología
52-24 A person who is engaged in *terminology*, either in general or in a particular *subject field*
DEF: 11-22, 12-31
REF: classficationist 52-06 (RT)

translator
F   traducteur
D   Übersetzer
R   переводчик
S   traductor
52-25 A person who translates *documents* from one *natural language* into another
DEF: 21-18, 15-18

UDC index

Sources:

Deutsche Gesellschaft für Dokumentation, Bibliothek und Dokumentationsstelle. *UDC-Code for documentation.* Frankfurt, 1969.

Deutscher Normenausschuss (ed.). *Dezimalklassifikation. DK-Handausgabe. Internationale Mittlere Ausgabe der Universellen Dezimalklassifikation.* 2 vols. Berlin-Köln, 1968.

Thompson, A. *Vocabularium bibliothecarii.* Paris, Unesco, 1962.

Alphabetical index

abridged document 21-01
abridgement 21-01
abstract 314-01, 314-13
  author's 314-06
  automatic 314-07
  encoded 314-14
  indicative 314-18
  indicative-informative 314-19
  information 314-21
  informative 314-21
  machine 314-07
  positioned 314-28
  skeleton 314-30
  slanted 314-26
  structural 314-28
  telegraphic 314-30
  telegraphic style 314-30
abstract bulletin 314-02
abstract journal 314-03
abstracting 31-01
  automatic 31-04
  machine 31-04
abstracting journal 314-03
abstracting service 314-04
  comprehensive 314-09
  selective 314-24
abstraction 38-01
abstraction relation 38-17
abstractor 52-01
acceptance rate 45-01
access 313-01
  arbitrary 313-28
  immediate 313-13
  multilevel 313-22
  multiple 313-23
  parallel 313-25
  random 313-28
  remote 313-30
  sequential 313-42

accession 31-02
accession list 32-01
accession number 310-01
accessions register 32-02
accuracy 42-01
acquisition 31-03
acronym 14-01
active dissemination 19-01
activity ratio 45-02
adaptability 45-03
adaptive control system 41-01
adaptive system 41-01
added copy 110-14
added entry 33-01
address 312-01
  direct 312-10
  indirect 312-17
  multilevel 312-17
  one-level 312-10
  symbolic 312-34
addressing system 312-02
advance copy 21-02
advances 21-43
affective relation 38-02
affix 14-02
alerting service 314-08
algorithmic language 15-01
allocation 34-01
  storage 312-29
almanac 21-03
alphabet 13-01, 13-02
alphabetic character set 13-04
alphabetic code 18-01
alphabetic notation 310-02
alphabetical arrangement 34-03
alphabetical bibliography 315-01
alphabetical-classed catalogue 34-02
alphabetical-classed filing system 34-02
alphabetical index 35-01

library of 51-07
    numeric 17-48
    row 17-51
    statistical 17-65
data bank 51-07, 51-08
data base 312-07
data centre 51-09
data code 18-12
data conversion 18-13
data documentation 31-14
data medium 17-13, 17-14
data processing 17-15
    automatic 17-02
    electronic 17-21
    integrated 17-36
data processing system 41-09
data reduction 17-16
data retrieval 313-05
data retrieval system 41-10
data storage and retrieval system 41-37
data transformation 18-13
data transmission 17-17
decentralized system 41-11
decimal classification 311-07
decimal notation 310-08
decoding 18-14, 18-15
definition 12-11
    contextual 12-08
    intensional 12-21
definition by genus and species 12-21
definition by intension 12-21
definition of context 12-08
definitive relation 38-15
demand, information 46-11
    user 46-32
demand study 46-05
denotative meaning 14-14
department library 51-10
dependent facet 39-28
deposit collection 312-08
deposit library 51-11
deprecated term 14-15
depth of indexing 35-18
derivate 14-16
derivative 14-16
derivative word 14-16
derived word 14-16
description 32-18
    analytical 33-02
    bibliographic
    class 39-17
    document 31-16
    full 33-18
descriptive abstract 314-13
descriptive cataloguing 32-18
descriptor 36-05, 36-06, 37-05
descriptor association list 37-06
descriptor language 15-07
descriptor network 37-07
design, logic(al) 44-15
    chronological 39-14
    operational 44-23
device, display 42-17
    geographical 39-43, 39-44

input 42-23
    octave 310-26
    output 42-30
    searching 313-39
    selecting 313-40
    storage 312-32
    storage retrieval 313-44
diacritical mark 13-17
diacritics 13-17
diagram 44-08
diagram, block 44-03
    flow 44-11
    logic 44-16
    Venn 44-38
dialect 15-09
dialogues search 313-06
diary technique 46-06
diazo-copy 110-06
diazo copying 110-06
diazo print 110-07
diazo process 110-06
dichotomized classification 311-08
dichotomized search 313-02
dictionary 16-03
    automatic 16-01
    bilingual 16-02
    etymological 16-05
    explanatory 16-06
    machine 16-01
    mechanical 16-01
    multilingual 16-10
    polyglot 16-10
    root 16-11
    special 16-12
    stem 16-11
    subject 16-12
dictionary catalogue 32-19
dictionary word 14-17
difference 39-07
    logical 12-25
differentia 12-25
differential facet 39-29
diffusion transfer process 110-08
digest 21-16
digit 13-18
    binary 13-06
digital computer 42-16
digital data 17-18
digital notation 310-25
dimensionality 39-30, 39-31
direct access storage 312-09
direct address 312-10
direct code 18-16
direct communication 17-19
direct copy 110-09
direct documentation 31-14
direct positive 110-10
directory 21-17
discrete data 17-20
discrete representation 13-19
disjunction 12-09, 12-10
display device 42-17
display, graphic 37-08
dissemination 19-04

Index alphabétique

Alphabetisches Register

Алфавитный указатель

Índice alfabético

WITHDRAWAL